THE PSYCHOLOGY OF ATTENTION

THE PSYCHOLOGY OF ATTENTION

Elizabeth A. Styles
Buckinghamshire College, Bucks, UK

Psychology Press
a member of the Taylor & Francis group

Psychology Press Ltd., Publishers
27 Church Road
Hove
East Sussex, BN3 2FA
UK

British Library Cataloguing in Publication Data

A catalogue record for this book is available from the British Library

ISBN 0-86377-464-4 (hbk)
0-86377-465-2 (pbk)

Printed and bound in the UK by TJ International Ltd.

Contents

Preface

I know from my students that cognitive psychology fills some of them with dread. They see it as the difficult side of psychology, full of facts that don't quite fit any theory. Cognition does not have the immediate appeal of social or developmental psychology to which, they say, they can relate more easily through personal experience. However, towards the end of a course, they begin to see how the pieces of the jigsaw fit together, and exclaim, " This is interesting. Why didn't you tell us this to start with?". The trouble is that, until you have put together some of the pieces, it is difficult to see even a part of what the overall picture is. Next, the parts of the picture have to be put in the right place. With respect to attention, no one yet knows exactly what the picture we are building looks like: this makes work on attention particularly exciting and challenging. We may have some of the pieces in the wrong place, or be thinking of the wrong overall picture. In this book I hope you will find some pieces that fit together and see how some of the pieces have had to be moved as further evidence is brought to light; and I hope you see, from the everyday example of attentional behaviour in the introduction, that we can relate to cognitive psychology just as well as to social psychology. Attention is with us all the time.

The primary motivation for this book was that my undergraduates were unable to find a suitable text on attention to support lectures, tutorials and seminars. My second motivation was that most chapters in general cognitive psychology texts tend to concentrate on the original early work on selective attention done in the 1960s, dual-task performance work from the 1970s and feature integration theory (FIT) from 1980. These aspects are important, but research on attention includes far more than this; in fact, so much more, that to gather it all into an undergraduate text is impossible. As cognitive neuroscience moves ahead, bringing together traditional experimental work, neuropsychological studies and computational modelling, the prospect for a better understanding of attention is coming nearer. At the same time, the range of evidence that needs to be considered has increased far beyond that which was accounted for by the original theories. However, I believe that in the end there will be a solution. As we understand more about the brain and the way it works, we are beginning to see how attentional behaviour may emerge as a property of complex underlying processing.

In choosing what to include, I have necessarily been selective and am sure to have omitted some work that others would see as essential. The selection of work I have made is bound to be influenced by the years I spent at the University of Oxford, first as a student and then as a colleague of two great thinkers in attention: Alan Allport and the late Donald Broadbent. Their energy, enthusiasm, wisdom and kindness inspired my own interest in attention. I acknowledge my debt to them here.

In writing the final version of this book I have been helped considerably by the extremely constructive comments of the reviewers. I should like to thank Alan Allport, Glyn Humphreys, Hermann Müller and an anonymous reviewer for their time and effort.

Liz Styles,
Oxford, 1997.

Introduction 1

What is attention?

Any reader who turns to a book with the word *attention* in the title, might be forgiven for thinking that the author would have a clear idea or precise definition of what attention actually is. Unfortunately, attention is a concept that psychologists have been particularly reluctant to define. Despite William James's (1890) oft-quoted remark that "Everyone knows what attention is", it would be closer to the truth to say that "Nobody knows what attention is" or at least not all psychologists agree. The problem is that attention is not a single concept, but the name for a variety of psychological phenomena.

We can easily see some of the many varieties of attention in the common usage of the word when we apply the same word to different situations and experiences. Let's take an everyday example. While we are out walking in a wood, I tell you that I have just seen an unusual variety of butterfly land on the back of the leaf in a nearby tree. I point out the tree and whereabout the leaf is, and tell you to pay attention to it. Following my instruction you are able to select one tree from many and then *attend to* a particular leaf, rather than the tree itself, so presumably you and I share some common understanding of what attention is. You continue to look carefully, hoping you will see the butterfly when it moves out from behind the leaf. Now, you will try to keep your attention on that leaf so as not to miss the butterfly when it appears. In addition, you will have some expectation of what the butterfly will look like and how it may behave and you'll be monitoring for these features. This expectation and anticipation will activate what psychologists call top-down processes which will enable you to be more ready to respond if a butterfly appears rather than some dissimilar animal—say, a caterpillar. However, if while you are selectively focusing attention on the leaf an apple suddenly falls out of another part of the tree, you will be distracted. In other words, your attention will be automatically captured by the apple. In order to continue observing the leaf, you must re-engage your attention to where it was before. After a time you detect the beautiful butterfly as it flutters round the leaf; it sits a minute and you watch it as it flies away.

In this example we have a variety of attentional phenomena that psychologists need to understand, and if possible explain, in well-defined scientific terms. We shall see that no single term is appropriate to explain all the phenomena of attention and control even in this visual task. Let's look at what you were asked to do. First of all, I asked you to attend to a leaf. In order to do this simple task, there had to be some kind of setting up of your cognitive system that enabled leaf rather than tree to become the current object of processing; and one particular leaf was selected over others on the basis of its spatial location. Once you are focusing on the leaf you are expecting butterfly-type shapes to emerge and may occasionally think you have detected the butterfly if an adjacent leaf flutters in the breeze. Here the perceptual input triggers, bottom-up, one of the attributes of butterfly (fluttering) that has been primed by your expectations, and for a moment you are misled. The idea of *mental set* is an old one. Many experiments on attention use a selective set paradigm, where the subject prepares to respond to a particular set of stimuli. The notion of selection brings with it the complementary notion of ignoring some stimuli at the expense of those that are selected for attentional processing. What makes selection easy or difficult is an important research area and has exercised psychologists for decades. Here we immediately run into the first problem: is attention, the internal setting of the system to detect or respond to a particular set of stimuli (in our example, butterflies), the same as the attention that you pay or allocate to the stimulus once it is detected? It seems intuitively unlikely. Which of these kinds of attention is captured by the unexpected falling apple? We already have one word for two different aspects of the task. A second issue arises when the apple falls from the tree and you are momentarily distracted. We said your attention was automatically drawn to the apple, so, although you were intending to attend to the leaf and focusing on its spatial location, there appears to be an interrupt process that automatically detects novel, possibly important, environmental changes outside the current focus of attention and draws attention to them. An automatic process is one that is defined as not requiring attention although, of course, if we are not certain how to define attention, this makes the definition of automatic processes problematic. Note now, another problem: I said that you have to return attention to the leaf you were watching. What does this mean? Somehow, the temporary activation causing the apple to attract attention can be voluntarily overridden by the previously active goal of leaf observation. You have remembered what you were doing and attention can then be directed, by some internal process or mechanism, back to the original task. To say that you do this direction voluntarily tells us nothing: we might as easily appeal to the little-man-in-the-head, or homunculus on which many theories seem to rely.

To continue with the example: if you have to sustain attention on the leaf, monitoring for the butterfly for more than a few minutes, it may become increasingly difficult to stop your attention from wandering. You have difficulty concentrating; there seems to be effort involved in keeping to the task at hand. Finally the butterfly appears: you detect it, in its spatial location, but as soon as it flies away, you follow it, as if your attention is not now directed to the location that the butterfly occupied but to the object of the butterfly itself. The question of whether visual attention is spatially based or object based is another issue that has recently begun to be widely researched.

Of course, visual attention is intimately related to where we are looking and to eye movements. Perhaps there is nothing much to explain here: we just attend to what we are looking at. However, we all know that we can "look out of the corner of the eye". If, while you fixate your gaze on this * you are able to tell me quite a lot about the spatial arrangement of the text on the page and what the colours of the walls are, it demonstrates that it is not the case that where we direct our eyes and where we direct attention are one and the same. Let's leave the example of looking for butterflies and consider other modalities.

In the case of vision there appears to be an obvious limit on how much information we can take in, at least from different spatial locations, simply because it is not possible to look in two directions at once—although, of course, there is the question of how we select from among spatially coincident information. Similarly, we cannot move in two directions or reach for different places at the same time. Auditory attention also seems to be limited. Even when there are several different streams of sound emanating from different locations around us—the traffic outside, the hum of the computer on the desk, the conversation in the room next door—we do not appear to be able to listen to them all at once.

We all know that we can selectively listen to the intriguing conversation at the next table in the restaurant even though there is another conversation continuing at our own table. This is an example of selective auditory attention, and a version of the "cocktail party" problem. Listening to a conversation in noise is clearly easier if we know something about the content. Some words may be masked by other noises, but our top-down expectations enable us to fill in the gaps; we say that there is redundancy in language, meaning that there is more information present than is strictly necessary. We make use of this redundancy in difficult conditions. If the conversation was of a technical nature, on some topic about which we knew very little, there would be much less top-down expectation and the conversation would be more difficult to follow. Although, we may be intent on the conversation at the next table, a novel or important sound will capture our attention, rather like the visual example of the apple falling out of the tree. However, as occurs in vision, we are not easily able to monitor both sources of information at once: if we are distracted, we must return our attention back to the conversation.

Now we have another question: is the attention that we use in vision the same as that we use in audition? Whilst it is difficult to do two visual or two auditory tasks concurrently it is not necessarily difficult to combine an auditory and a visual task. What about other modalities? While most research has been involved with vision and hearing, we can of course attend to smells, tastes, sensations and proprioceptive information. To date we know little about these areas and they will not concern us here. However, the question of why some tasks do interfere with each other while others seem capable of independence, and how we can share or divide attention, may crucially depend on the modality of input and output as well as on the kind of information processing that is required in the two tasks.

An important question in attentional research is why some tasks or kinds of processing require attention but others do not. While you were looking for butterflies, we may have been walking and talking at the same time. It is possible to continue eating dinner in the restaurant at the same time as listening to a conversation. Walking, talking and eating seem to proceed without attention—until the ground becomes uneven, a verbal problem is posed or your peas fall off your fork. At these moments, you might find one task has to stop while attention is allocated to the other. Consider learning a skill, such as juggling. To begin with, we seem to need all our attention (ask your self which kind of attention this might be) to throw and catch two balls. The prospect of ever being able to operate on three at once seems rather distant! However, with practice, using two balls becomes easy; we may even be able to hold a conversation at the same time. Now, introduce the third ball. Gradually this too becomes possible, although to start with we cannot talk at the same time. Finally, we can talk and juggle three balls. So, now it seems that the amount of attention needed by a task depends on skill, which is learned through practice. Once attention is no longer needed for the juggling we can attend to something else. However, if the juggler goes wrong, the conversation seems to have to stop while a correction is made to the ball-throwing. It is as if attention is being allocated or withdrawn according to the combined demands of the tasks. In this example, attention seems to be either a limited "amount" of something, or some kind of "effort". Some theorists have likened attention to resources or effort, while others have been more concerned with where a limiting attentional step operates within the processing system to select some information for further processing.

Memory is intimately related to attention. We seem to remember what we have attended to: "I'm sorry I was not paying attention to the colour of her dress. I was listening to what she said". Although you must have seen the dress, and in fact assume that she was wearing a dress, you do not remember anything about it. If we want to be sure someone remembers what we are telling them, we ask them to pay attention. How attentional processing affects memory is another important issue. However, there is increasing evidence that considerable processing is carried out without attention being necessary or the subject having any memory of the event. Although the subject may not be explicitly able to recall, at a conscious level, that some particular information was present, subsequent testing can demonstrate that the "unattended" stimuli have had an effect, by biasing or priming, subsequent responses.

Note that for a stimulus to be apparently "unattended" it seems to have to be "unconscious". This brings us to another thorny question: what is the relationship of attention to conscious experience? Like attention, consciousness has a variety of meanings. We usually say we are conscious of what we are attending to. What we are attending to is currently in short-term or working memory. What is in short-term memory is what we are consciously thinking about at that moment in time. Here, I hope you see the problems of definition: if we are not careful we find ourselves ensnared in circularity. Memory and attention are also closely interwoven in the planning and monitoring of day-to-day activities. Have you ever gone to make a cup of tea and poured the tea into the sugar bowl? The correct actions have been performed but not on the correct objects. This sort of "slip of action" often arises when we are "not paying attention" to what we are doing. When we engage in a complex sequentially ordered set of actions to achieve a goal, like making a cup of tea, not only do we have to remember the overall goal, but we must also monitor and update the steps that have been taken towards goal completion, sometimes updating goal states as we go. In this example, we may have to stop and wash out the sugar bowl before continuing, but will not have to go right back to beginning of the goal sequence where we filled the kettle. Attention in the control of action is an example of another kind of attention, driven by goals or what we intend to do. The question of the intentional, voluntary control, where behaviour is planned according to current goals and instructions, has been largely ignored in the attentional literature, but we shall discuss later what is known.

Rather than labour the point further, let us accept that to try to define attention as a unitary concept is not possible and to do so would be misleading. Perhaps the best approach is to look at experimental situations that we all agree involve one or another application of some sort of attention and from the data obtained, together with what we now know about the organisation of the underlying neurophysiology and the breakdown of normal function following brain damage, try to infer something about the psychological processes or mechanisms underlying the observed behaviour.

Is attention a causal agent or an emergent property?

From the way I have been talking about attention, it might sound as if it is a "thing" or a causal agent that "does something". This is the problem of the homunculus to which I have already referred. Of course it might well be that attention is an emergent property; that is, it appears to be there, but plays no causal role in information processing. William James (1890) pointed out this distinction when he asked "Is attention a resultant or a force?". Johnston and Dark (1986) looked at theories of selective attention and divided them into cause theories and effect theories. Cause theories differentiate between two types of processing, which Johnson and Dark call Domain A and Domain B. Domain A is high capacity, unconscious and passive and equates with what various theorists call automatic or pre-attentive processing. Domain B is small capacity, conscious, active processing system and equates with controlled or attentive processing. In cause theories, Domain B is "among other things an attentional mechanism or director, or cause of selective processing" (1986, p.66). They go on to point out that this kind of explanation "betrays a serious metatheoretical problem", as, "if a psychological construct is to explain the intelligent and adaptive selection powers of the organism, then it cannot itself be imbued with these powers" (1986, p.68). We shall meet many examples of cause theories as we move through the chapters; for example, Broadbent (1958,1971), Kahneman (1973), Posner and Snyder (1975), Shiffrin and Schneider (1977), Norman and Shallice (1986). However, as I said, it might just be the case that attention is an "effect" that emerges from the working of the whole system as inputs interact with schemata in long-term memory: an example of this view is Neisser (1976). Johnson and Dark (1986, p.70) think that it would be "instructive to see how much we can understand about selective attention without appealing to a processing homunculus". As has already been argued, attention seems so difficult to define that it is intuitively likely that these different forms of attention arise from different effects rather that reflecting different causal agents.

Preview of the book

There is a familiar joke about asking someone the way to a destination and getting the reply, "Oh, if you want to go there, you don't want to start from here!". The trouble is, you can't change where you start from. If we were to begin to research attention today with all the knowledge that has accumulated along the way, we might ask questions rather different from those initially posed. Allport (1993) has eloquently put all these points before. Today, the joint venture of cognitive science, as cognitive psychology is now called, takes account of biological, neuropsychological and computational factors, as well as following the traditional experimental route. When attention research began in the 1950s, cognitive psychology did not even have a name. Since this initial work on attention, research has taken a long and winding road, sometimes going down a cul-de-sac, sometimes finding a turning that was missed. Posner (1993) divides work on attention into three phases. Initially, in the 1950s and 1960s, research centred on human performance, and on the concept of "the human as a single channel processor". In the 1970s and early 1980s the field of study had become "Cognition" and research was most concerned with looking for and studying internal representations, automatic and controlled processes and strategies for focusing and dividing attention. By the mid 1980s "Cognitive Neuroscience" was the name of the game and psychologists were taking account of biology, neuropsychological patients and computing. Posner points out that, although there has been a shift of major emphasis, all the strands of research continue, and are represented in the 1990s. Looking forward to the future, Posner proposes that advances in understanding the underlying neuroanatomy and the use of computer simulations in neural networks will accelerate our understanding of attention if used in conjunction with experimental studies. Allport (1993) thinks that the uses of the term *attention* are too many to be useful, but Posner (1993) believes that if we think of attention as a system of several brain networks, the concept is valid. Whoever is right, we have seen that attention is applied to rather disparate situations, and whether there are many or just a few kinds of attention, there is certainly not only one.

It is difficult to know how to make this complex field of study digestible. I have chosen to follow the development of ideas. So, to a large extent the chapters follow the chronology of attentional research because the design of new experiments is usually driven by the outcome of previous ones. If different experiments had been done first, different questions might have been asked later and the whole picture taken on a different complexion.

We start, in Chapter 2, with some of the initial studies of auditory attention and the first models proposed by Broadbent (1958), Treisman (1960), Deutsch and Deutsch (1963). These models and others shaped the argument on the early–late debate, which came to dominate psychology for many years. Generally these models assumed a single channel, limited capacity, general-purpose processing channel, which was the bottleneck in processing. Prior to the bottleneck, processing was parallel and did not require attention, but after the bottleneck, processing was serial and required attention. Theorists argued about where in the processing continuum the bottleneck was located. The following four chapters are all concerned with selection, mainly from visual displays. In Chapter 3, we begin to consider selective report from brief visual displays involving iconic memory, including the classic work by Sperling (1960), as well as selective report in bar-probe tasks, especially the one devised by Eriksen and Eriksen (1974). In these experiments, the same questions concerning the level of processing achieved prior to selective attention are continued, together with an exploration of how exclusively selective the visual attention process can be. By the end of Chapter 3, it will have become apparent that the brain codes different attributes of the stimulus, such as identity, colour and location in parallel, and arguments are given to suggest a resolution to the early–late argument.

The theme of visual attention continues in Chapter 4, when we consider the evidence for a spotlight of visual attention, and work by Posner and others on attentional cueing effects. The importance of neuropsychological studies is demonstrated by considering how visual neglect can help us to understand both normal attentional orienting and attentional deficits. We also examine experiments aimed at discovering how visual attention moves, and whether it is more like a zoom lens than a spatial spotlight. A major question asks whether attention is directed to spatial locations or to the objects that occupy those locations. We find that object-based attention is important, and this leads us to ask: how are objects constructed from their independently coded components? The theme of Chapter 5 is visual search and code coordination. Here, feature integration theory (Treisman, 1993) is introduced and again the question of whether visual attention is spatially-based or object-based continues to be raised. Alternative theories to feature integration such as Duncan and Humphreys' (1989) attention engagement theory are discussed, together with computational models of visual search and visual attention. Chapter 6 changes the emphasis, for, although the theme of attentional selectivity continues, we move on to consider selection for action. Much of the evidence presented in this chapter is taken from visual selection experiments, but the central question we shall be concerned with now is: what is attention for? Seminal ideas put forward by Allport (1987) and Neuman (1987) are used to illustrate the role played by selective attention in guiding actions. Moving on from selectivity, Chapter 7 addresses the question of how attention is divided when tasks are combined. Attentional resource theory is evaluated and the importance of stimulus response compatibility between tasks is illustrated. Although in many cases tasks can be combined provided the input/output relations do not demand concurrent use of the same sub-system, we shall see that recent work by Pashler (1993) on the psychological refractory period (PRP) suggests that there remains a fundamental limit at the final stage of processing, when responses are selected. Chapter 8 continues the task combination theme, with a discussion of experiments about automaticity, skill and expertise. Here automatic and controlled processing is explained in terms of Shiffrin and Schneider's (1977) two-process theory. However, Neuman's (1984) critique reveals that the distinction between automatic and controlled processing is at best blurred. We attempt to explain how expertise and skill emerge with practice in Anderson's (1983) ACT* production system. By the end of these chapters it will be clear that a very large amount of information processing is carried out automatically, outside conscious control. Not only does this raise the problem of how to distinguish between tasks that do or do not need attention for their performance, but it also raises the question: if there is a distinction, how is "attentional" or "conscious" control implemented? This is the question we turn to next, when theories of attentional control are debated in Chapter 9. Starting with an examination of the breakdown of normal intentional behaviour exhibited by patients with frontal lobe damage, we try to explain both normal and abnormal behaviour in terms of Norman and Shallice's (1986) model of willed and automatic behaviour, and Duncan's (1986) theory of goal-directed behaviour. Only recently has intentional control been studied experimentally on normal subjects, and we shall discuss work by Allport, Styles, and Hseih (1994) and Rogers and Monsell (1995). Finally, our discussion of conscious control leads on, in Chapter 10, to a consideration of what is meant by the term *consciousness*, what processing can proceed without it and how it might be defined. Following Holender's (1986) review of experiments on semantic activation without conscious identification in normal subjects, it becomes clear that there are many methodological problems with such work. Possibly, the greatest is determining criteria for conscious awareness (Merikle & Cheesman, 1984). Neuropsychological patients offer a promising inroad to this problem and we look at a few dissociations between processing and consciousness in patients with blindsight (Weiskrantz, 1988), patients with prosopagnosia (inability to recognise faces) (De Haan et al., 1987), and amnesia (Schacter, 1987). Finally, we shall look at a variety of arguments about the nature of consciousness. Each chapter includes, where appropriate, data from neuropsychological patients, something on the neurophysiology of the brain and computational models of attentional behaviour.

Summary

Attention is not a unitary concept. The word is used to describe, and sometimes—which is more of a worry—explain a variety of psychological data. Although we all have some subjective idea of what we mean when we say we are "attending", what this means is different in different situations. As research has progressed, old theories have been modified or abandoned, but as science is driven by testing theories, the path followed by the psychology of attention has been strongly influenced by the initial assumptions. Today, account is taken of biological, neuropsychological, computational and functional considerations of attentional behaviour which will, we hope, bring us closer to finding an answer to the question: what is attention?

Further reading

Allport, (D.)A. (1993). Attention and control: Have we been asking the wrong questions? A critical review of 25 years. In D.E. Meyer & S. Kornblum (Eds.), *Attention and performance XIV: A silver jubilee* (pp.183–218). Cambridge, MA: MIT Press. This paper, as its title suggests, reviews the direction of research on attention and is very critical of the assumptions that have driven research for so long. It is, however, quite a difficult paper, incorporating aspects of neurophysiology and neuropsychology which we shall meet later in this book.

Allport, (D.)A. (1980b). Attention and performance. In G. Claxton (Ed.), *Cognitive psychology: New directions* (pp.112-153). London: Routledge & Kegan Paul. Although now rather old, this is a weaker and more approachable version of the 1993 paper.

Posner, M.I. (1993). Attention before and during the decade of the brain. In D.E. Meyer & S. Kornblum (Eds.), *Attention and performance XIV: A silver jubilee* (pp.343–351). Cambridge, MA: MIT Press. This chapter is really an overview of the chapters on attention contained in the book; it provides a brief history of the development of attentional research.

The series of books called *Attention and performance* began in 1967 and have subsequently been published every two years. They contain the history and evolution of work on attention by major contributors of the time.

Early work on attention 2

Beginnings

During the Second World War it had become clear that people were severely limited in their ability to act on multiple signals arriving on different channels. Pilots had to try to monitor several sources of concurrent information, which might include the numerous visual displays inside the cockpit, the visual environment outside the plane and auditory messages coming in over the radio. Ground staff confronted difficulties when guiding air traffic into busy aerodromes and radar operators suffered from problems in maintaining vigilance. Psychology had little to say about these problems at the time, but researchers were motivated to try to discover more about the limitations of human performance.

Welford (1952) carried out an experiment which showed that, when two signals are presented in rapid succession and the subject must make a speeded response to both, reaction time to the second stimulus depends on the stimulus onset asynchrony (SOA) between the presentation of the first and second stimulus. When the second stimulus is presented after only a very short SOA, reaction time to the second stimulus is slower than when there is a long SOA between stimuli. Welford called this delay in response to a second stimulus in the short SOA condition the psychological refractory period (PRP). He was able to show that for every millisecond decrease in SOA there was a corresponding increase in reaction time to the second stimulus.

Welford argued that this phenomenon was evidence of a "bottle-neck", where the processing of the first stimulus must be completed before processing of the next stimulus can begin. At long SOAs the first stimulus will have had time for its processing to be completed before the arrival of the second stimulus and so no refractoriness will be observed. We shall examine more recent research on PRP when we discuss dual-task performance in Chapter 7. For the present we shall note that at the time Welford's work seemed to provide good evidence for a central limit on human processing capability.

Dichotic listening: Early experiments on selective attention

Almost all the early experiments on attention used auditory stimuli. Apart from the fact that multi-channel tape recorders became available at the time and provided an elegant way of presenting stimuli, Broadbent (1971) explained that there were very good reasons for investigating audition rather than vision. We cannot move our ears in the same way as we move our eyes, neither can we close our ears to shut out unwanted inputs. Although we said in Chapter 1 that our attention is not necessarily directed to where we move our eyes, this is usually the case. With auditory stimuli any selectivity of processing must rely on central or neural rather than peripheral or mechanical processes.

A popular experimental paradigm was the dichotic listening task. This involved presenting two simultaneous (usually, but not always, different) messages to the two ears via headphones and asking the subject to do one of a variety of tasks. In a selective attention task the instruction is to attend to the message presented to one ear and to ignore the other message which is simultaneously presented to the other ear. This mimics the cocktail party situation, where you selectively listen to one speaker rather than another. In ordinary life, the speech message we attend to will be in a particular voice (with its own characteristic physical quality) and be coming from a different direction from other voices. Under laboratory conditions it is possible to present two different voices, or two messages in the same voice to the same spatial location (i.e. to the same ear) or to deliver two messages in the same voice, or two messages in different voices to the two ears. In a divided attention experiment, the subject would be required to attend to both messages at the same time.

Most of the first studies were of selective attention. Results from studies by Broadbent (1952, 1954), Cherry (1953) and Poulton (1953, 1956) showed that both the physical acoustic differences between voices and the physical separation of locations were helpful for message selection. The most effective cue was physical separation. These results were taken to confirm that a listener can selectively attend to stimuli that possess some common physical feature and can reject stimuli that do not possess that feature. Cherry (1953) also showed that performance was better when subjects were told beforehand which channel was to be responded to, rather than when they were given instructions afterwards about which channel to report. Further, it was discovered that, when selective listening is compelled by requiring the subject to repeat the relevant message out loud as it arrives (this is called *shadowing*) subsequent recall tests revealed that subjects had virtually no memory for the information that had been presented to the unattended ear. Although there was very little memory for the content of the ignored message in terms of its meaning, or the language in which it was spoken (subjects did not notice if the unattended message changed from English to German), subjects did notice if the speaker's voice changed from that of a man to a woman, or if a bleep or tone was presented.

Taking all the evidence into account, Broadbent (1958) interpreted the data as demonstrating that stimuli that do not need response are, if possible, discarded before they have been fully processed, and that, as physical features of the input are effective cues for separating messages, there is a filter which operates at the level of physical features, allowing the information characterised by that feature through the filter for further processing. In unattended messages, only physical properties of the input seemed to be detected and it is these properties that can guide the setting of the filter.

Broadbent's (1958) book, *Perception and communication*, turned out to be extremely influential. With its publication, research into attention was resurrected, having been virtually ignored for many years. Part of the problem of investigating something like attention is that it is hard to observe. Attention is an internal process, and, as such, had been abandoned to philosophy when the behaviourist tradition dominated psychology. Part of Broadbent's contribution was to provide a means of conceptualising human performance in terms of information processing. Based on his own research and other contemporary evidence, Broadbent proposed a new conception of the mind, in which psychological processes could be described by the flow of information within the nervous system. Broadbent's model was to prove the starting point for modern theorising on attention, and the structure and underlying assumptions of the model have shaped the pattern of subsequent work. He drew three main conclusions. First he concluded that it was valuable to analyse human functions in terms of the flow of information through the organism. He believed it was possible to discuss information transmission in the abstract, without having to know the precise neural or physical basis of that transmission. This conception of the nervous system as an information processor was an extremely important and influential idea, signalling the beginning of the information-processing approach to psychology.

(See Eysenck & Keane, 1995, for an introduction to approaches in psychology).

The concept of information had arisen from communication theory (Shannon & Weaver, 1949). Information can be described mathematically, and not all signals carry the same amount of information. As uncertainty increases so does the amount of potential information. Fitts and Posner (1973) provide an accessible introduction to the topic, giving the example of tossing a coin: the statement "It will be either heads or tails" does not contain any information because knowing this does not reduce our uncertainty over which way the coin will come down. However, if we are told "It is tails" we have no uncertainty and have gained information. So, information reduces the amount of uncertainty present in a situation. Fitts and Posner use another everyday illustration to explain how the amount of information in a statement varies with the degree of uncertainty: if we are told which way a dice has fallen, we gain more information than when we are told which way a coin has fallen—this is because there are six possible outcomes for rolling the dice but only two possible outcomes for tossing the coin.

Broadbent was concerned with the transmission of information within the nervous system. Information transmission is maximal when a given stimulus always gives rise to the same response. When this happens, there is no uncertainty between the stimulus input and the response output. However, if a different response were to occur on some occasions, the amount of information transmitted would be reduced. If the amount of information transmitted is calculated and divided by the time taken to make the response, then the rate of information transmission can be found. The attraction of this information-processing approach to studying human performance is its ability to provide measures of otherwise non-observable internal processes.

Related to these measures of information is the measure of *redundancy*. In any situation where there is less than the maximum amount of information, there is redundancy. A good example is English spelling because there are different transitional probabilities between letters in words. When reading poor handwriting, our prior knowledge allows us to disambiguate the letters we find difficult to read. Thus, the presence of some letters predict, or constrain the possible letters that might follow. The most obvious example is that q is always followed by u: here, u is redundant because it is predicted by q. When redundancy is high, information is low and vice versa. Redundancy in language is also useful when we try to listen to something in a noisy situation because even if we hear only part of the input there is enough redundancy for us to understand the message. (Noise can also be mathematically expressed in information-processing terms.) Later, when we consider some results of experiments on dual-task performance in Chapter 7, and unconscious processing in Chapter 10, we shall see how the amount of information or redundancy in the messages can affect performance.

Broadbent borrowed the idea of the transmission of information within a telecommunications channel, and this brought with it a number of corollary assumptions, which led to Broadbent's second conclusion, that, as a communications system, the whole nervous system could be regarded as a single channel which was limited in the rate at which information could be transmitted. Third, for economy of mechanism, Broadbent concluded that the limited capacity section of the nervous system would need to be preceded by a selective filter, or switch, which protected the system from overload and passed on only some small, selected portion of the incoming information. All other information was blocked. These major conclusions were largely accepted, together with the necessity for a short-term buffer store that preceded the selective filter. This buffer was a temporary memory store in which the unselected information could be held, in parallel, for short periods of time. The model became known as Broadbent's Filter Theory. It is important to note that in this model, although information enters the system in parallel it is held only temporarily in the buffer memory. Unless information is selected to pass through the filter for further processing, that information is lost. Only when information passes through the filter into the limited capacity channel, which is a serial processor, is it identified. This means that selection from the parallel input is made at early levels of processing and is therefore an *early selection model*. Note also that this model is structural, in that it posits a sequence of information flow through a series of stages and transformations that are limited by structural properties of the proposed system.

Digressing for a moment, let us look at what has just been suggested. First, Broadbent has made the tacit assumption that, if a cue aids selection, the nature of the cue represents the level of analysis that has been achieved by the information that is selected. There is in fact no real reason to suppose that, because physical cues are effective in guiding selection of one message rather than another, that the messages have been processed only to the physical level. It is perfectly possible that there is much fuller processing of all inputs, but physical cues happen to be the best way of selecting channels. The assumption that an effective cue tells us about the degree of analysis of what is selected was not seriously challenged until van der Heijden (1981, 1993), whose ideas will be considered in Chapter 3. Second, almost all of the studies at this time were limited to studying selection of information within a single sensory modality; i.e. audition. Although the problems encountered by aviators were often in situations where information was coming in via both visual and auditory modalities and responses were having to be made as either motor outputs to control the plane, or spoken responses to give messages, the first model of attention is concerned with a very simple situation such as, "Repeat the message in one ear and ignore the other". Nothing else has to be done. In daily life we routinely find ourselves in far more complex situations than the dichotic listening task and should pause to consider how safely we can generalise the results of these experiments to life in the real world. In fairness, most psychology experiments have to be concerned with small-scale, well-controlled experiments, because otherwise it is difficult to know which variables are affecting behaviour and performance. However, to build a general theory of attention on attention in a single modality might be judged dangerous. We shall, however, see in the next chapter to what extent selection in audition experiments is like selection in vision experiments.

Returning to Broadbent (1958), here then was an elegantly simple model. The human information-processing system needed to be protected from overload and was therefore preceded by a selective filter which could be switched to whichever channel was required on the basis of some physical characteristic of the sensory input. Exactly how this switching was achieved is not clear. If attention needed to be divided, say, between both ears to monitor both messages at once, then the filter was said to be able to switch rapidly between channels on the basis of the spatial location or physical characteristics of information in the sensory buffer.

Broadbent (1954) experimented on the division of attention using simultaneous, dichotic presentation, in what became known as the *split-span* technique. The listener is presented with six digits, arranged into three successive pairs. In each pair, one digit is heard through a headphone to the right ear, with the other digit presented simultaneously to the left ear. When all three pairs (i.e. six digits) have been presented the subject is asked to recall as many digits as they can. The interesting finding here is that when all digits are reported correctly, it is usually the case that the subject reports the three items from one ear before the three items from the other ear. Thus, Broadbent argued, selection is ear by ear, and the second set of digits is waiting in the buffer store, to be output when the channel is switched. Even in this simple task it seemed that people could not simultaneously attend to both channels (ears) at once.

One of Broadbent's most important contributions was that he was one of the first people to produce a diagram of the flow of information through the nervous system. If we look at Fig. 2.1 we see there is parallel processing, indicated by multiple arrows, through the senses and short-term store as far as the selective filter. All processing beyond the selective filter is strictly serial. Broadbent believed that only information that passes through the limited capacity channel becomes conscious and can modify or become part of our long-term knowledge. He believed that in this way the filter controls what we know at a conscious level about the perceptual input. Our ability to apparently do two things at once can be explained by time-sharing, or multiplexing.

According to the theory, which allows only strictly serial processing, combining tasks that require continuous parallel processing is not possible. We only seem to be able to do two tasks at the same time, when those tasks can proceed momentarily without attention, allowing time for rapid switching between them. As the evidence stood at the time, the theory seemed to be perfectly plausible.

Modifications of filter theory

One of the good things about a rigid theory is that it generates strong predictions. In the new decade of the 1960s the search was on for experimental results that challenged Broadbent's original theory.

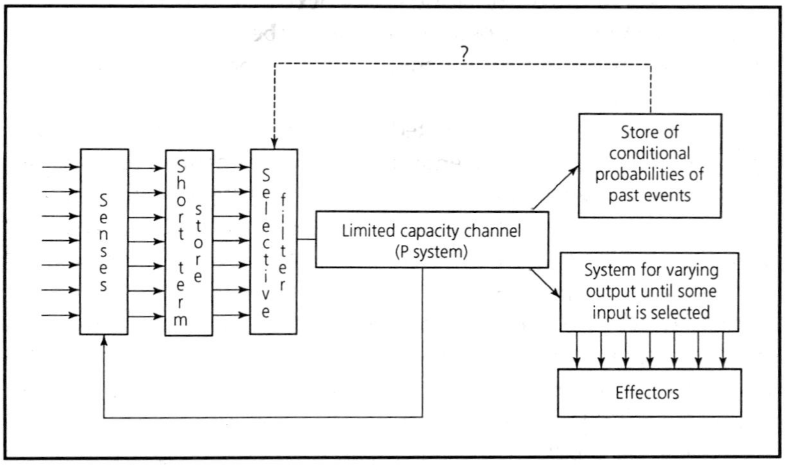

FIG. 2.1. Diagram of the flow of information within the nervous system, as conceived by Broadbent (1958) (reprinted by permission of Academic Press from Broadbent, 1971).

Note that many of the original assumptions were retained, such as the notion of some limit on computational capacity of the brain and the notion of a selective filter at which there was a bottleneck in processing. In general terms much of the new research was concerned with the search for the bottleneck. Research still continued with auditory stimuli using the tried and tested *split-span* and *shadowing* techniques. Some psychologists, most notably Sperling (1960), were beginning to try out new methods of studying selective visual attention, using the tachistoscope. We shall consider Sperling's work along with other experiments on selective visual attention in Chapter 3.

An immediate challenge to the 1958 version of filter theory came from a series of studies by Moray (1959). Using shadowing experiments Moray showed that when the same small set of words was repeated on the unattended ear, recognition memory for those words was very poor, even a few seconds after presentation. If the unshadowed words had received attention, they should have been easily recognisable. This result is predicted by filter theory and appears to support it. However, some of Moray's results were not consistent with the predictions of Broadbent's theory. For example, Moray found that listeners often recognised their own name when it was presented on the unshadowed, and, in theory, unattended ear. This was quite contradictory to the notion of a selective filter that allowed input to the serial, limited capacity channel only on the basis of physical attributes. Remember, it is only when information gains access to the limited capacity system that the subject becomes consciously aware of its occurrence. Moray's results suggest that there is more analysis of unattended information than Broadbent thought. In particular, there must be some parallel semantic processing prior to conscious identification. We should note, however, that in Moray's experiment subjects were not generally able to recognise words from the unattended message, only particularly relevant words, such as the subjects' name, were likely to break through the filter. Recently, Wood and Cowan (1995) have replicated Moray's original experiment under much more tightly controlled conditions and found very similar results. Wood and Cowan found that 34.6% of subjects recalled hearing their name on the unattended channel (Moray's result was 33.3%) and that subjects who detected their name, monitored the irrelevant channel for a short time afterwards. So, although some of the early experiments may have had methodological flaws, their results are still robust.

Breakthrough of the unattended was studied in more detail by Anne Treisman (1960). Treisman has continued to work on attention right up to the present day, and we shall examine her feature integration theory (FIT) of visual attention in Chapter 5. Just remember that when people talk about Treisman's theory of attention, you need to know which one they are referring to. Back in the 1960s Treisman provided more experimental evidence that was inconsistent with original filter theory. She showed that, even if a subject is attending to the stream of events on one channel, there may be information breakthrough from the unattended message, especially if there is a meaningful relation between what is currently being attended and what is coming in on the unattended channel. Subjects were told to shadow a story (story 1) on one ear and to ignore the other story (story 2) that was concurrently presented to the other ear. Whilst the subject was shadowing story 1, story 1 was switched to the other, presumably unattended, ear; story 2 ceased to be presented to the unattended ear and a new story (story 3) came in to replace story 1 on the attended ear. According to Broadbent's initial theory, subjects would have their selective filter set to the attended ear, or channel, and would have no knowledge about the meaning of information on the channel that was blocked off. So when the stories were switched, they should have immediately carried on, shadowing the new story, story 3. However, Treisman found that, as soon as the stories were switched, subjects shadowed a few words from story 1 from the unattended ear before picking up story 3 from what should be the attended ear.

The difficulty of selecting one message on the basis of its content, when two messages in the same voice were presented to the same channel, initially studied by Cherry (1953), was further examined in a series of studies by Treisman (1964a,b,c). She asked her subjects to shadow one message and ignore the other. The relevant message was always a female voice reading a passage from a novel, and the irrelevant message was sometimes in the same voice, sometimes in a different voice. In one condition, Treisman compared performance when the unattended message was a passage from the same novel with the case where the unattended message was a technical passage about biochemistry, a message in a foreign language, or nonsense syllables. The subjects' ability to shadow the attended message was significantly affected by the content of the material in the unattended message, with the most difficult condition being when the same voice was reading two passages from the same novel. Shadowing the passage from a novel was easier when it was concurrently presented with the biochemical passage. When the unattended passage was in a foreign language, it made a difference whether the subject knew the language or not. Overall, these experiments showed that a difference in the semantic content of the two messages could be used to aid selection, but that a content difference is much less effective than a physical difference. These results are inconsistent with a strict filter that operates only on the physical characteristics of the input, and they are in accordance with the previous experiment by Moray. It was now clear that selection from the parallel stages of processing could be much later, or further along the processing continuum, than Broadbent had initially thought. This new evidence led Deutsch and Deutsch (1963) to propose a rather different view of selective attention which could account for semantic effects of the "unattended" message.

Is selection later rather than earlier?

This theory from Deutsch and Deutsch has been interpreted as the first *late-selection theory*. Here the bottleneck was still present but the limit on parallel processing was much nearer the response stage than the identification stage. Collecting together evidence from experiments such as those by Moray (1959) and from studies that showed EEG (electroencephalogram) changes, during sleep, to the presentation of a subject's name, they suggested that "a message will reach the same perceptual and discriminatory mechanisms whether attention is paid to it or not; and such information is then grouped or segregated by these mechanisms" (Deutsch & Deutsch, 1963, p.83). They suggested that incoming signals were weighted for importance and in some way compared to determine the currently most important signal. At the time they felt that any comparison mechanism that had to compare every possible incoming signal with all other possible signals would make decision times extremely slow, if not impossible. Connecting every possible incoming signal to all other possibilities seemed out of the question. Today, with the advent of connectionist, parallel distributed computational methods, this multiple comparison process is no longer considered difficult, but in the early 1960s the brain was likened to computers which were serial limited capacity devices. Deutsch and Deutsch therefore suggested a simple analogy. Imagine you wanted to find out which boy in the class was the tallest. You could measure each one individually, but this would take time. However, if you gathered all the boys together and placed a board over their heads, the boy whose head touched the board would be the tallest, and he would immediately know that fact. If you took that boy out of the group, the board would come to rest on the next tallest boy's head. The same system could compare signals. If, as each signal arrived, it pushed up some "level" that reflected its own "height" or importance, then any other signal that would be of less importance, would be below this level. However, if the most important signal ceases, the level will then fall to that of next most important signal. Thus the level is determined by the signals present, and Deutsch and Deutsch suggested that only the most important signals switch in other processes like memory storage and motor output.

The model assumes that all sensory messages are perceptually analysed at the highest level. When the subject is at normal levels of arousal, the signal that is at the highest level will enter memory or evoke a response. However, if the individual is drowsy or asleep a signal will evoke a response only if it crosses the current level of a fluctuating arousal system. Thus Deutsch and Deutsch (1963) propose that in all cases the signal of the highest importance will be responded to, or the subject alerted by it, provided its activity is above the current arousal level. In this way the most important message will have been selected, not at an early level, but after full processing.

Additional evidence consistent with the idea that selection could proceed on the basis of meaning was supplied by a modification of the split-span experiment, done by Gray and Wedderburn (1960). Remember that, when Broadbent had presented pairs of digits to both ears simultaneously, the preferred order of report was ear by ear. Gray and Wedderburn presented the following kind of stimulus pairs: *mice, one, cheese,* to the right ear, while simultaneously presenting *four, eat, two* to the left ear. Subjects in this experiment did not preferentially report ear by ear, but grouped the information by meaning; so they reported, *mice, eat, cheese* and *four, one, two.*

The early–late debate begins

Although Treisman has provided some of the evidence that led to Deutsch and Deutsch proposing their late-selection view of attentional selection, she herself considered that a modification to Broadbent's original theory was more appropriate. Breakthrough of the unattended happened only occasionally, and in fact rather infrequently. In 1960, Treisman showed that on only 6% of trials subjects reported a word from the unattended channel if that word was highly probable. Put another way this shows that on 94% of trials there is no breakthrough at all. If all incoming information was processed fully it seemed unlikely that there could be so little breakthrough. Treisman (1964a) proposed that the filter was not such an all-or-nothing affair as Broadbent had said. Rather than blocking out all information that does not meet the selection criterion for attention, the filter attenuated or reduced the strength of the unattended channels. If incoming information was not totally blocked off, then partial information that was consistent with current expectations (e.g. the continuation of the stories in Treisman's shadowing tasks) or personally relevant (e.g. the subject's name in Moray's 1959 study) might be sufficient to raise the activation of those words above the threshold of consciousness. See Fig. 2.2.

Treisman (1964, 1969) put forward ideas similar to those best known as Morton's logogen model (Morton, 1969, 1979), which is concerned with interactive processes in reading. Morton (1969) proposed that word recognition was mediated by *logogens*. Each word that we know has a logogen which collects both perceptual and semantic evidence. When there is sufficient evidence to raise the logogen above its threshold, the logogen fires and becomes available for response; in some sense we "know" about it. When we listen to a sentence, the words at the beginning of the sentence will lead us to expect certain other words to follow. These expectations, based on semantic knowledge, prime or raise the activation level of the logogens for the most likely words. For example, "The cat sat on the...........?" If "rainbow" is the next word, you will be slower to read it than if "mat" were the next word. "Mat" is quite clearly printed here but if the print were indistinct, or had coffee spilt over it, the perceptual input would be degraded and top-down processes would help disambiguate the bottom-up input, making it more likely that you could read "mat" than "rainbow".

Rather than logogens, Treisman initially proposed that the nervous system contained a set of dictionary units, each of which corresponded to a word. Different words have different thresholds depending on their salience and probability. If the attenuator has the effect of reducing the perceptual input from the unattended channels, then only when words are highly probable or salient, will their thresholds be sufficiently low for the small perceptual input to make the dictionary unit fire. Thus the attenuator can account quite neatly for breakthrough of the unattended at the same time as providing almost perfect selection most of the time.

In his next book on attention, *Decision and stress*, Broadbent (1971) modified his original theory somewhat, although he said that as the 1958 model was so general, the changes were not major. To meet the challenge of the data since 1958 he expanded the role of the filter and

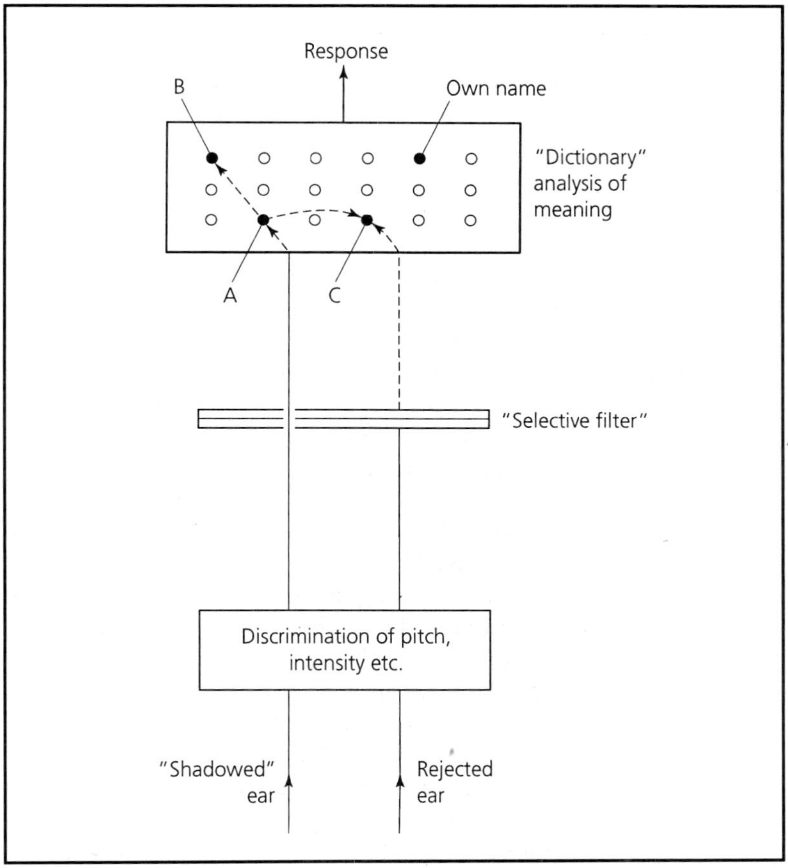

FIG. 2.2. Modified theory of attention, introduced by Treisman (1960) (reprinted by permission of Academic Press from Broadbent, 1971). Following occurrence of word A, the thresholds of words B and C are lowered because they are very probable following word A. If word C is activated by the attenuated signal from the rejected ear, it may be heard.

added two new selection processes; pigeon-holing and categorising. Filtering was seen as grouping the input on the basis of simple characteristics and this information passes to higher levels. The results of filtering only represent "evidence" for the stimulus from the outside world. So, although the evidence may suggest that one state of the environment, or stimulus, is more likely than another, this is not certain. However, although there may be ambiguity over the state of the outside world, the output of the limited capacity channel must be either one state or the other. Broadbent named this the *category state*. To determine which category state is best fitted to the evidence, a decision is required, and rather than information theory which was the basis for the 1958 model, Broadbent (1971) frames his explanation in terms of statistical decision theory. This allows for the concept of noise, or uncertainty, to be incorporated into the system.

So, firstly, selective filtering links the stimulus states to states of evidence. Rather than the all-or-nothing filter of the 1958 model, Broadbent accepted Anne Treisman's modification of the original filter theory which allowed some stimuli to be responded to on the basis of less evidence than others. Now, as he explained in his 1982 paper, the filter was seen as a strategy to allow performance under conditions where interference would otherwise occur. Filtering did not block out everything about the unattended: some features could break through and other features could trigger other later processes. Another concept introduced in 1971 was *pigeon-holing*. This refers to the process which relates the evidence from the filter to a category state. Pigeon-holing alters the number of states of evidence which lead to any particular category state. Broadbent (1982) says pigeon-holing is rather like filtering, except instead of selecting on the basis of features, selection operated by biasing the threshold of a category state, which has the effect of allowing some categories to be triggered by less evidence than would normally be needed. So, for example, if you were asked to listen for the name of an animal, you would very rapidly respond to animal words irrespective of the voice in which they were spoken and you would be more responsive to animal words than, say, words to do with fruit.

Bundesen (1990) put forward a unified theory of visual recognition and attentional selection in which he explicitly modelled these two attentional mechanisms, filtering and pigeon-holing, proposed by Broadbent (1971). Bundesen's paper is rather mathematical and contains detailed mathematical modelling of many visual attention tasks. However, the maths need not concern us here; we shall simply consider the concepts of filtering and pigeon-holing. Bundesen defines filtering as the selection of elements from the visual field and pigeon-holing as the selection of categories. The filtering mechanism increases the probability of elements from the target category being selected "without biassing perception in favour of perceiving the elements as belonging to a particular category" (Bundesen, 1990, p.525). This is achieved by using attentional weights derived from pertinence values. Selection of elements belonging to one category are favoured over elements belonging to other categories by increasing the attentional weights of elements belonging to the pertinent category. For example, Bundesen explains that in a task where red digits are to be selected in favour of black digits, the pertinence values of the perceptual category *red* would be high and the pertinence values of *black* would be low. The difference in pertinence values has the effect of speeding the perceptual processing of red elements and as a process is filtering, in that it changes the probability that a red element is detected. However, to recognise the identity of the red digits, pigeon-holing is necessary to bias the system to recognise identity rather than another attribute of the stimulus, such as size. According to Bundesen, pigeon-holing is "a pure categorical bias mechanism, complementary to filtering" (Bundesen, 1990, p.525). So, to identify a red digit, perceptual bias parameters would be set high for digits and low for all other pertinence values. This biasing speeds the categorisation process for digit relative to other attributes. In this example, the categorisation *digit* is favoured by the categorical bias mechanism. Bundesen's (1990) theory of visual attention (TVA) is incorporated by Logan (1996) into another mathematical theory of attention, CTVA, which is covered later in Chapter 5.

In his last review of task combination and selective attention Broadbent (1982) was still in favour of the attenuation alternative to the all-or-none filter, and held to the view that selection was early, saying that late-selection models "are driven by the need to explain breakthrough and have not developed explanations for these other phenomena" (Broadbent, 1982, p.261). These other phenomena included problems of task combination, the question of why unattended events do not provide context for attended events, and why false percepts are provoked by unattended information. Broadbent believed that if all unattended events were fully analysed these problems should not arise.

However, by the end of the 1960s there was sufficient evidence for at least some parallel processing up to higher levels of analysis for experimenters to begin to try to distinguish more clearly the precise location of the rate limiting stage or bottleneck. Psychologists at this time were deeply entrenched in their belief that the nervous system was, indeed, as Broadbent had suggested a serial processor of limited capacity, and that some processes were logically *earlier* or *later* than others. These kinds of assumptions have been challenged by Allport (1980, 1993) who points to the increasingly clear evidence that the brain computes information in parallel over multiple specialised processing systems and that we should be considering what attention is designed to achieve in the control of coherent human behaviour. We shall examine these ideas in much more detail in Chapter 6. For the moment, you should also note that what might have started out as rather general questions about attention, such as what causes some messages to be difficult to select, seems to have become crystallised into a single question about where, in some kind of structural system, the change from parallel to serial processing happens. This question is, of course, important. Parallel processes proceed "automatically" without the need for attention, whereas attentional processing does seem to be limited. Psychologists did want to be able to characterise those processes which were attentional and which were not, and so the search for the processing bottleneck continued. Remember, though, that discovering precisely where selection occurs is only one small part of the issues surrounding attention, and finding *where* selection takes place may not help us to understand *why* or *how* this happens. Nevertheless, any theory has to account for the experimental results, and in the search for the bottleneck psychologists certainly collected plenty of data!

The search for the bottleneck

Rather like Deutsch and Deutsch (1963), Norman (1968) believed that sensory inputs were extensively processed automatically and unconsciously before we consciously know about them. He believed that this processing relied heavily on the permastore of information in long-term memory. Sensory features of the input automatically addressed their location in semantic memory so that if the input matched some stored representation, the meaning would be accessed. If the input was a nonsense word—had no pre-existing representation—no meaning would be found, indicating that the input was not a word. In Norman's model, selection comes after semantic memory has been accessed, and both attended and unattended sources of information have automatic and effortless access to semantics. Once semantics have been activated, pertinence values are assigned to those activations according to current ongoing cognitive activities. Pertinence is determined by the context of the inputs and activates nodes, or locations in semantic memory. Selection is then based on the summation of activation in semantic memory from both sensory input and context. This account may seem rather like Treisman's attenuator, in that highly probable inputs are more likely to be selected because of an interaction between priming and input. However, Treisman placed the attenuator at the beginning of the system, prior to the place where long-term knowledge is stored, whereas Norman placed the selective, attentional process after parallel access to semantic memory. Also, Norman's model has some aspects in common with that of Deutsch and Deutsch (1963); but rather than complete analysis of all inputs to the highest level, Norman allowed attention to be a matter of degree. Pertinence values are assigned at all levels of processing, and the pertinence value may change with further processing. A message that initially seems of low pertinence, may be found to be more pertinent following further processing. Finally, most messages will have been rejected, leaving only the most pertinent to become most deeply processed. Norman's model can easily account for the effects of semantics that were troublesome for original filter theory. Highly probable words that are presented to the unattended ear will be attended because of the effect of context-determined pertinence. Lewis (1970) did an experiment that showed how the relation between the shadowed or attended message and the unshadowed or unattended message affected shadowing rate. Words presented to the unattended ear were semantically related, associatively related, or unrelated to the message being shadowed. Although subjects were unable to remember anything from the unattended ear, the time it took them to say the shadowed words was greater when there was a semantic relation between the two. This effect is predicted by Norman's model, as the unconscious semantic processing slowed the processing of the attended words.

A number of other experiments were devised to measure the effects of unattended semantic information. For example, Corteen and Wood (1972) and Corteen and Dunn (1973) did some intriguing experiments using galvanic skin response (GSR). When subjects expect to get a small electric shock, their skin resistance changes. This is what GSR measures. Corteen and colleagues conditioned subjects to expect a shock in association with a particular set of words; in this case words to do with the city. These subjects were then given a dichotic listening task and asked to attend to one ear while ignoring information on the other ear. Every so often, one of the shock-associated words was presented on the unattended channel, and the subjects showed a clear GSR, although they claimed that they did not detect any of those words. Interestingly, these subjects also showed a GSR to other city words that had not been included in the training set. This result suggests that not only was there semantic access of the unattended words, but there was also semantic generalisation. Other experimenters have found similar results. Lackner and Garrett (1972) demonstrated that the interpretation of an ambiguous sentence could be biased by the presentation of an unattended sentence that suggested one particular interpretation of the sentence. McKay (1973) presented ambiguous sentences in a dichotic listening task. Subjects shadowed sentences like, "They threw stones at the bank yesterday". Here bank was ambiguous, in that the sentence would have been equally sensible if you were thinking of a river bank or a high street money bank. McKay found that if the word "river" was presented on the unattended channel, subjects did not remember having heard "bank", but interpreted the sentence in terms of river bank rather than money bank. Experiments like these can be interpreted as providing more evidence that the selective processes in attention come after the meaning of words has been accessed.

Other proponents of late selection put forward their own versions of attentional theory. These theories are still structural, and are concerned with the location of a bottleneck, where parallel processing stops and serial processing begins. Johnston and Heinz (1978) allow the bottleneck to move in a flexible way, so that selection will take place as early as possible in processing, but exactly where selection happens will depend on current task demands and prevailing circumstances. They suggest that the more stages of processing that are required prior to selection, the greater will be the demands on processing capacity. Duncan (1980) suggested that selection involved passage between two levels, where that passage is controlled by a "selector". Only information which is passed through the selector gains awareness or the ability to control a response, but all stimuli are fully identified at level 1. The limit in Duncan's model is entry to level 2, where awareness can deal efficiently only with one stimulus at a time.

It began to seem as if the bottleneck metaphor was wearing thin. As soon as the bottleneck can be moved around, or can be hypothesised to be located at either end or almost anywhere in the processing continuum, perhaps it ceases to be a bottleneck after all. However, remember Welford's (1952) evidence on the psychological refractory period (PRP)? This clearly showed some limit on simultaneous processing. We shall meet PRP again in Chapter 7, where Pashler (1990) provides evidence that this limitation is real. But next, in Chapter 3, we shall discover that there is some evidence from experiments on visual attention that the level of processing at which selective attention operates might depend on the task being performed. At the time it was beginning to look as if a different metaphor from the single channel processor was needed. Norman (1968) proposed that there was no fixed, structural point where the system was limited; rather, the system is limited by having only a fixed amount of processing *resources*. The concept of resource limitation began to gain popularity: psychologists began to experiment on the limits of task combination and examine how these resources could be shared between tasks. We shall look at resource theory in Chapter 7.

Summary

Initial research suggested that the human information-processing system was limited in its ability to perform multiple tasks. Broadbent (1958) proposed that the human could be likened to a single channel for processing information. The single channel selected information to be passed through a protective filter on the basis of physical characteristics. Only this selected information was passed on to be identified. Evidence of semantic processing for material presented on the unattended channel led to the suggestion that all information was preattentively analysed for meaning but only the most important signals were passed on to the response stage (Deutsch & Deutsch, 1963). Treisman (1964) introduced a compromise theory in which the unattended information was attenuated, so that only the most important signals were able to break through the filter. Other theories suggested that the selective bottleneck between preattentive parallel processing and serial attentive processing could move according to different circumstances and task demands (Johnston & Heinz, 1978; Norman, 1968). New ideas (to be dealt with in Chapter 4) which viewed attention as a pool of processing resources, began to gain popularity.

Further reading

Every introductory book on cognition has a section on early-attention experiments and theory. Here are a few examples.

Hirst, W. (1986). The psychology of attention. In J.E. LeDoux & W. Hirst (Eds.), *Mind and brain: Dialogues in cognitive neuroscience.* London: Cambridge University Press.

Eysenck, M.W., & Keane, M.T. (1995). *Cognitive psychology: A student's handbook* (3rd ed.). Hove, UK: Lawrence Erlbaum Associates Ltd.

Hampson, P.J., & Morris, P.E. (1996). *Understanding cognition*. Oxford: Blackwell.

Selective report and interference effects in visual attention 3

Introduction

We now turn to selective attention experiments using visual stimuli. There is such a large literature on visual attention that I have chosen to break it down into three chapters. To a great extent the issues raised in Chapter 2—what kinds of information can be used to guide selective attention, what limits selectivity, and where in the continuum of processing selection is made—will continue here. Other related issues concerning visual attention—what visual attention actually does, how it is directed, and whether it is directed to coordinates in space or to objects—will be addressed in Chapters 4 and 5.

The division of material between chapters is somewhat arbitrary and, really, these chapters need to be read together. However, to maintain some structure, I have tried to break up the issues. For the present we shall examine some of the data on selective reports from brief visual displays and see how this can help us to understand the nature of information made available to the rest of the processing system. Unlike auditory information, which is a pattern of frequencies distributed in time, visual information is distributed in space and usually endures over time. In visual experiments the whole display can be presented simultaneously in parallel, which allows different kinds of experiments. Not only can we look at selective filtering from brief visual displays, but we can control the time for which a stimulus is available and manipulate the physical and/or the semantic relationship between targets and distractors.

Selective filtering and selective set

Kahneman and Treisman (1984) made an important distinction between two broad categories of visual attention task, selective filtering and selective set. They point out that most of the early experiments involved tasks where subjects have to select a message or stimulus from a quite complex environment and select a response from a wide choice. For example, when shadowing a message the words to be spoken might come from a wide vocabulary, rather than being simply "Yes" or "No". Accuracy of report is generally taken as the dependent measure. From about 1970 onwards a rather different kind of experiment became the norm, which Kahneman and Treisman call *selective set* experiments. Here, the stimulus set is usually small, the stimuli are simple, and they require a response from a small set of possibilities. In these experiments the usual measure of performance is reaction time. We shall see in the following experiments that some involve selective filtering, while others might be better considered as selective set experiments. The difference in demand of the two paradigms might explain some of the conflicting evidence that emerges from them.

Selective filtering from brief visual displays

Sperling's experiments

In a classic series of experiments George Sperling (1960) investigated peoples' ability to selectively report items from very brief visual displays. Sperling presented stimuli using a tachistoscope. The tachistoscope was invented in the 1880s, but modern ones are essentially the same except they are automatically, electronically controlled. In essence a tachistoscope is a light-proof box. The subject looks in one end and the stimulus is placed in the other end. However as the box is light-proof and dark inside, the subject cannot see the stimulus until a light is switched on. Using special lighting tubes, which onset and offset extremely quickly, the duration of the light and hence exposure duration, can be carefully controlled to an accuracy of a few milliseconds (ms). By using half-silvered mirrors, a number of viewing fields can be added to the box, each field having its own lighting control. The most usual tachistoscope has three fields, one for the stimulus, one for a fixation point, where the subject looks in preparation for the stimulus, and the third field can have a *probe* that marks the stimulus position to be reported, or a *mask* which functions to disrupt, degrade or terminate stimulus processing. (For an accessible review of masking, see Humphreys & Bruce, 1989.)

Sperling (1960) found that when subjects were presented with visual arrays lasting 50ms, containing twelve letters, they were able to report only about four or five items. However, subjects said they could "see" the whole display for a short time after the display was terminated. The data suggested that, although all items were initially represented in a brief visual memory, there was some limit on the rate at which items could be retrieved from this store before they had decayed. Sperling believed the pattern of results was evidence for a high capacity, fast decay, visual memory store which faded over a short time and that, unless this rapidly fading memory for visual information was transformed into another, more permanent state, it was lost. This brief visual information store was subsequently named by Neisser (1967) *iconic memory*.

Sperling then introduced an important modification: instead of asking the subject to report the whole display, he gave them a cue immediately after display offset, which indicated which row they were to report selectively. When the cue was a tone (three different pitched tones corresponded to the three rows) subjects could report virtually all the items from the cued row. Note that the subjects had no idea which row would be asked for. This showed that they must have perceived all twelve items in the display and could selectively report the cued subset.

The partial report superiority effect

Next, Sperling investigated what happened if he delayed presenting the tone. As the delay between display offset and tone presentation increased the proportion of items that could be reported decreased, until after a delay of 500ms, subjects' performance was no better than in the whole report (WR) condition, as presumably, iconic memory had completely decayed away. The advantage that cueing gives is called the partial report (PR) superiority effect and suggests that the cue (in this case a tone) can be used to allow a subset of items to be selectively transferred to a later stage of processing. In effect, this is the same as using a physical location cue, such as left or right ear, to select one auditory message from another. Although Sperling was investigating the nature of what we now call *iconic memory*, his results are of importance in studies of attention, because they can tell us something about which cues are, or are not, effective for guiding selective attention among a complex display of visual stimuli. In the partial report (PR) condition, selective attention allows the stimuli indicated by the cue to be preferentially reported: see Fig. 3.1.

As the PR advantage was found when a tone indicated which row to report, it seemed evident that the spatial locations of the items in the display must have been represented in iconic memory. Subsequent

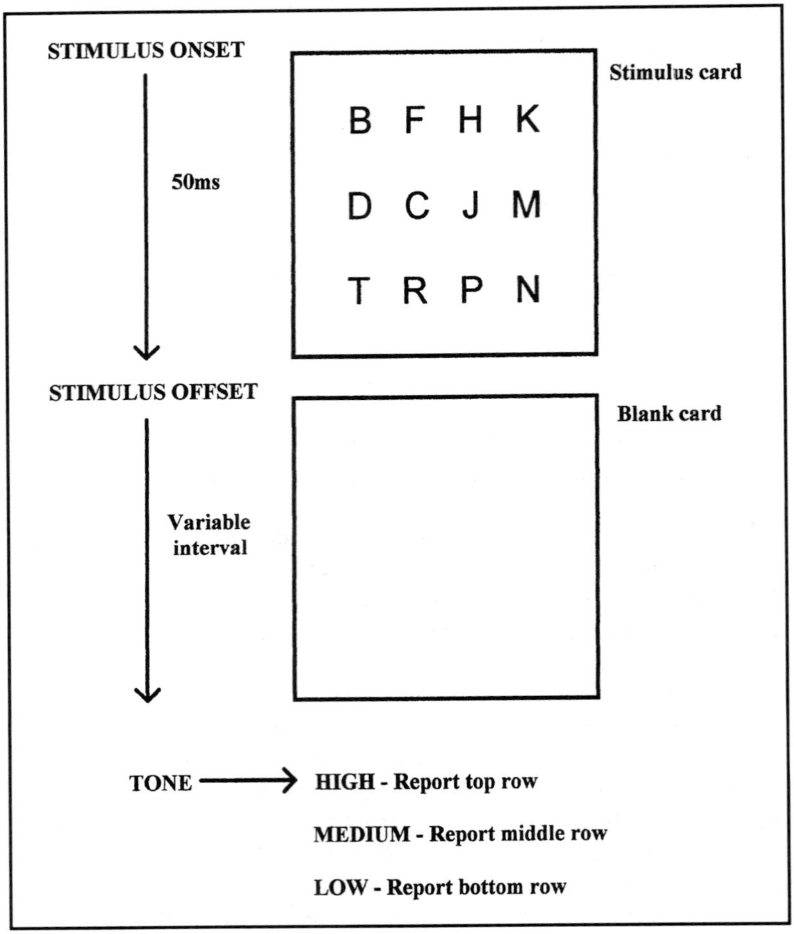

FIG. 3.1. Diagram of the sort of display used by Sperling (1960). In whole report, the subject reports non-selectively from the display; in partial report, the row indicated by the cue (tone) is to be reported. In both conditions report is after the display has terminated.

experiments have shown that other cues such as colour (Dick, 1969; Von Wright, 1969, 1970), size or shape (Turvey & Kravetz, 1970), will also allow selective processing. A bar-marker, or probe, can also be used to indicate visually which location in a row is to be reported. Averbach and Coriell (1961) carried out a similar experiment to Sperling's, but they presented only two rows of letters, followed at varying intervals by a bar-marker to probe a given location in the row. They found that when the probe was presented immediately after display offset, report of the probed letter was very good, but as the probe delay increased, there was a corresponding decrease in the probability of the correct letter being reported. This result is analogous to the PR advantage declining with cue delay.

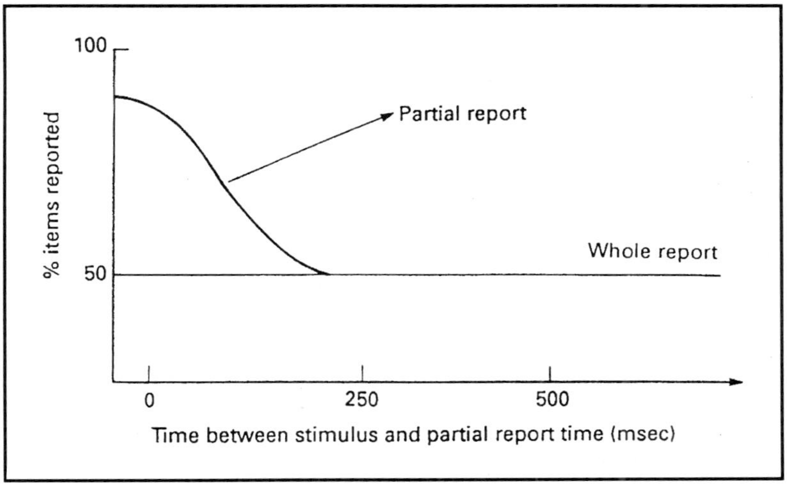

FIG. 3.2. Schematic description of results from partial report experiment, showing partial report superiority and loss of this advantage as the stimulus–cue interval increases (reprinted by permission of Psychology Press from Humphreys and Bruce, 1989).

Rather like auditory filtering experiments, it seems as if physical cues are effective in allowing selective report. Another potential cue for selection is the category of the item: for example, whether the target is a letter or a digit. However, Sperling found that if item category was given as the post-exposure cue there was no PR advantage and hence argued that the representation from which selection was made was pre-categorical; i.e. before category membership had been determined. If category membership was not represented in iconic memory, then, of course, it could not act as a basis for selection. This is the same assumption made by Broadbent (1958) in his auditory selection experiments. We shall see, however, that this assumption may in fact be false.

An interesting experiment was done by Mewhort (1967) who presented his subjects with two rows of letters and used a post-exposure tone to indicate which row to report. Sometimes the information in the uncued, irrelevant row was just a string of letters, like YRULPZOC; and sometimes the row was more like a word: for example, VERNALIT. Mewhort found that the content of the irrelevant row had an effect on the number of letters reported from the cued row: when the row was VERNALIT, subjects reported more from the cued row than when the uncued row was not like English. This result shows that subjects must have been processing the uncued row, otherwise it could not have affected performance. Subjects could not have been completely ignoring the irrelevant row, just as we saw that subjects were affected by information on the ignored, or unattended channel in dichotic listening experiments. Mewhort's data indicated that the meaning of unattended items can "breakthrough" to influence processing of attended information. Thus, iconic memory could not be a purely visual store containing solely the visual properties of colour and location: if it were, semantics should have no effect. The puzzle here is that while there is evidence of semantics influencing processing, subjects cannot use semantics as a PR cue.

We do, now, have evidence that semantic and categorical properties of the stimulus can act as a basis for selective report. Dick (1974) reviewed the usefulness of various cues for selective report from iconic memory. If a cue declines in efficiency over time, the assumption is that its representation fades and is lost with time. Partial report for colour and location decline with instruction delay, but a category cue (letters or numbers) does not show this decline. Further, Dick (1971) analysed a number of experiments using partial report, in terms of accuracy as a function of response position. He found that when order of report was scored, whole report accuracy was always greater than partial report accuracy, for all response positions. Graves (1976) investigated whether more items were identified than could be reported from a tachistoscopic array and found that when position of report is required, the number of items identified together with their correct position was no greater in partial report than in whole report. Item identity and the position of the item in the display seemed to separate out. Later experiments by Merikle (1980) showed that if the letters to be reported from amongst digits were formed into a perceptual group, either by the spatial arrangement of the display or by a colour difference, then there was an added advantage of having the category difference which was larger than the physical difference on its own, Merikle argued that the reason a category cue (e.g. "Report the letters not the digits") does not easily produce a PR superiority effect was because a category difference does not form a perceptual group. Later we shall see that experimenters are now convinced that perceptual grouping is an important factor in selective attention.

In summary, the results of these experiments demonstrate that, although subjects say they have seen all the items from a brief display, they are severely limited in their ability to report them all. However, it is the case that more items can be reported than can be accurately integrated with their position in the display. Only when partial report is of identity alone, does it exceed whole report. Physical attributes such as colour or location act as efficient cues for selection, and as such would seem to support an early selection account of visual attention. However Mewhort's (1967) and Merikle's (1980) results show that there is breakthrough of categorical information which affects selection, suggesting that a late interpretation—in which both visual and semantic properties of the visual display are represented in iconic memory—is a better interpretation.

The experiments so far have been investigating how much of the information in a brief visual display is processed and how selection of a subset of that information is achieved. The next experiments are more concerned with how little can be processed; i.e. how selective can selective visual attention be.

Selective set experiments

The Eriksen paradigm

In 1974 Eriksen and Eriksen introduced an experimental paradigm which has been widely adopted by many later experimenters as a useful selective visual attention task. We shall encounter the Eriksen task several more times with respect to interference effects and selective attention: for example, Lavie (1995) later in this chapter; in Chapter 4, Driver and Baylis (1989); in Chapter 7, with the psychological refractory period, Fagot and Pashler (1992). There have been many other experiments by Eriksen and his colleagues, some of which we shall review here, which are all versions of the same task. Eriksen (1995) provides a short review of the usefulness of his task for investigating a variety of cognitive problems.

According to Kahenman and Treisman's definition, the Eriksen task is closer to a selective set experiment than a filtering experiment. Subjects are presented with only a few items, which have well-defined responses from a small set, and performance is measured by reaction time. Remember, a filtering experiment usually involves many items, a large response set, and accuracy is the dependent measure. In the original version of the Eriksen task, subjects are instructed that there are two sets of letters which are to be responded to by moving a lever in either one direction or another. For example, H and K are mapped onto one direction, but S is mapped onto the other. The subjects' task is to respond as quickly as possible to the central letter of a row of five. Eriksen and Eriksen (1974) showed that when two letters (H and K) are assigned to the same lever response, a target H is responded to more slowly in displays like SSHSS, where lever responses are incompatible, than in KKHKK displays where lever responses are compatible. This effect is called the flanker compatibility effect (FCE). The data clearly implicate response competition as the source of interference between the letters in the display, for, unless the distractors had been analysed to the point where their responses were activated, no response level differences in interference should arise. Here, then, we have further evidence that identity information from the to-be-ignored, response-irrelevant stimuli is available to the processing system, even though in some selective report conditions (e.g. Sperling's selective filtering experiment) this identity information cannot control selective report. Of course there is another difference between the two studies. Sperling showed the display for a very short time, and in the partial report condition subjects did not know which row they would have to report until after the display had terminated and would not have had time to make eye movements around the display to search each location. In the Eriksen experiment, subjects know where the target will appear and what they have to do before stimulus onset. Clearly these tasks place very different demands on the subject and therefore may be tapping quite different kinds or levels of attentional operation. We shall return to this point at the end of the chapter.

Eriksen and Eriksen (1974) also discovered that interference from response incompatible distractors was dependent on the spatial separation of the distractors from the target, and that, once the distractors were within one degree of visual angle of the target, they could not be ignored. As selective attention seemed unable to exclude distractors within this region, the notion of a minimum width *spotlight* emerged, with stimuli falling under the spotlight being fully processed. In the next chapter we shall review a variety of evidence regarding the nature of the attentional spotlight and what processing goes on within it. For the present we shall continue the debate on the level of processing achieved by attended and unattended stimuli in visual displays.

A completely contradictory result to that of Eriksen and Eriksen (1974) was found by Bjork and Murray (1977) who showed that the best inhibitor for a target letter is another example of the same letter. For example, if the target is B, the strongest inhibition is found when the flanker is another B. Let's call this the BB effect. According to the Eriksen experiments, as B and B have the same response there should be no interference between them. However, Bjork and Murray argue that, in this case, interference is due to feature specific interference between signal and noise elements in a display, which results in competition at an early level of feature extraction. Bjork and Murray's (1977) feature specific theory of interference effects in visual attention is an extension of Estes' (1972, 1974) theory, in which it is assumed that there are separate feature detectors for separate features and that associated with each feature detector are a number of input channels distributed over the visual field. When a visual array is presented, the elements of that display are processed in parallel, and if a feature set comprising a target is present with sufficient accuracy, a primary detection response is made. If there is no primary detection response, there may be a secondary detection response, which is slower and less likely to be correct. Input channels associated with the target can be put into a state of heightened excitability, and this excitation exerts an inhibitory influence on other channels going to the same or other feature detectors. The net result is a limited capacity bottleneck at the point where the parallel input reaches the feature detectors, due to the inhibitory influence of input channels on each other. Bjork and Murray's theory states that interference is more specific, in that the strongest inhibition on a specific feature detector comes from another detector for the same feature. Thus, when detectors for the same feature are activated close to each other, competition is at its greatest, which will make B most difficult to detect when it is adjacent to another B. This result is difficult for any late, or post-categorical theory of attention, because according to the late view, if both the Bs were concurrently active, there should be a facilitation of the response to B.

Further experiments by Eriksen and colleagues (Eriksen & Schultz, 1979) contradicted Bjork and Murray (1977) again. These experiments showed that in the display HHHHH where the response is the same for both lever movement and letter identity, the response to the central H was faster than when only the lever movement was compatible; for example, if the display was KKHKK when both K and H are mapped onto the same lever response. This result demonstrates a FCE for the letter names as well, and we shall call this the HHH effect. Again, we have clear evidence for response level interference effects rather than feature level interference effects and we can see an early–late argument arising in visual attention. Results from Sperling and Bjork and Murray support an early selection view, while Mewhort and Eriksen and Eriksen's results support a late view. At the same time Sperling's subjects showed a partial report superiority (so must have perceived all display items) yet Estes' model suggests that there is a limit on feature extraction at a perceptual level. Clearly there is a paradox here.

Of course, it is very often the case that the featural and the categorical properties of an item are confounded. Say, for example, you ask your subject to respond as quickly as they can to a letter that is flanked by either digits or other letters. If the result shows that subjects are slower to respond to a letter when it is surrounded by other letters, is this because at the featural level, letters are more similar to each other and so compete at an early level, or, is it because the responses to letters are from the same category, and so compete for response at a later level? Jonides and Gleitman (1972) did a clever experiment to try to separate out these factors. Jonides and Gleitman presented two, four, or six items for 100ms. Subjects were asked to search for a letter embedded in either letter or digit distractors (or vice versa). The most interesting manipulation was to use O as either a letter or a digit. So, while the featural properties remained exactly the same, the category membership could be changed. Previous experiments had shown that there appears to be a parallel search (i.e. no response time (RT) cost for increasing display size) for between-category search, but a linearly increasing cost for within-category search. (Egeth, Jonides, & Wall, 1972). Jonides and Gleitman found that depending on whether subjects were told to search for an "oh" or "zero" the physically identical figure behaved either as a letter or a digit.This provides strong evidence that all array items are categorised prior to selection. If the effects were featural, the ambiguous O should behave the same in both conditions.

Before we try to resolve the discrepant results from these experiments let's look at some other theories put forward at the time.

Some early-selection theories of interference

We have already encountered theories proposed by Estes (1972, 1974) and Bjork and Murray (1977) to explain how signal and noise items interact to produce lateral masking during visual information processing. According to these theories the limited capacity bottleneck is at the point where the parallel input reaches the feature detectors, due to the inhibitory effects of input channels on one another. This model can account for Bjork and Murray's data, but not the "oh", "zero" effect found by Jonides and Gleitman (1972).

Wolford (1975) put forward a perturbation model to explain FCE and retinal position effects in tachistoscopic report. Estes had used response time data, but Wolford used accuracy of report. Wolford and

Hollingsworth (1974a,b) presented lines of nine letters over 18 different retinal locations. The number of letters reported peaks at about four items on foveal-centred displays and decreases to about two letters for arrays toward the periphery. This result was taken to show that the limit that allows only about four items to be reported from a multi-element display (Sperling, 1960) is not due to a memory limitation. If subjects were seeing more than they could report, the number of items they report should be the same in either case.

Wolford (1975) suggests that selection is affected by more variables than explained in Estes' model. A study by Wolford and Hollingsworth (1975b) looked at retinal location effects on rows of letters. It was found that while retinal location had an effect on all positions in the row, the retinal location effect was most reduced at the end positions in the string. By inserting spaces in the row either before or after the target, they found that a space on the peripheral side of the target was more beneficial than on the foveal side. Wolford suggested features are extracted independently and this information is held in a sensory information store. The probability of a feature being extracted is a function of factors like retinal location, size, and contrast. Spaces between features are extracted like any other feature. In the sensory store there is serial identification of letters, by a processor which first parses the feature bundles into groups. Decision criteria used to identify the letters depends on the task, and the time it takes to identify a letter depends on the amount of information required. In this model interference occurs because all the features and spaces are assumed to have a spatial ordering, and over each moment in time perturbations in ordering can occur. The probability of the perturbation of a particular feature depends on retinal location and inter-letter spacing: the wider the spacing the less likely the perturbation. According to this account, the main reason that letters interfere with each other during processing is because of perturbations, and only to a lesser extent because of interactions at the feature extraction level.

Wolford's perturbation model of interference in visual selection moves the locus of interference away from the feature level which is where Estes had said interactions occurred, but still puts selection prior to identification, making explanation of the Eriksen effects difficult. However, the model was specifically designed to account for whole report experiments, more like those of Sperling; and as we have seen there are differences in the apparent level of processing achieved by letters in the two paradigms.

Some models placing selection later in processing

Eriksen and Eriksen (1974) proposed a model that places the interaction between letters at the stage of *incipient response*, a late-selection model of the kind first suggested by Deutsch and Deutsch (1963). Whilst the BB effect of Bjork and Murray (1977) suggests perceptual interference, the HHH effect shows the opposite; i.e. response interference. In Eriksen and Eriksen's model, it is assumed that two or more items can complete processing at the same time, and begin to evoke their responses. Thus the interference between target and distractors arises because only one response can be made at a time, and a further decision mechanism is required to determine which of the two responses corresponds to the target. The production of competing data and competing explanations over whether interference and selection occurs early or late does not really seem to have moved us any further forward in understanding attention. We sometimes feel we are at the pantomime where "Oh, yes it is", "Oh, no it isn't" is about as far as the argument goes. Perhaps we need to consider more carefully what might actually be required for different computations within the information-processing system to be achieved if we are to understand the attentional behaviour that emerges. For the moment, an important factor we have not addressed is that not only does the processing system need to know *what* something is, which will arise from computing the features and mapping them onto internal representations, but also, some experiments require the subject to know *where* that object is.

Evidence for the separability of identity and location information

Eriksen and Rohrbaugh (1970) performed a bar-probe experiment. They found that accuracy of report declined with cue delay, as had Averbach and Coriell (1960); but, the important finding was that, as the probability of reporting the correct letter in the correct position declined, the probability of reporting an item adjacent to the true target increased. When subjects made an error, they were most likely to report another item that had been present in the display. We call this type of error a *mislocation error*. Note here that subjects were not simply reporting any old letter that was in the array, which might be expected if they opted to select a location at random; rather, they reported a close neighbour, not an item from further away at the end of the row. If the store from which subjects were making their selection was some kind of fading image of physical information, we would have expected subjects to begin to make intrusion errors; that is, reporting an item that was not in the display. Perhaps reporting F rather than E, or O rather than G. So Eriksen and Rohrbaugh's results suggest that both identity information and location information were available, in parallel, at the time of selection.

This idea is consistent with a model of processing that assumes parallel analysis of all inputs to the level of identification, with serial selection for response. This is a theory of the kind proposed by Deutsch and Deutsch (1963) that we looked at in Chapter 2. The problem for selection seems to be that more identities are available than can be reported, and a decision must be made to determine which of the competing responses corresponds to the target. Townsend (1973) proposed that the problem is not *what* the target is but *where* it is. This idea is consistent with Dick's re-analysis of the whole/partial report data and Eriksen and Rohrbaugh's results. Graves (1976) had shown that more items were identified than could be reported from a tachistoscope array and that when the position of report is required, the number of items identified together with their correct position is no greater in partial report than whole report. Again this points to the possibility that positional information decays, but identity information does not.

Selective masking experiments reported by Mewhort, Marchetti, Campbell, and Campbell (1981) show that different properties of a stimulus are selectively disrupted by different types of mask. Their results provide further evidence for the independent coding of identity (*what* the stimulus is) and stimulus location (*where* the stimulus is). Styles and Allport (1986) reported a series of experiments in which subjects were told to write down the identity of the central letter from a display and also, if they saw any other letters, write them down as well in the appropriate position on the response sheet. The duration of the display was manipulated by pattern masking, and the relationship between the target and distractors was manipulated in a variety of ways. With this procedure we were able to watch the time course of selectivity of report and the development of location information in each condition.

A target letter was presented in the centre of a group of four distractors, with the group appearing either above or below fixation, so that the target was not preferentially processed because it was in fixation. Feature level distractors were: simple hatchmarks; letter-like flankers made up from components of letters but not representing any actual letter, so having no meaning; digit flankers offering meaning but from a different category; letter flankers from a different response set from the target; and lastly, letter flankers from the target set: see Fig. 3.3.

In the last condition, when a target is surrounded by other letters from the target set, the only way to distinguish a target from a non-target is by knowing not only *what* the identity is, but also *where* that identity is. All the other conditions could have been performed by priming the target set and selecting the letter most strongly activated by the display. We found a hierarchy of interference effects: see Fig. 3.4. Any distractor causes interference, as indicated by a reduction in accuracy by the hatchmarks; digits produced more interference than hatchmarks, while letter-like features and letters from the non-target set were more disruptive, but not different from

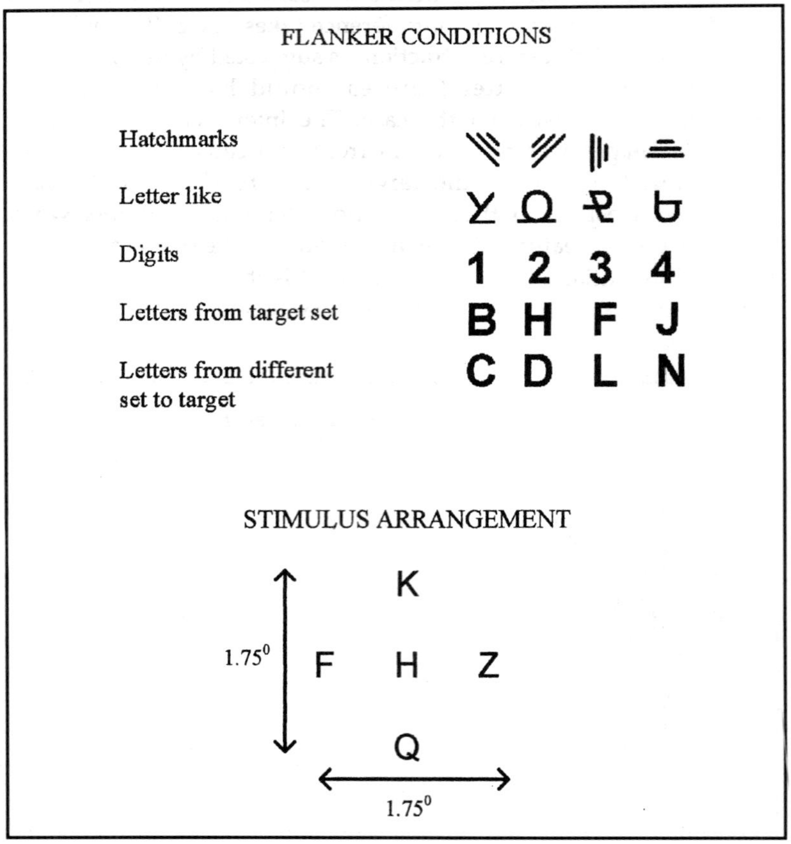

FIG. 3.3. Examples of some of the different distractors used as flankers by Styles and Allport (1986). Depending on the experimental condition, distractors were chosen to flank the target stimulus (the central letter) as shown in the stimulus arrangement. Here, the stimulus arrangement shows the target flanked by other letters from the target set; the letters same condition.

each other. Letters from the target set were most interfering. In all conditions, except where the target was flanked by distractors from the target set, the target could be selected by simply reporting the most active member of the primed, target, set. In every condition targets began to be accurately reported at a short stimulus onset asynchrony, (SOA) well below 100ms. However, in the last condition, when both identity and location were needed for accurate report, we found that, at SOAs below 100ms, although target letters could be reported, they were put in the wrong position; i.e. most errors were mislocations. As more time became available, accuracy of reporting the correct letters at their correct location increased. There seemed to be a critical period of about 100ms, before which the identity of the target was available, but it was not accurately localised. This is evidence for the independent representation of *what* something is and its other attributes like location.

Evidence from this experiment also bears on the question of the level in processing at which interference takes place. If interference were at the level of feature extraction, as suggested by Estes (1974) for example, then any letter features should have caused equal interference. This was not the case. The interference effects from letter-like shapes was no different from that caused by non-target letters, but letters from the target set were significantly more disruptive. Despite all these conditions having distractors which comprised letter features, it was the identity of the distractors which caused differential interference. Clearly it is the identities of letters, rather than their featural components that interact with response to the target.

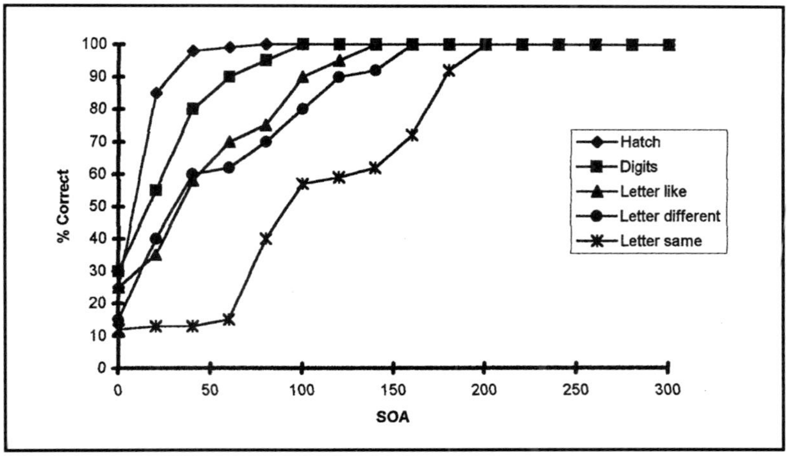

FIG. 3.4. Typical accuracy of target report for letters set amongst the different flankers, showing the hierarchy of interference effects (adapted from Styles and Allport, 1986, reproduced by permission of Springer Verlag).

Other evidence that the physical attributes of a stimulus are represented independently of its identity come from studies where experimenters manipulate the surface appearance of words that are to be reported. Johnston and McClelland (1976) found that although subjects were accurate at reporting the identity of a word, they were able to say whether it was written in upper or lower case only 52% of the time. Adams (1979) also found identity to be separate from physical form and McConkie and Zola (1979) found that alternating the case of letters during eye movements (saccades) did not influence reading.

Attentional dyslexia

Further evidence for the separability of *what* and *where*, as well as for categorisation prior to selection, is reported by Shallice and Warrington (1977). Two patients with tumours in the left parietal lobe were tested for reading ability. Shallice and Warrington found that these patients could read whole words perfectly well, but were very inaccurate when asked to selectively report single letters from a specified letter position within a word. However, the letters which the patients did report were not random errors, but mislocations; i.e. patients reported a letter that was present in the display, but from the wrong location. These patients seemed to be performing in a similar way to subjects doing bar-probe tasks, where errors were most likely to be reports of letters adjacent to the target; see, for example, Eriksen and Rohrbaugh (1970). The letter identities were available for report, but not accurately integrated with their correct location. Attentional dyslexic patients also show behavioural similarities to experimental subjects engaged in lateral masking experiments (e.g. Eriksen & Eriksen, 1974), in that when there is a categorical difference within the display, so that the letter to be reported is flanked by digits, performance is almost perfect. The categorical difference between the target and distractors, allows selection on the basis of the "most active letter" and does not require the integration or stabilisation of location and identity. Another finding was that when several words were presented simultaneously these patients mixed words together. So, for example, given "WIN FED" the patient might report "fin fed". Again, a similar effect can be found in subjects without neurological damage, when words are briefly presented and followed by a pattern mask; e.g. Allport (1977). Letters are not mixed up randomly, but keep their word position. These errors are called *migration errors*. There would appear to be some conflict between the finding that, when report of a single letter is required, the attentional dyslexic has difficulty making a within-category discrimination on the basis of location, but when given multiple words, letters migrate according to their position in the word. Yet the errors of an attentional dyslexic patient can be produced in the ordinary subject under experimental manipulations. Within words, higher level knowledge can constrain letter position so although the letters migrate they do so to preserve "wordness", producing migration errors. When selection is required from within the word, on the basis of an external verbal cue, accurate selection demands accurate localisation to coordinates outside the word. The underlying reasons for the pattern of impairment is not as yet clear but the fact that similar results can be found in both patients and neurologically intact subjects supports the view that categorical information is available prior to attentional selection.

Neurophysiological evidence for independent codes

Advances in neurophysiology have revealed quite clear specialisations in cells, pathways and regions of the brain. Evidence from cognitive neuropsychology, points to a variety of quite specific deficits of attentional processing. In this chapter we have seen evidence, from normal subjects and patients, for a dissociation of identity, colour and location information in selective report experiments. There is good evidence for two parallel streams of visual information analysis in association cortex. One, a ventral stream, projecting to the inferior temporal lobe, is responsible for analysing *what* an object is; and a second, dorsal stream, projecting to parietal cortex which is responsible for analysing *where* an object is located (Ungerleider & Mishkin, 1982; Posner & Petersen, 1990; Zeki, 1980, 1991). Goodale and Milner (1992) propose that the main function of the dorsal stream of the visual cortex is to guide actions. They believe that rather than a *what* and a *where* stream, the streams should be considered as a *what* and a *how* stream. One problem to be solved is how attributes belonging to the same object in a visual display are accurately combined to control response. In the next two chapters we shall consider, amongst other things, feature integration theory (FIT) and the importance of selection for action. There were, however, some theorists, notably Allport (1977) and Coltheart (1980), who were already considering the problem of combining multiple codes and how an understanding of this process might help us to understand why early attributes were good selective cues while, despite all the evidence for its availability, late semantic codes were poor selective cues.

A resolution?

Coltheart (1980) proposed a cognitive theory of iconic memory, that would predict the result of response interference like the HHH effect found by Eriksen and Shultz (1979) and the "oh", "zero" effect found by Jonides and Gleitman (1972). It also accounts for the differential effectiveness of position and identity in selecting information from brief visual displays. Coltheart suggested that the identity of an item is stored early in the lifetime of the display and this *semantic* representation is relatively stable, decaying more slowly than the physical attributes of the letter. The physical *episodic* information is unstable and will decay rapidly unless processed further. Although the precise nature of this further processing is not clearly specified by Coltheart, it involves the integration of the semantic and episodic information (i.e. *what* and *where*) by something called the "lexical monitor". The lexical monitor coordinates the episodic and semantic memories relating to a particular item. Unless these two sources of information are stabilised together, the identity information, which is considered to be rather like the activation of a lexical entry or logogen, dies away and cannot be reported. However, the fact that the lexical entries have been accessed and hence activated, means that residual unconscious activation can still lead to semantic facilitation or interference effects.

In a partial report experiment, the lexical monitor can stabilise a subset of the array on the basis of the physical information tagged to the identities, but, as the lexical monitor can stabilise only four or five items before the physical information has decayed, this limits whole report performance. Coltheart's model explains the effect of category differences on report in that when the lexical entries are semantically close, from the same category, there are several competing entries vying for the attention of the lexical monitor, which must decide on the basis of physical information which is the target letter, and therefore which lexical entry to stabilise. When there is a category difference between the target and distractors the decision is much easier, because as the subject is primed to detect a letter, and as only one letter is activated from the display, the lexical monitor has no choices to make. According to Coltheart, patients with attentional dyslexia have a faulty lexical monitor, which means that, when selection necessitates integrating physical and lexical information, in the case where one letter must be reported from amongst other letters, the patient cannot do the task. However, when a category difference in the display allows selection on the basis of the most active member of the target set, selection is possible. Migration errors are also a result of poor integration between where the letters are and what they are. When the only constraint is top-down lexical knowledge, letters will move to appropriate word positions, but not necessarily in the correct word.

Here we have a model within which all letters are processed to a post-categorical stage, but selection is based on physical information. It does not have to assume that an effective selection cue is a reflection of the degree of processing that has been achieved by what is selected. This is an important conceptual point, and a similar view was put forward by Allport (1977). If letters are categorically processed prior to selection, but selection is effected by physical information, then these different sources of information must be combined or bound together in some way. Coltheart's lexical monitor is not very concrete, but we shall see in Chapter 4 that the means by which the brain binds different attributes of the same object together is a topic of much current research.

Van der Heijden (1981), called the process by which categorised information is selected on the basis of early perceptual information *post-categorical filtering* (for a more recent review of this view, see van der Heijden, 1993). If we take this view of selection to be correct, the early–late debate could be resolved. Items are fully processed to a late stage, but selection can be based on early physical features like position or colour, which, as we have seen, need to be coordinated or bound together with the identity. Can this model also explain why there are, under certain conditions, interference effects that suggest feature level interference (like the BB effect of Bjork & Murray, 1977)? Presumably, here, the lexical monitor has two similar responses which are also closely similar at a featural level. In this case only spatial separation or location can be used to distinguish the target from the non-target and a fine, time-consuming discrimination will be required to determine which is which, so increasing reaction time.

Recent work on flanker compatibility: The argument continues

We have seen that, when subjects must respond to a relevant letter that is flanked by irrelevant items, the nature of the information in the flankers produce a response compatibility effect. Many experiments have been done and theories proposed but there is still basic disagreement about the mechanisms and locus of attentional selection. Two contradictory, but well-established findings are in direct contradiction: the first, which we called the BB effect, where the encoding of features from the display is inhibited by adjacent, featurally similar elements; and the second, the HHH effect, which suggests that the featural encoding of display items is independent of adjacent featurally similar items. Santee and Egeth (1982a,b) review the conflicting evidence and attempt to resolve the conflict in terms of experimental differences. Their conclusions are that when a mask is used, perceptual interactions between features will be found, but when the location and the identity of the target are required as the response, there will be interference related to the identity of the distractors. In one of their experiments they found that if target location was not required, there was no effect of interletter separation in the range 0.2°–1.8° of visual angle.

Miller (1991) has reviewed and summarised the evidence on the flanker compatibility effect (FCE) and conducted experiments to determine the boundary conditions under which the effect could be found. Eriksen and Eriksen (1974) found that when a subject must attend to the central letter that is flanked by letters having either a compatible or incompatible keypress response, the flanker letters produce large response compatibility effects, showing that the flankers have been identified even though they are unattended. The FCE can also be found in cueing tasks, where a bar-marker is presented, before display onset, to direct the subject's attention to the relevant location (Eriksen & St. James, 1986). Eriksen and Rohrbaugh (1970), Styles and Allport (1986), and Mewhort et al. (1981) found mislocations. These data among others provide evidence for the identification of unattended letters prior to selection and so support a late-selection account of visual attention.

Miller (1991) manipulated five factors that he thought might be responsible for the processing of unattended stimuli. These were:

1. Poor spatial resolution of attentional focus.
2. Inability to hold attentional focus on a fixed location.
3. Inability to focus completely on an empty display location.
4. Inability to filter out stimuli that onset during the task (we shall see later that objects that onset somewhere else in the visual field have a tendency to grab attention).
5. Inability to prevent analysis of all stimuli when there is insufficient demand by the attended items.

Miller found that he was unable to eliminate the FCE by manipulating any of these factors. His conclusion was that "early selection rarely, if ever, completely excludes unattended stimuli from semantic analysis" (p.270). He also concluded that spatial separation is especially important in visual selective attention. However, the separation may depend on the target distractor relationship. Eriksen, Pan, and Botella (1993) showed that the interfering effect of incompatible distractors was inversely proportional to their distance from the attended area and suggested this reflected an inhibitory field surrounding the attended area. LaBerge et al. (1991) argued that the gradient of attention around a target, and hence the area within which interference would or would not be found, varied with the attentional demand of the task. Further, Yantis and Johnston (1990) were also able to manipulate the distance over which flanking distractors had an effect on response to the target. The distance over which distractors interfere within the visual field is an important consideration when trying to determine if visual attention is a spotlight of fixed or variable width, or more like a zoom lens. We shall return to this evidence in the next chapter. For the present we shall stay with the question of the level of processing achieved by both target and distractors in these experiments.

Perceptual load and selective attention

It is now becoming increasingly clear that the degree of processing achieved by information in visual displays is dependent on a variety of factors and that a clear-cut distinction between early selection and late selection may be inappropriate: recall the differences between selective filtering and selective set experiments pointed out by Kahneman and Treisman (1984) who concluded that these different paradigms may require different attentional mechanisms. In a typical filtering task the subject has a large target and response set and has to select one stimulus from a subset of many. The response measure is usually accuracy. Here the memory load is high and results suggest early selection with very limited processing of unattended stimuli. A typical example of this kind of filtering task is that of Sperling (1960), discussed at the beginning of the chapter. In a selective set task the subject usually makes a speeded response to a target from a small set and chooses from a restricted response set by pressing a button. The response measure is usually reaction time. Here the memory load is low, and results suggest that selective attention speeds response to expected targets, resulting in late selection. A typical example of a selective set task is the Eriksen and Eriksen (1974) experiment. Thus these two experimental paradigms are very different in terms of the demand made on the information-processing system and Kahneman and Treisman (1984) believe it is unlikely that the same type of perceptual processing is required in the two tasks.

Picking up on Kahneman and Treisman (1984), and the fifth point in Miller's (1991) paper discussed above, Lavie (1995) reviews evidence for the effect of load on performance in a variety of selective attention tasks. Lavie proposes that whether attention is early or late depends on the demands of the task. Basically if the attentional demand of the task is low, irrelevant distractors will be processed, as there is still some attentional capacity left over. Therefore, as long as the task of selecting the target does not use all available attentional resources, there will be interference. On the other hand, when target selection requires full use of all attentional resources, there will be no possibility of distractors being processed. Kahneman and Chajczyk (1983) demonstrated that the Stroop effect is diluted when other information is presented in the visual array. The Stroop effect was first demonstrated by Stroop (1935) who found that when the name of a colour is written in a conflicting ink colour, subjects are slower to read the word than when the ink colour does not conflict with the colour represented by the word. Kahneman and Chajczyk's argument is that in their experiment the irrelevant information draws on attentional resources so reducing the amount available for processing the conflicting ink colour. The Stroop effect is discussed in more detail in Chapter 9.

In a series of experiments using versions of the Eriksen and Eriksen (1974) task, Lavie systematically manipulated perceptual load to gauge its effect on interference from irrelevant distractors.

First, Lavie (1995) varied the set size of possible targets from one to six and found that interference effects from a distractor with an incompatible response to the target, was significant only in the low-load condition. In another experiment, processing demands were manipulated by requiring two different forms of processing for a coloured shape presented next to the target. Depending on the combination of colour and shape the subject was to respond or not to the target, in what is called a *Go, No-go* situation. In the low-load conditions subjects were to respond if the shape was blue but not if it was red. In the high-load condition, *Go* was signalled by either a red circle or a blue square and *No-go* by either a red square or a blue circle. Assuming attention is needed to correctly integrate the colours and shapes in the display, as well as there being a memory load, Lavie (1995) predicted that the high-load condition would reduce interference from an incongruent distractor also present in the display. Results confirmed that interference from incompatible distractors is found only in the low-load condition.

Lavie claims that "perceptual load plays a causal role in determining the efficiency of selective attention" (1995, p.463). The experiment by Eriksen and Eriksen (1974) was a low-load experiment and so there was attentional capacity left over to process the distractors, leading to the appearance of late selection. In Sperling's (1960) experiment the load was high and hence all the attentional capacity was required for target processing, leading to the necessity for early selection. This argument might account for the discrepancy and resolve the debate over whether selective attention is early or late. But, there is a problem. Remember Bjork and Murray (1977) used displays which were as low in load as those of Eriksen and Eriksen (1974): how can the difference in results be accounted for? Lavie concedes that the "load" hypothesis does not really bring us any closer to solving this discrepancy in the data and has to assume that in certain conditions feature level interference will occur. Other problems arise out of the difficulty in defining exactly what "load" and "perceptual capacity" are. These problems are usually associated with dual-task experiments and divided attention, which we address in Chapter 7. Despite some problems, Lavie's work offers a promising compromise between a strict early or late selection theory.

Does no interference mean no processing?

In numerous experiments discussed so far, we have seen that interference effects are taken as evidence of whether or not information in the visual field, has been processed. For example, Eriksen and Eriksen (1974) assumed that, as incompatible distractors outside the 1° of visual angle did not slow target response, those distractors were not processed. Driver and Tipper (1989) use a different index of processing to show that this assumption may not be valid. The measure of processing used by Driver and Tipper is called *negative priming*. In order to understand their experiment we need to explain what negative priming is.

Negative priming

Priming paradigms have been widely used in cognitive psychology. In the more usual, facilitatory priming experiments, response to a second, probe stimulus is speeded, if either the same, or a semantically associated stimulus is presented first. So, for example, prior experience of a semantically associated word such as "doctor" speeds up naming, or lexical decision to a subsequent related probe word such as "nurse" (Meyer & Schavaneveldt, 1972).

Negative priming has been extensively used by Tipper and his colleagues to explore both the level of processing achieved by unattended stimuli and mechanisms of selective visual attention (Allport, Tipper, & Chmiel, 1985; Tipper, 1985; Tipper & Cranston, 1985; Tipper & Driver, 1988). In the original form of the experiment, subjects were presented with pairs of overlapping line drawings and had to name one of them. The target stimulus was specified by colour. So, for example, the subject may be presented with a drawing of a dog in green ink, overlapped by a drawing of a spanner in red ink. As the stimuli overlap, spatial separation is not possible, both stimuli fall in the attended area, and the target must be selected on the basis of the colour difference. The relation between the target and distractor stimuli on the first, prime trial, and the second target stimulus on the probe trial can be manipulated. So, for example, the target on the prime trial may be repeated as the target on the probe trial: this is called *attended repetition*. When this happens, response to the probe is facilitated as in the usual priming experiment. The interesting effect happens when the distractor on the prime trial is presented as the target on the probe trial. Now the probe response is slowed down, relative to a neutral control condition, in which the ignored distractor is unrelated to the probe. The effect is found when stimuli are presented so briefly that although subjects are able to report the target on both prime and probe trials, they are unable to report the distractors. Negative priming can be taken as evidence for semantic processing of the unattended stimulus, even though the subjects are unable to report its identity. Further, Tipper has argued, that in order for the target to be selected, the distractor must be actively inhibited. This inhibition results in a slower response to an identical or categorically related item presented on the probe trial.

Driver and Tipper (1989) used both interference and negative priming as measures of distractor processing. For their first experiment they used a version of an experiment originally performed by Francolini and Egeth (1980). Francolini and Egeth asked their subjects to count the number of red items in a display consisting of both red and black items. When the red items were digits inconsistent with the counting response, there was interference, but when the black, to-be-ignored, items were digits inconsistent with the counting response there was no interference. (This is a version of the Stroop task, but rather than the conflict being between ink colour and colour word, the conflict is between the numerical value of the digits and the number the subject has to count.) Francolini and Egeth (1980) claimed that the lack of interference between the red and black items showed that the unattended stimuli were filtered out at an early stage of processing before any identification had taken place. Driver and Tipper reasoned that if the unattended items in Francolini and Egeth's experiment were not processed sufficiently to produce interference they could not produce negative priming. To test this, Driver and Tipper presented their subjects with successive pairs of displays where the first (acting as a prime) was of the same type used by Francolini and Egeth. The second display was a probe to measure priming. The relation between the black items in the prime display and the number of red items in the probe display was manipulated so that sometimes the black items in the prime were congruent with, and at other times, incongruent with the probe response.

The results were quite clear. Data from the prime trials replicated Francolini and Egeth's results in that the ignored black digits did not interfere with the counting response to the red items. However, although the black digits had produced no interference in the prime trial, they did cause negative priming on the probe trial. Similar experiments reported in the same paper led Driver and Tipper to conclude that the non-interfering distractors are identified and inhibited. If the demonstration of no interference is not equivalent to demonstrating no processing, then any theoretical interpretation of experiments that rely on this assumption may be flawed.

Summary

Sperling (1960) found evidence for what he believed to be a high capacity fast decay visual memory, which faded within half a second. When presented with displays of brief duration, subjects can typically report only four or five items. However, early in the lifetime of the display, all items were available for report, as demonstrated by the discovery that when subjects were cued by colour or location to selectively report a subset of the display, they could report any of the items. This is called the partial report (PR) superiority effect. As selection on the basis of alphanumeric category seemed impossible, it was thought that categorical information was not encoded in iconic memory. However, just as in auditory experiments, evidence soon accumulated for semantic effects in visual attention tasks (Mewhort, 1967). The question arose as to why selective report on the basis of semantics was so difficult if semantic information was, in fact, available. Merikle (1980) found that selective report was enhanced by a category difference provided the category formed a perceptual group. While Sperling had been concerned to discover how much could be processed in a multi-element display, a new wave of experiments was aimed at discovering the extent to which attention could be selective within a multi-element display. Selective set experiments using the Eriksen paradigm (Eriksen & Eriksen, 1974) demonstrated response level interference effects between a target and incompatible distractors, but other experiments suggested interference was at an early level of feature extraction (Bjork & Murray, 1977). Overall, this issue is unresolved, but the bulk of evidence seems to support selectivity operating after the identity, colour and position have been analysed. Many experiments show that errors in selective report are due to identity and position not being correctly combined. This evidence is consistent with the neuroanatomical organisation of the brain, in which there is one system that knows *what* something is and another system that knows *where* something is (Ungerleider & Mishkin, 1982). It has been proposed that selection is usually made on the basis of physical information, but from identified stimuli which only evoke a conscious experience once integrated (Allport, 1977; Coltheart, 1980). Van der Heijden (1981) calls this process "post-categorical filtering". Recent work on the interfering effects of incompatible distractors shows that there are different effects which depend on task demand. Treisman (1993) and Lavie (1995) believe the results found depend on the perceptual load of the task. When perceptual load is high, as in selective filtering experiments, evidence for early selection is found, but when perceptual load is low, in selective set experiments, selection can be late. When distractors interfere with a target this is taken as evidence of distractor processing. However, it was also assumed that when distractors caused no interference this reflected the fact that they had not been processed. This assumption was tested by Driver and Tipper (1989) who were able to show that "ignored" distractors which produced no interference did give rise to negative priming. As negative priming results from the inhibition of identified distractors, the argument that no interference is a measure of no processing is flawed, as are theories which rely on interference as a measure of processing.

Further reading

Carlson, N.R. (1994). *Physiology of behaviour (5th ed.).* Needham Heights, MA: Allyn & Bacon. Provides an accessible account of the neurophysiology of vision.

Coltheart, M. (1972). Visual information processing. In P.C. Dodwell (Ed.), *New horizons in psychology.* Harmondsworth, UK: Penguin. This is an overview of selection in vision to that date.

Coltheart, M. (1984). Sensory memory: A tutorial review. In H. Bouma & H. Bouwhuis (Eds.), *Attention and performance X.* Hove, UK: Lawrence Erlbaum Associates Ltd. Following on from the previous item, this chapter updates the position and gives a clear account of Coltheart's theory of selection from brief visual displays.

Humphreys, G.W., & Bruce, V. (1989). *Visual cognition: Computational, experimental and neuropsychological perspectives.* Hove, UK: Lawrence Erlbaum Associates Ltd. Chapter 5, includes some of the issues raised here.

Allport, (D.)A. (1989). Visual attention. In M.I. Posner (Ed.), *Foundations of cognitive science.* Cambridge, MA: MIT Press. Covers much more than this chapter including neuropsychological aspects and broader conceptual issues.

The nature of visual attention 4

The attentional spotlight

Usually, we move our eyes to an object or location in space in order to fixate what we are attending to. However, as early as 1866, Helmholtz noted that attention and fixation were not necessarily coincident. In the introduction we noted that if you fixate in one place (for example, on the asterisk here *) you are able to read nearby words without shifting fixation to the location occupied by those words. Further, if you are attending and fixating in one place, you may find your attention drawn to a familiar word, such as your name or home town, elsewhere on the page, or by a movement in peripheral vision. It is as if there is some kind of breakthrough, or interrupt mechanism caused by information outside fixation.

One of the most popular metaphors for visual attention is that it is like a spotlight that allows us to selectively attend to particular parts of the visual environment. William James (1890) described visual attention as having a focus, a margin and a fringe. We have already seen in the previous chapter that there is disagreement over the degree of processing that stimuli receive with and without attention. To some extent the same arguments will continue through this next section, but we shall mainly be concerned with the question of whether a spotlight is a good metaphor, how it knows where to go, to what it can be directed, and what kinds of processing go on inside and outside the spotlight.

Spatial cueing

The effects of cueing a position in retinal space where a visual target might appear have been studied by many psychologists including Posner (1978, 1980), Posner, Snyder, and Davidson (1980). Posner's technique is elegant and simple. Subjects are asked to make a speeded response as soon as they detect the onset of a light in their visual field. Just before the target is presented, subjects are given a cue which can be one of two types. The first type, called a *central cue,* is an arrow which points towards either the left or the right, indicating that the target will appear to the left or the right of fixation. A central cue, although usually presented centrally on fixation, is so-called because it is a symbol representing direction and as such requires central processing by the cognitive system for its interpretation. The alternative type of cue, called a *peripheral cue,* is presented outside, or peripheral to, fixation and involves a brief illumination of one of a number of box outlines which mark the possible locations at which a target may appear. A peripheral cue is not symbolic in the same way as a central cue, because no interpretation is needed to determine its location; a peripheral cue indicates position directly.

Posner manipulated the validity of visual cues to try to determine the manner in which such cues could be used to summon or direct attention. Validity is the probability that the cue does, in fact, indicate where a target is to be presented. That is, although the cue was usually a valid indicator of where the target would appear, on some trials the cue was invalid, indicating a location different from that where the target would be presented. In order to compare the costs and benefits of valid and invalid cues, Posner included a baseline control in which a central cross was presented to indicate that a target was about to be presented, but did not provide any information about where the target was going to appear.

When the cue was valid, subjects were faster to respond to the target than in the control condition. It seemed as if subjects were able to use the cue to direct, or orient, attention because, when the cue was invalid, their response was slower than control, suggesting that attention had moved in the wrong direction. These results were the same for both central and peripheral cues.

Further experiments have shown that there are differences between the cueing effects of a central cue, such as a directional arrow, and a cue such as a flash of light that appears in the periphery. When the cues are only valid on a small proportion of trials, it would be advantageous for the subject to ignore them, as most of the time they would be misleading. However, Posner has shown that whilst central cues can be ignored, peripheral cues cannot. If the subject believes that the central arrow is pointing in the invalid direction, they can ignore it. On the other hand, even if the subject has good reason to believe that a peripheral cue is invalid, a response time (RT) cost still occurs, showing that, despite intention, attention is directed to the cued location: see Fig. 4.1.

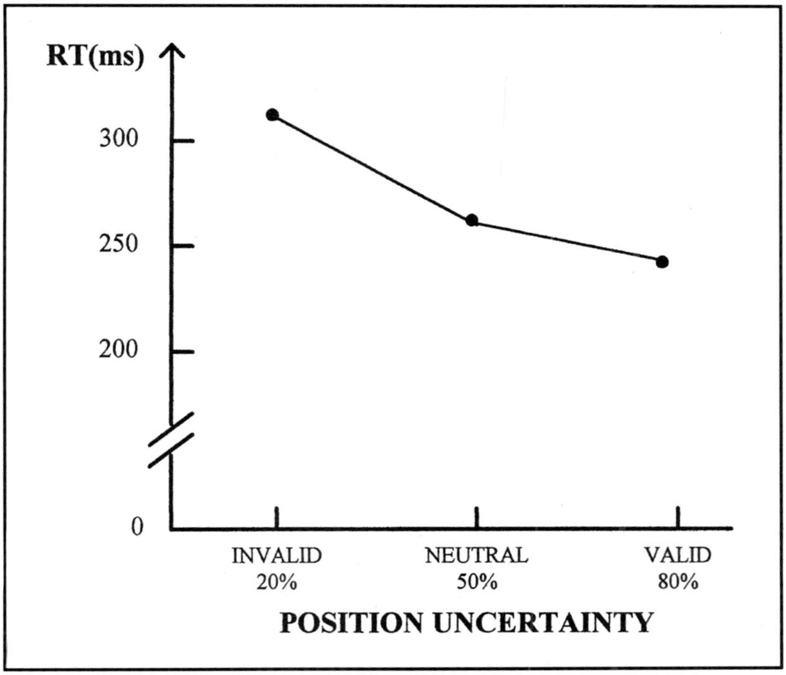

FIG. 4.1. Response times (RT) to targets according to the validity of the spatial location cue (adapted from Posner, Snyder, & Davidson, 1980, copyright © American Psychological Association, adapted with permission).

Endogenous and exogenous orienting of attention

Posner (1980) showed that directing attention to a valid stimulus location facilitates visual processing, and this led him to suggest that "attention can be likened to a spotlight that enhances the efficiency of the detection of events within its beam" Posner et al. (1980, p.172). It is important to note here that attention is not synonymous with looking. Even when there is no time to make a voluntary eye movement to the cued location, facilitation is found. Thus, it seems, visual attention can be covertly directed to a spatial location other than the one we are fixating. Posner (1980) proposed two ways in which attention is oriented to a stimulus. He distinguished between two attentional systems: an *endogenous* system, which is overtly controlled by the subject's intentions (for example, when an arrow cue is believed to be informative or not); and an *exogenous* system, which automatically shifts attention according to environmental stimuli, is outside the subject's control, and cannot be ignored. Posner gave the term *covert visual orienting* to the effect of the exogenous orienting system.

Further evidence from neurophysiological studies on monkeys, studies on neurologically normal subjects using positron emission tomography (PET) and cerebral blood flow and experiments with brain-damaged patients, led Posner and Petersen (1990) to propose two independent but interacting attentional systems. The posterior system is involved in directing attention to relevant locations using the operations of engaging, shifting, and disengaging. Three areas of the brain show enhanced response when a monkey attends to the location of a stimulus rather then some other spatial location: the parietal lobe (Mountcastle et al., 1978); part of the pulvinar (Petersen, Robinson, & Morriss, 1987); and the superior colliculus (Goldburg & Wurtz, 1972). Using PET studies, similar activity has been observed in humans (Petersen, Fox, Miezen, & Raichle, 1988; Corbetta, Miezen, Shulman, & Petersen, 1993). Lesions in these areas produce symptoms of attentional neglect which we shall consider a little later. The posterior system is specialised for covert orienting to location information, but not for other features of the stimulus such as colour. When subjects must select on the basis of these other cues, different areas of the anterior part of the brain are involved. This difference between the brain circuits involved in selectivity to different stimulus attributes may, according to Posner (1993), account for the finding that location is a more effective cue for visual selection than cues such as colour or form. Experiments showing the differential effectiveness of cues were discussed in Chapter 3; see, for example, Sperling (1960).

Posner and Petersen (1990) note there are strong connections between the posterior parietal lobe and parts of pre-frontal cortex. When a task requires monitoring for targets which may be presented in any input modality or during a Stroop task, the anterior cingulate gyrus is active (Pardo, Pardo, Janer, & Raichle, 1990). The pattern of connectivity between these anterior areas of the frontal lobes which are involved in planning, and the posterior attentional system, suggest the anterior system is involved in controlling the posterior system. Posner and Petersen (1990, p.10) suggest there is "a hierarchy of attentional systems in which the anterior system can pass control to the posterior system when it is not occupied with processing other material".

Overt and covert orienting: One system or two?

In experiments using neurologically normal subjects, Jonides (1981) showed that although covert orienting to peripheral cues is unaffected by a secondary memory task, voluntary orienting to central cues is affected by a secondary task. As already mentioned, a central cue needs interpretation by central mechanisms to ascertain the direction in which attention should be moved and requires controlled processing, whereas peripheral cues provide direct information on the to-be-attended location and orient attention automatically. A memory load competes with the interpretation of a central cue but not with a peripheral cue. (For a discussion of the distinction between automatic and controlled processing, see Chapter 7.)

Like Posner, Jonides (1981) interpreted these two varieties of attentional orienting as reflecting two different modes of controlling the same attentional orienting system. However, Müller and Findlay (1989) and Müller and Rabbitt (1989), argued that this might be the wrong interpretation. They termed exogenous orienting "reflexive" and endogenous orienting "voluntary". Müller and Findlay (1989, reported in Müller & Rabbitt, 1989) found that there were different time courses for the costs and benefits produced by peripheral and central cues. Peripheral cues produced a fast automatic orienting response which was strongest between 100 and 300ms after cue onset, peaking at 150ms. Central cues took 300ms to reach their maximum effect, but last longer. At a stimulus onset asynchrony (SOA) of less than 300ms the costs and benefits for peripheral cues were greater than for central cues, but after 300ms peripheral and central cues had the same effect. Müller and Findlay had argued that as the effects of the different cues had different time courses this could be evidence for two separate orienting mechanisms.

Müller and Rabbitt (1989) did a series of experiments aimed at refining and clarifying the question of whether there was only one attentional orienting mechanism controlled in different ways, as Posner had proposed, or whether there were two distinct mechanisms, one reflexive and the other voluntary. Their experiments pitted peripheral and central cues against each other to determine the difference in their time courses and whether they were equally susceptible to interruption. Results were consistent with an automatic, reflexive mechanism which is strongly resistant to competing stimuli and a second, voluntary mechanism which can be interfered with by the reflexive orienting mechanism. In their second experiment Müller and Rabbitt found that when peripheral and central cues were compatible, facilitation of cued locations was greater than when the cues were incompatible, and that the inhibitory effects of peripheral cues were lessened when they were in unlikely locations. It appeared that voluntary orienting to central cues could modify orienting in response to reflexive, peripheral cues. Müller and Rabbitt (1989, p.328) claim, "This pattern is consistent with the idea that the reflexive and the voluntary mechanism can be active simultaneously".

The fact that the "automatic" reflexive orienting can be modified by voluntary control processes, suggests that reflexive orienting is less than truly automatic. (Automatic processes cannot be voluntarily controlled; see Chapter 8.) However, according to the two-mechanism model of attentional orienting this can be explained. Reflexive orienting is triggered and proceeds automatically, and if both reflexive and voluntary orienting mechanisms are pulling in the same direction they have an additive effect. However, if they are pulling in different directions, their effects are subtractive.

Inhibition of return (IOR)

Although a valid cue usually facilitates processing, there are conditions in which inhibition can arise. If there is a delay of 300ms or more after a peripheral cue, target detection at that location is slowed down. That is, the normally facilitatory effect has reversed to become inhibitory. This effect is called *inhibition of return* and, although Wolfe and Pokorny (1990) failed to replicate the effect, inhibition of return (IOR) has been demonstrated several times; e.g. Posner and Cohen (1984); Maylor (1985). A plausible suggestion for why the visual system might require this kind of inhibition, is that it allows efficient visual search (Klein, 1988). Once attention has been directed to a location, that location is tagged so that there is no need to return to search that place again. Without such a record, the search process would be in danger of revisiting the same places over and over again. IOR can be observed in a variety of tasks; for example, it can be associated with an object's colour (Law, Pratt, & Abrams, 1995) and with moving objects (Tipper, Weaver, Jerreat, & Burak, 1994). The issue of whether it is the spatial location or the object which occupies the location that is tagged will be discussed in more detail a little later when we consider whether attention is directed to objects or the space they occupy.

The question of how many successively cued spatial locations can be tagged for inhibition of return is the subject of some debate. Pratt and Abrams (1995) found that IOR is associated only with the most recently cued location and they suggested that IOR has a very limited memory. However, Tipper, Weaver, and Watson (1996) claimed to find IOR for as many as three successive locations and argued that Pratt and Abram's experiment was inappropriate, as it included only two possible target locations. Pratt and Abrams (1996) replied that in fact, Tipper et al. (1996) had tested only a special case in which subjects could segregate the display into two spatial regions, and as such did not capture the complexity of real-world environments. When Pratt and Abrams (1996) made the display more complex, they again found that only the most recently cued location was inhibited. There appears to be no resolution to this debate at present, but it is clear that factors such as expectation and perceptual grouping have marked effects on IOR.

Movement of the spotlight

Given that cues can direct attention, another question arises: how does attention move over the visual field? Is it an instantaneous shift or does it take time? Is it initially spread over the whole field, narrowing down when the cue indicates a location, or does a small spotlight travel to the cued location? Experiments by Posner and his collaborators have been taken to suggest that the spotlight takes time to move over visual space. When the cue indicates only the direction in which the target is likely to appear, rather than the precise location, it is better to have a longer time interval between cue and target when the target is distant from the currently attended point. Tsal (1983) showed that reaction time to a target gets faster as the interval between the cue and the target increases, suggesting that it takes time for the spotlight to travel to the cued location. It appeared as if there was a point of maximum selectivity moving through space, as if it were indeed a spatial spotlight. In a similar experiment, Shulman, Remington, and McLean (1979) obtained data on near and far, expected and unexpected targets. It was found that response times to targets at far cued locations was equal to near uncued locations. This result is not consistent with the concept of an attentional spotlight moving through space.

Rather than time being used for spatial movement of the spotlight, this time might be better explained by the difference between early visual processing on the fovea and in the periphery. Downing and Pinker (1985) investigated the effect of cueing targets that were presented to different regions of the retina. Subjects were given cues at ten positions, distributed over peripheral, parafoveal and foveal regions. Downing and Pinker discovered that when the cues were closest to fixation, response times for a valid trial were fast, but on invalid trials there were rapid increases in costs as the target appeared further from the cued location. When cues were presented at more peripheral locations, the costs and benefits were less sharply graded. These results are consistent with the notion that the attentional spotlight can be focused more sharply at foveal locations than in the periphery and that when subjects know in advance where a target will appear, and have time to make an eye movement which allow the target location to be foveated, interference from adjacent distractors will be minimal. At the fovea, we are able to focus attention much more narrowly than in the periphery, so the size of the spotlight is larger or smaller, depending on whereabouts in the visual field the stimulus appears. This ties in with the lateral masking effects we covered in Chapter 3. As targets are presented further into the periphery they are interfered with by flankers at a greater distance than targets on the fovea, (Bouma, 1970). These effects are related to the size of receptive visual fields, which are larger in the periphery than in the foveal region. Supporting evidence was found by Humphreys (1981) (mentioned in the last chapter) who showed that when subjects fixate a target, distractors as near as only 0.5° of visual angle from the target could be successfully ignored.

Variable spotlight or zoom lens?

If there were only a single spotlight, dividing attention in the visual field would be difficult. Eriksen and Yeh (1985) were interested to see whether subjects could attend to more than one position in a visual display. They used a cueing experiment, with letters distributed around a circle, or clockface as the targets. Some positions could contain target letters and the other positions were filled with distractor letters. Stimulus displays were shown for only 150ms which is too short for any re-fixation during the lifetime of the display. The cue indicated where the target would appear with a given probability. On some trials the cue indicated the target position, but on other trials the cue would appear directly opposite the target. There were three cueing conditions. First where there was an equal probability that the target would be at the cued position on 40% of trials or opposite it on 40% of trials. In the second condition, it was more likely that the target would be where the cue indicated (70%) than opposite the cue (30%). For the third condition the cue reliably indicated the position of the target on all trials (100%). The control condition had no pre-cue at all.

When there was a pre-cue for the target, subjects responded more quickly than the no-cue control. Also, as the probability that the target would be at the cued location increased, so did the benefit of cueing, but only for the primary cue location where the cue actually appeared. Responses to the secondary location, which was opposite the actual cue, did not show the same benefit, and were slower, even when there was an equal probability that the target would appear in that location (in the 40%, 40% case). However, there was a benefit for the secondary location over the other non-cued location. Eriksen and Yeh interpreted their results as demonstrating that the spotlight could not be divided between the two equally probable locations, but could be rapidly moved from one location to the next. Recently, Castiello and Umiltà (1992) have shown that subjects can split focal attention and simultaneously manipulate two independent attentional foci when objects are located in opposite hemi-fields.

There is evidence that the spotlight can change the width of its focus depending on the task to be performed. LaBerge (1983) used a probe to indicate which letter in a five-letter word was to be reported. Subjects' spread of attention was manipulated. In one condition they had to categorise the central letter in the row, which was expected to make them focus attention in the middle of the word. In the other condition they were to categorise the word, which was expected to encourage them to distribute attention over the whole word. LaBerge found that response to a probe was affected by whether the subject was attending to the central letter or to the whole word. When attention was focused on the centre letter, responses to that letter were faster than to any other letter, but when the whole word was attended, responses to any letter position were as fast as that to the centre letter in the focused condition. This result seems to show that the beam of the spotlight can be adjusted according to the task and is not of a fixed size.

Broadbent (1982, p.271) summarised the data on the selectivity in visual displays and suggested that we should "think of selectivity as like a searchlight, with the option of altering the focus. When it is unclear where the beam should go, it is kept wide. When something seems to be happening, or a cue indicates one location rather than another, the beam sharpens and moves to the point of maximum importance." Evidence consistent with this view came later, from an experiment by Eriksen and Murphy (1987). In this experiment subjects were to decide whether the underlined target letter was an A or a U.

The target and the distractor could be the same or different (e.g. AA or AU) and the separation between target and distractor was varied. We know from all the work on flanker compatibility effects discussed in Chapter 3, and especially the work of Eriksen and colleagues, that when the target and distractors have incompatible responses there will be interference unless the separation between target and distractor is more than about 1°. In Eriksen and Murphy's (1987) experiment, on some trials, subjects were given a pre-cue indicating where the target would appear, but on other trials there was no pre-cue. When subjects were given a pre-cue, a response incompatible distractor close to the target caused more interference than one further away, as we would expect, because near incompatible distractors usually do cause interference. However, when there was no pre-cue, incompatible distractors interfered whether or not they were near or far. Eriksen and Murphy (1987) proposed that a better metaphor for visual attention would be a *zoom lens*. Initially attention is widely distributed with parallel processing of all elements in the display. In this case all distractors will activate their responses. However, with a pre-cue, the lens, or attention can be narrowed down so that only the elements directly in the focus of the lens will activate their relevant responses. Incompatible items outside this area do not, therefore, interfere. Recent experiments by Lavie (1995) led her to suggest that the size to which the spotlight closes down could depend on the perceptual load of the whole task. When the perceptual load is high, evidence for a narrow spotlight will be found, but in easier, low-load tasks distractors much farther from the target will be processed automatically.

Local and global processing

In everyday life we sometimes want to attend to a whole object or to a small part of a larger object. We can attend to a tree, a branch on a tree, or a leaf on a branch, but do we have to attend to the tree before its local details? Navon (1977) presented subjects with large letters made up of small letters: see Fig. 4.2. The large letter is the global shape and the small letters are the local shapes. With such stimuli it is possible to arrange for the local and global properties to be *congruent* (for example, an E composed of small Es), or *incongruent* (an E composed of small Ss).

Navon showed that in the incongruent condition response to the small letters was interfered with by the global letter identity, but local letter identity did not interfere with global letter identification. This

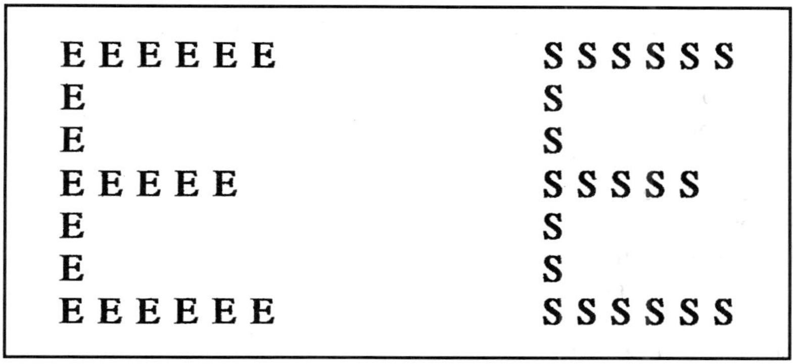

FIG. 4.2. Examples of compound figures with local and global properties. In the *congruent* stimulus the global property (large E) is the same as the local property (small E). However, in the *incongruent* stimulus the global property (E) is incongruent with the local property (S).

result was interpreted as showing that attention is directed to the coarse-grain global properties of an object before it is directed to analysis of fine-grain local properties. However, Martin (1979) manipulated the sparsity of the local elements in the global shape and discovered that in some cases it is possible for local processing to take precedence. Evidence seems to suggest that perceptual factors are important in determining whether local or global properties take precedence in attentional processing. Whichever is the case, there are data to indicate that it is difficult to divide visual attention between the local and global attributes of an object. Sperling and Melchner (1978) showed that subjects found it more difficult to divide visual attention between large letters surrounding small letters than between large letters surrounding degraded large letters. Shiffrin (1988) suggests attention focuses on one size or another and time is required to switch between size settings. Shiffrin views the data regarding global or local precedence as equivocal and thinks that, although both levels are generally processed in parallel, precedence may vary with experimental conditions.

Stoffer (1993) examined the time course of changing attention between the local and global levels in compound stimuli. He proposed that attention not only has to change spatial extent, but also has to change between representational levels. Clearly if attention changes from operating on the global shape to a local element there will have to be a zooming up or down of attentional focus. Stoffer compared the RT–SOA function in two conditions where subjects were to attend to either the local or the global property. In one condition, involuntary shifts were cued by an abrupt onset which specified the spatial extent of the area to be attended; and in the other, voluntary changes were indicated by a symbolic instruction. Thus the task is analogous to

Posner's (1980) spatial cueing experiments using a peripheral or central cue (see the beginning of this chapter). Validity of the cues was manipulated and a cost–benefit analysis was performed. Results showed that attentional zooming and attention shifting are similar at a functional level in that they can both be controlled either involuntarily (exogenous cue) or voluntarily (endogenous cue). However, zooming to the local level took longer than zooming to the global level. Stoffer suggests that the global level is usually attended to first and this additional time reflects an additional step which is required to reorient to the local level of representation. There are many studies directed to discovering the variables involved in local and global processing. Luna, Marcos-Riuz, and Merino (1995) provide a recent review of the current evidence.

Hemispheric differences in attention

Studies of patients have shown that the right cerebral hemisphere is biased toward global processing, while the left hemisphere is biased toward local processing. Robertson, Lamb, and Knight (1988) demonstrated that patients with right hemisphere lesions found attention to the global level most difficult while patients with left hemisphere lesions had most difficulty processing local attributes of a stimulus. Posner and Petersen (1990) argue that the hemispheres are individually specialised in the level of detail to which attention is allocated. Further specialisation is reviewed by Posner (1993) who points out that unilateral visual neglect, which we discuss in detail in the next section, is much more likely to follow right than left parietal lesions. This finding has led to the assumption that the right hemisphere controls attention to both sides of space. Corbetta, Miezen, Schulman, and Petersen (1993) studied visual attention using PET. They found that the right superior parietal cortex is activated when attention is shifted to both the right and the left. However, the left parietal cortex is active only during shifts to the right. It is also believed that, in spatial cueing experiments, not only does the cue serve to orient attention, but it also acts as a warning signal which increases the efficiency of, or enhances, signal processing. The right hemisphere is thought to be involved in maintaining enhancement because patients with right-sided lesions have difficulty maintaining alertness during sustained attention tasks and vigilance tasks.

Visual neglect

A great deal of evidence for the importance of orienting visual attention has come from studies of neuropsychological patients who have difficulty with the normally simple orienting task. As we saw above, patients with visual neglect usually have parietal damage in the right hemisphere, as discussed earlier.

Imagine a patient who bumps into objects in the left-hand side of visual space, who eats the food only from the right-hand side of the plate. It would be easy to imagine that this person is blind to one side of visual space, and that there is a visual defect underlying the problem. When asked to copy a picture or draw an object, patients draw only one half of the picture or objects within the picture: see Fig. 4.3a.

FIG. 4.3a. Copying performance of a flower and spontaneous drawing of a clock that a typical neglect patient might produce.

Given a page of lines to cross, they cross lines on only one half of the page (Albert, 1973): see Fig. 4.3b. The intriguing thing about patients with visual neglect is that they do not notice anything odd about their drawings or performance on crossing out tasks.

If it can be shown that such a patient is not blind in the neglected region of space, there has to be another reason why they do not acknowledge the presence of objects placed there. These patients are not visually blind, but act as if they have not perceived one side of visual space. The very term "neglect" suggests that the explanation may lie in the patients' inattention to the contra-lateral side of space. If inattention is the explanation then theories of attention should be able to account for the behaviour observed in these patients.

Earlier we discussed Posner's work on endogenous and exogenous attention. We saw that attention can be facilitated by a cue which appears to automatically orient attention to the cued side of space; e.g. Posner (1980). Posner and his colleagues carried out a number of experiments on patients with unilateral visual neglect using the cueing technique. It was demonstrated that with valid cues—those which reliably predicted where the target would appear—there was no great difference between targets presented in the neglected or non-neglected side. However, when the cue was invalid—appeared on the opposite side to where the target was presented—performance was very much more severely impaired than in normal subjects. Posner et al. (1984) proposed that three components of visual attention were needed to explain these results. First, the ability to engage visual attention on a target; second the ability to disengage attention from

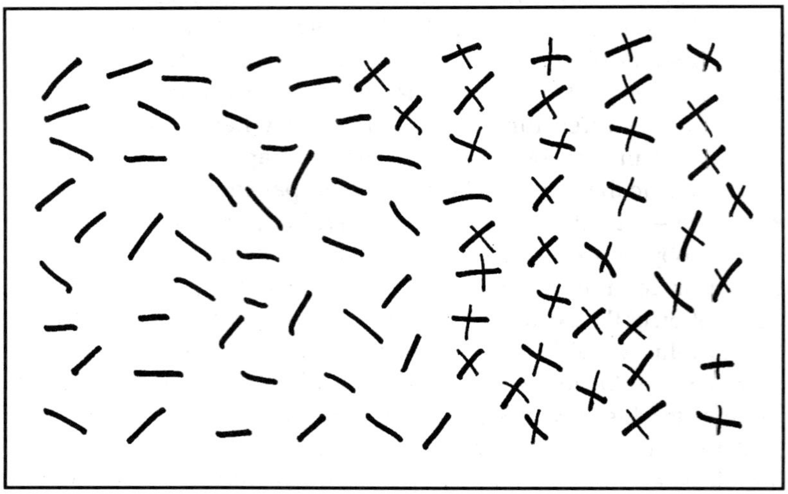

FIG 4.3b. Idealised performance of a neglect patient on the lines cancellation test.

the target; and third, to shift attention to the new target. As there was no difference in effect of a valid cue in either visual field, Posner argued that patients with neglect have no problem with the engagement of attention. Patients also seem to be able to shift attention, but when the cue is to the neglected side and the patient had previously been engaged on the non-neglected side it appeared that visual attention could not be disengaged to move into the neglected area of space. Further studies have tested patients with thalamic lesions, specifically the pulvinar nucleus, who do appear to have difficulty engaging attention to the side of space contralateral to the lesion; e.g. Rafal and Posner (1987). This belief is supported by PET studies by LaBerge and Buchsbaum (1990) which indicated increased activity in the pulvinar nucleus during attention tasks in which ignoring a stimulus is important. Therefore, the pulvinar is involved not only in engaging attention, but also in preventing attention from being directed to other unwanted stimuli.

Another deficit often associated with unilateral visual neglect is visual extinction. Patients with this problem have parieto-occipital lesions and have no difficulty in identifying a single object presented visually. However, if two objects are presented simultaneously, they do not seem to "see" the object presented contralateral to the lesion. In this condition patients can name an object presented to their visual field contralateral to the lesion, but only when there is nothing presented to their good side. When two stimuli are presented concurrently to both the good and bad side, the patient is able to report only the stimulus appearing in the good side of visual space. It is as if the presence of a stimulus in the good field extinguishes the response to the stimulus in the damaged field. However, Volpe, LeDoux, and Gazzaniga (1979) provide evidence that patients who exhibit extinction do not have a visual deficit but are experiencing a higher-order attentional problem. Even when two objects are presented simultaneously—for example, an apple to the good field and a comb to the damaged field so that the patient reports seeing only the apple—the patient can make accurate judgements about whether the two objects are the same or different. When questioned about the basis for their judgement, the patient cannot give any verbal description of the extinguished stimulus; they claim not to know what the stimulus was although they know it is not the same as the stimulus that they are able to report from the good field. Of course, it might be possible for this comparison to be made on basic perceptual properties of the pair of objects: an apple and a comb have different shapes. A simple shape discrimination judgement would support accurate performance. However, Berti et al. (1992) investigated the level of processing achieved by the stimuli to be compared in patients who showed extinction. They demonstrated that same/different judgements can still be made in conditions where "same" is two different photographic views of the same object. As the photographs have different perceptual properties but the same conceptual properties, it seems clear that extinction is affecting high level representations of the objects rather than earlier perceptual levels. Volpe et al. (1988) thought that patients are able to reach a level of processing for the extinguished stimulus which allowed the comparison between objects to be made, but could not support conscious awareness. This evidence suggests that, despite "inattention" to the neglected side, semantics are available but do not allow overt response. We shall discuss these findings again in Chapter 10 when we consider the nature and possible functions of consciousness.

Neglect of imagined space

So far, we have considered neglect in terms of what the patient sees, either in terms of high or low level representations, based on analysis of a visual input from the external environment. What about internal representations of the imagination? Bisiach and Luzatti (1978) argue that neglect is the result of the subject failing to construct an internal representation of one side of visual space. They asked two patients with neglect to describe a scene that they knew very well, the Piazza del Duomo in Milan. When asked to report the scene as if they were standing on the steps of the cathedral, the patients reported only one side of the piazza, not mentioning any of the buildings that lay on their neglected side. Then the patients were asked to imagine that they had crossed the piazza and report what they could see when facing the cathedral. Now they reported all the buildings they had omitted from the other perspective and omitted all those previously reported. This demonstration is clear evidence against visual neglect being a result of a visual deficit. Further evidence for neglect operating at different levels of representation are found in patients with neglect dyslexia, to be covered shortly.

Objects, groups, and space

In the last chapter we saw that Driver and Tipper (1989) used both interference and negative priming as measures of distractor processing. Although Driver and Tipper (1989) found negative priming from stimuli that produced no concurrent interference on target identification, it is still true to say that spatial separation between objects in a display can allow efficient selection? Both the zoom lens and spotlight metaphors discussed earlier consider focal attention as something that is shifted and directed in space. Whether or not selection is early or late, and relies on a spotlight or a zoom lens, there seemed until recently to be a consensus that visual attention operates on contiguous regions of the visual field. However, some psychologists have suggested that attention is directed to perceptual groups according to Gestalt principles. Prinzmetal (1981) looked at how people grouped features in simple displays. He tested two hypotheses: firstly, that features from the same or neighbouring locations in space are likely to be joined; and secondly, that features from the same perceptual group are likely to be joined. In all his experiments, he found that the perceptual group principle predicted performance best. The experiment by Merikle (1980), discussed in Chapter 3, showed that perceptual grouping can influence the partial report superiority effect in an iconic memory experiment. Merikle suggested that spatial cues like a particular row, or a cue such as colour were effective for partial report because they formed a perceptual group that was easily selected. There is no partial report superiority on the basis of a category distinction, he argued, because a category difference does not produce a perceptual group. Merikle found that when categorically different items in a display also form a perceptual group, they can act as an effective cue for selective report.

Driver and Baylis (1989) thought that distractors that are close to a target may cause interference, not simply because they are close to the target, but because items that are close together form a good perceptual group. They did an experiment to distinguish between the spatial spotlight and perceptual grouping hypotheses. The task they chose was a version of that used by Eriksen and Eriksen (1974) in which we have seen that response compatibility effects are found for flankers near the target, but not for flankers more distant than 1° of visual angle. Driver and Baylis's manipulation involved grouping distractors with the target by common movement. It is a well established Gestalt principle that items that move together are grouped together. The task was to respond to the central letter in a horizontal display of five letters where the central letter moved with the outer letters of the array but the intermediate letters remained stationary. Two alternative predictions are made by the two hypotheses. A spotlight account predicts that distractors nearer the target will cause most interference, whereas the grouping hypothesis predicts that flankers grouped with the target will interfere most although they were farther away.

Results supported the perceptual grouping hypothesis: distant distractors that moved with the target produced more interference than stationary distractors that were close to the target. (Unfortunately, Kramer, Tham, & Yeh, 1991, were unable to replicate this result.) Driver and Baylis believe that it is better to think of attention being assigned to perceptual groups rather than to regions of contiguous space because in the real world we need to attend to objects moving in a cluttered environment. Imagine watching an animal moving through undergrowth. Here we can see only parts of the animal distributed over space, but we see the animal as one object because we group the parts together on the basis of common movement.

There is increasing evidence that we do attend to objects rather than regions of space. Duncan (1984) showed that subjects found it easier to judge two attributes that belonged to one object than to judge the same attributes when they belonged to two different objects. The stimuli in Duncan's experiment were a rectangle with a gap in one side over which was drawn a tilted line. Both the rectangle and the line had two attributes. The rectangle was long or short with the gap either to the left or the right of centre. The line was either dotted or dashed and was tilted either clockwise or anticlockwise. Duncan asked subjects to make one or two judgements on the possible four attributes. When two judgements were required—say, gap position and tilt of line—subjects were worse at making the second judgement. However, when both the judgements related to the same object—say, gap position and the length of the box—performance was good. Duncan proposed that we attend to objects, and when the judgements we make are about two objects, attention must be switched from one object to another, taking time.

Object-based inhibition of return

Object-based attention is clearly very important. But, if you remember, Posner (1980) showed that the attentional spotlight could be summoned by spatial cues and covertly directed to locations in space. An associated effect, inhibition of return, was hypothesised to result from the tagging of spatial locations. What if you were searching for an object, found it, but then the object moved? If attention was spatially based, you would be left looking at an empty location! Tipper, Driver, and Weaver (1991) were able to show that inhibition of return is object based. They cued attention to a moving object and found that the inhibition moved with the object to its new location. Tipper et al. (1991) propose that it is objects, not space that are inhibited and that inhibition of return ensures that previously examined objects are not searched again.

Object-based visual neglect

The attentional explanation for unilateral visual neglect given earlier assumed that it was space that was neglected rather than objects. However, there is an increasing body of evidence in favour of the suggestion that attention can be object based. Indeed the amount neglected by a patient will depend on what they are asked to attend to. In Bisiach and Luzatti's (1978) experiment, the object was the Piazza del Duomo. What if the object had been the Duomo itself? Or if the patient had been asked to draw a single window? Then the patient would have neglected half of the building or half of the window. Driver and Halligan (1991) did an experiment in which they pitted environmental space against object-centred space. If a patient with visual neglect is given a picture of two objects about which to make a judgement and that picture is set in front of the patient so that both the environmental axis and object axis are equivalent, then it is impossible to determine which of the two axes are responsible for the observed neglect. Driver and Halligan (1991) devised a task in which patients had to judge whether two nonsense shapes were the same or different. If the part of the one shape which contained the crucial difference was in neglected space when the environmental and object axes were equivalent, the patient was unable to judge same or different: see Fig. 4.4.

Driver and Halligan wanted to discover what would happen when the paper on which the stimuli were drawn was rotated so that the crucial part of the object moved from neglected space, across the environmental axis, into what should now be non-neglected space. Results showed that patients still neglected one side of the object, despite the object appearing in the good side of environmental space. This experiment demonstrates that neglect can be of one side of an object's principal axis, not simply of one side of the space occupied by that object.

Behrmann and Tipper (1994) and Tipper and Behrmann (1996) have recently demonstrated the importance of object-based attentional

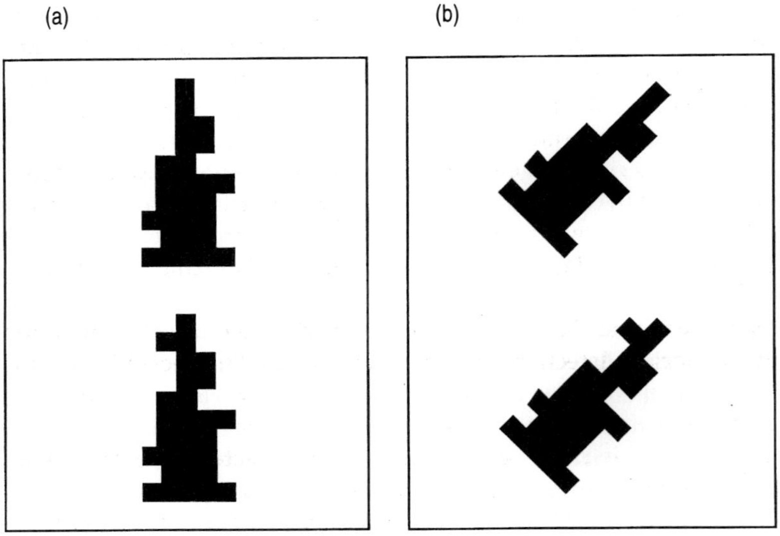

FIG. 4.4. Stimuli used by Driver and Halligan (1991, reprinted by permission of Psychology Press). In (a) the object-centred axis and midline are identical and therefore confounded, but in (b) the feature distinguishing the two shapes lies to the left of the object-centred axis, but to the right of the midline.

mechanisms in patients with visual neglect. In their experiments they presented the subjects with an outline drawing of two circles connected by a horizontal bar, a barbell, which was arranged across the midline of visual space. A target might appear in either ball of the barbell, so that it was in either neglected or non-neglected space. As expected, patients with neglect showed very poor performance when targets appeared on the left, in their neglected field. Control patients were able to do the task equally well in either visual field. The question that Behrmann and Tipper were interested in was: what would happen to patients' performance when the barbell rotated? If attention is object based rather than environmentally based, would visual attention move with the barbell if it was rotated? In the rotating condition the barbell appeared on the screen, remained stationary for a short while, and then rotated through 180°. This rotation took 1.7 seconds. The experimenters predicted that if attention was directed only to the left and right of environmental space, then performance in the rotating condition would be exactly the same as in the stationary condition. However, if attention is directed to the left and right of the object, then, as rotation moves the left of the object to the right of space and vice versa, performance in the rotating condition should be the reverse of that when the barbell was stationary. Although not all patients showed exactly the same effects, it was discovered that in the rotating condition there was an interaction between condition (static versus moving) and the side on which the target appeared. For controls there were no differences in target detection rates in the static and rotating condition and no left–right asymmetries. Two patients failed to detect the target on 28% of trials despite its arriving on their "good" side. Two other patients showed equivalent performance for both left and right targets, but overall, patients were slower to detect the target when it ended in the right-hand position (that is the good side) and four showed significantly better performance on the left side (the neglected side) in the moving condition. Remember, that in the static condition all patients showed poorer performance for the left (neglected) side. The results show that when the object of attention moves target detection can be better on the "neglected" than the "good" side of visual space. If the basis for visual neglect was environmental space, then irrespective of any movement of the object, targets falling in neglected space should be detected far less well than those falling in attended space. Behrmann and Tipper's results cast doubt on this explanation of visual neglect. The performance of these patients might be explained by an attentional cueing effect. As discussed earlier, Posner et al. (1984) have argued that neglect patients have difficulty disengaging their attention from the right side of space. Possibly, when the barbell rotates patients have difficulty disengaging from the right side of the object and attention is drawn into left-sided neglected space, so when a target appears there, response is faster. Behrmann and Tipper (1994) argue that while this explanation may hold for improved performance in the neglected field, it cannot account for impaired performance on the "good" side, as attention should always be biased to right-sided space in these subjects. Instead, Behrmann and Tipper propose that attention accesses both environmental and object-based representations of space. In the static condition, both reference frames are congruent, with good attention directed to the right and poor attention to the left. However, when the barbell moves, attention is drawn with the object so that the "poor" attention which was directed to the left of the object moves to the right and the "good" attention which was directed to the right of the object moves to the left. This explanation could account for both left-side facilitation and right-sided inhibition in the rotating condition. As in the experiment by Driver and Halligan (1990), these data demonstrate that neglect may be based on different frames of reference in different conditions.

While there does seem to be some evidence for visual neglect having an object-based component, Behrmann and Moskovitch (1994) point out that object-based effects are not always found. They suggest that environmental space is usually the dominant coordinate system and that object-based effects may be found only under conditions where stimuli have handedness or asymmetry in their representations which require them to be matched in some way relative to the object's main axis.

Neglect in Balint's syndrome

Patients who exhibit Balint's syndrome usually have posterior parietal lesions. A classical description was given by Balint (1909) but up-to-date evidence can be found in Jeannerod (1997). Patients have severe deficits in spatial tasks. Not only do they have difficulty orienting to visual stimuli, but they fail to orient their arm and hand correctly when reaching and do not make normal adjustments to finger shapes when grasping. They may also fail to orient in other modalities, such as hearing. When eye–hand coordination is required in a task the deficit in these patients is most pronounced. Optic ataxia, as this difficulty is called, has been discovered to follow damage to the superior parietal lobule (Perenin & Vighetto, 1988). Patients often have difficulty judging length, orientation and distance and may have lost the ability to assemble parts into a whole. Generally, object-oriented actions are severely impaired. We have already discussed neglect and extinction in the preceding sections, but will now add two patients with Balint's syndrome, studied by Humphreys et al. (1994).

In this study, patients were presented with either two words or two pictures simultaneously above and below fixation. Both patients showed extinction when presented with two words or two pictures, but when a picture and a word were presented, pictures tended to extinguish words. In another condition, stimuli were presented in the same location so that they were overlapping. When a single stimulus was presented, the patients were, as expected, always correct, but one patient, G.K., reported both the picture and the word on 16/40 trials and only the picture the rest of the time. In their second experiment, Humphreys et al. (1994) presented stimuli in a vertical arrangement, with the target on fixation and the other stimulus either above or below it. Spatial selection should have favoured the fixated word, but again, although a word on its own could be reported, when a picture was simultaneously presented, G.K. showed extinction of the word by a picture.

Humphreys et al. conjectured that pictures might dominate words because they are "closed" shapes. Displays were constructed in which the shapes of a square and a diamond differed in their degree of closure. This was achieved by drawing only parts of the shapes. In the good closure condition the corners specified the shapes but the sides were missing, while in the other, weaker closure condition, the lines of the sides specified the shape, with the corners missing. The task was to detect whether a square was present. Results showed that both patients showed a preference for squares with good closure; i.e. those made up from the corners. However, the patients were at chance when asked to decide if the square had been presented above or below fixation. Despite detecting the square, its spatial location was unknown to the patients. Humphreys et al. argue that extinction can be based on properties of the object, in this case closure. Pictures have shape closure but words do not, hence pictures dominate words. Further, even when spatial selection and localisation are poor, these object properties can mediate selection from the visual display.

These patients had suffered damage to the brain areas in the parietal lobes which are normally involved in spatial perception. However, there was no damage to those areas in the occipito-parietal region which process the properties of objects. Humphreys et al. suggest that closed shapes dominate over open shapes and without spatial information to guide a shift between objects, extinction occurs. In an intact system, they suggest, "there is normally coordination of the outcomes of competition within the separate neural areas coding each property, making the shape, location and other properties of a single object available concurrently for the control of behaviour" (Humphreys et al., p.359).

Explicit in this quotation is the next question we have to address: how are the multiple sources of information pertaining to an object brought together in order for us to perceive a world of unified objects and how is the visual environment segregated into those objects?

Summary

Visual attention has been likened to a spotlight which enhances the processing under its beam. Posner (1980) experimented with central and peripheral cues and found that the attentional spotlight could be summoned by either cue, but peripheral cues could not be ignored whereas central cues could. Posner proposed two attentional systems, an endogenous system controlled voluntarily by the subject and an exogenous system, outside the subject's control. Müller and Rabbitt (1989) showed that exogenous, or in their terms automatic "reflexive", orienting could sometimes be modified by voluntary control. Although a cue usually facilitates target processing, there are some circumstances in which there is a delay in target processing (Maylor, 1985). This inhibition of return, has been interpreted as evidence for a spatial tagging of searched locations to help effective search. There is some debate over how many locations can be successively tagged. Inhibition of return can also be directed to moving objects (Tipper et al., 1994). Other experimenters have tried to measure the speed with which the spotlight moves (e.g. Downing & Pinker, 1985). The apparent movement of the spotlight might be more to do with the speed with which different areas of the retina can code information. Other researchers asked whether the spotlight could be divided but concluded that division was not possible. It was suggested that a zoom lens might be a better analogy than a spotlight as it seems that the size of the spotlight depends on what is being attended (LaBerge, 1983). Lavie (1995) argued that the size to which the spotlight could close down depended on the perceptual load of the task.

Visual attention can also be cued endogenously and exogenously to change between levels of representation when either the local or global attributes of a stimulus are to be attended (Stoffer, 1993). The right cerebral hemispheres are specialised for global processing and the left for local processing. The hemispheres are also specialised for orienting (Posner & Petersen, 1990), with the right parietal area able to orient attention to either side of space, but the left parietal area able to orient only to the right. Thus right parietal lesions often give rise to visual neglect of the left side of space. Posner et al. (1984) believed that normally there are three components of visual attention: disengage, shift, and engage. According to Posner et al. patients with visual neglect have no difficulty engaging or shifting attention, but if attention is cued to the neglected side they have difficulty disengaging from the non-neglected side. Volpe et al. (1979) and Berti et al. (1992) have demonstrated that patients can make judgements about stimuli in neglected space, even when the stimuli can be judged only on a semantic property. Despite no awareness of the stimulus on the neglected, or extinguished side, and visual "attention" not being directed there, semantics on the neglected side have been processed. Neglect can also be of one side of imagined, or representational, space (Bisiach & Luzatti, 1978). Rather then focusing on space *per se*, psychologists are becoming increasingly interested in object-based effects in attention. Driver and Baylis (1989) showed that objects which formed a group by common movement were attended to despite not being spatially contiguous. This is evidence against a purely spatial spotlight account of visual attention. Further, neglect can be to one side of object-centred space (Driver & Halligan, 1991), and inhibition of return can apply to objects rather than their spatial location (Tipper et al., 1991). Extinction in patients with Balint's syndrome, who have severe spatial deficits, was shown to be based on the perceptual property of closure. As these patients have no location information, the coordination of perceptual codes which normally allows selection was not possible, and the perceptually stronger representation dominated, leading to extinction (Humphreys et al., 1994).

Further reading

Allport, (D.)A. (1989). Visual attention. In M.I. Posner (Ed.), *Foundations of cognitive science.* Cambridge, MA: MIT Press. A detailed review of the biological, neuropsychological, and psychological evidence.

Humphreys, G.W., & Bruce, V. (1989). *Visual cognition: Computational experimental and neuropsychological perspectives.* Hove, UK: Lawrence Erlbaum Associates Ltd. Chapter 5 on visual attention reviews theories of visual attention and provides a detailed criticism of feature integration theory (FIT) as it stood in 1989.

Parkin, A.J. (1996). *Explorations in cognitive neuropsychology.* Oxford: Blackwell. A good introduction to studying patients. Chapter 5 is on visual neglect.

Robinson, D.L., & Peterson, S.E. (1986). The neurobiology of attention. In J.E. LeDoux & W. Hirst (Eds.), *Mind and brain: Dialogues in cognitive neuroscience.* Cambridge: Cambridge University Press. This chapter provides an introduction to the neurophysiology of attentional mechanisms.

Combining the attributes of objects and visual search 5

Putting it all together

We have already seen that there is overwhelming evidence that the brain computes multiple sources of information over multiple channels. In preceding chapters we have reviewed studies that provide evidence for the independence of colour, identity, and location. We have considered the way in which attention might move over the visual field and noted that attention is affected by perceptual grouping and that objects rather than locations can be attended to. What we have not yet considered is how the separate codes are combined into objects. Clearly, this is crucial. We do not inhabit a world of fragmented colours, shapes and meanings, but interact with meaningful objects which are segregated such that the correct attributes of individual objects are combined. In addition to the question of how attributes are combined, there is another question concerning visual search: how does attention find a designated target in a cluttered visual field? It is to these questions that we now turn.

There are many competing and complementary theories of visual search and visual attention. For example, Bundesen (1990) presented a mathematical model, which we touched on in Chapter 2 and shall meet again later in this chapter; Schneider (1995) put forward a model which incorporates neuropsychological evidence, the control of segmentation, object recognition and selection for action, all in one theory of visual attention; van de Heijden (1992) has a detailed theory of selective attention in vision and Wolfe, Cave, and Franzel (1989) suggest a "guided search model". Here I shall concentrate on only a few theories, beginning with one of the most influential theories of visual search with focal attention.

Feature integration theory

Treisman's feature integration theory (FIT) is a model for the perception of objects. The theory is constantly being updated but was originally proposed by Treisman and Gelade (1980). Treisman (1988) and Treisman (1993) provide useful summaries of the status of FIT at those dates. Feature integration theory is in a state of constant evolution, frequently being updated to take account of fresh data, and new ideas are constantly being tested in new experiments. There is therefore an enormous volume of work which would need a book to itself for a complete review. However, here we shall look at how FIT started out and summarise the position as seen by Treisman in 1993. The initial assumption of the model was that sensory features such as colour, orientation and size were coded automatically, pre-attentively, in parallel, without the need for focal attention. Features are coded by different specialised *modules*. Each module forms a feature map for the dimensions of the features it codes; so, for example, the distribution of different colours will be represented in the colour map, while lines of different orientations will be represented in the orientation map. Detection of single features that are represented in the maps takes place pre-attentively, in parallel. However, if we need to know whether there is a line of a particular orientation and colour in the visual scene, the separately coded features must be accurately combined into a conjunction.

Conjunction of separable features can be achieved in three ways. First, the features that have been coded may fit into predicted *object frames* according to stored knowledge. For example, we expect the sky to be blue and grass to be green: if the colours blue and green are active at the same time, we are unlikely to combine green with the position of the sky. A second way is for attention to select within a *master map* of locations which represents where all the features are located, but not which features are where. Figure 5.1 is an illustration of the framework, from Treisman (1988). When attention is focused on one location in the master map it allows retrieval of whatever features are currently active at that location and creates a temporary representation of the object in an *object file*. The contents of the object file can then be used for recognising the object by matching it to stored knowledge. Treisman (1988) assumes that conscious perception depends on matching the contents of the object file with stored descriptions in long-term visual memory, allowing recognition. Finally, if attention is not used, features may conjoin on their own and although the conjunction will sometimes be correct it will often be wrong, which produces an "illusory conjunction".

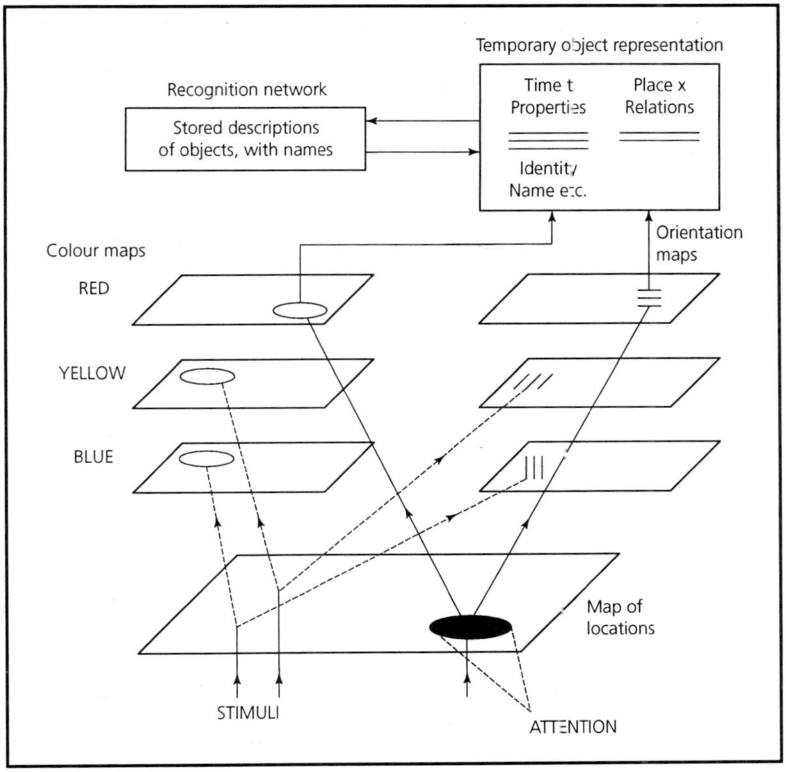

FIG. 5.1. Framework proposed to account for the role of selective attention in feature integration (from Treisman, 1988, reprinted by permission of the Experimental Psychology Society).

Evidence for feature integration theory (FIT)

Early experiments by Treisman and Gelade (1980) had shown that when subjects search for a target defined only by a conjunction of properties—for example, a green T amongst green Xs and brown Ts—search time increases linearly with the number of non-target or distractor items in the display. When search is for a target defined by a unique feature—for example a blue S set amongst green Xs and brown Ts—search time is independent of the number of distractors. This difference in search performance was taken as evidence that, in order to detect a conjunction, attention must be focused serially on each object in turn, but detection of a unique, distinctive feature could proceed in parallel. Treisman suggests that the unique feature can "call attention" to its location. This is sometimes called the attentional *pop-out* effect.

As distinctive features automatically pop out, there is no need for an attentional search through the display to find the target, and display size will have no effect on search time. When the display does contain a target, and that target is defined by a conjunction, the very first or the very last object conjoined may contain the target, but on average half of the items in the display will have been searched before a target is detected. On the other hand, when there is no target present, every possible position must be searched. If we plot search times for present and absent responses against display size, we find that there is a 1:2 ratio between the search rates for present: absent responses. Data of this kind are shown in Fig. 5.2. Results like these suggest that conjunction search is serial and self-terminating and is consistent with the idea that in conjunction search, focal attention moves serially through the display until a target conjunction is found. Conversely, targets defined by a single feature are found equally quickly in all display sizes, which fits with the idea of a parallel pre-attentive search process. If activity for the relevant feature is detected in the relevant feature map, a target is present; if not, there is no target.

Treisman and Schmidt (1982) presented subjects with brief visual displays in which there was a row of three coloured letters flanked by two digits. The primary task was to report the digits and second to report the letters and their colours. As the display was very brief there was insufficient time for serial search with focal attention on the letters. Treisman and Schmidt found that subjects made errors in the

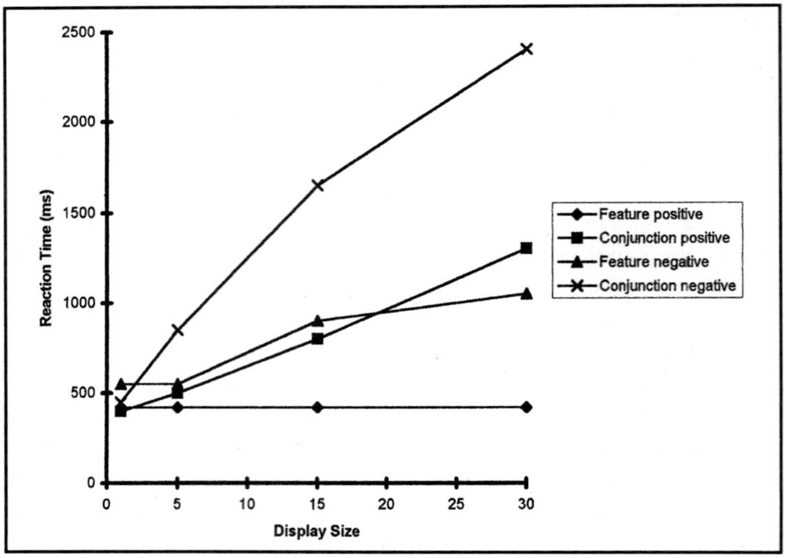

FIG. 5.2. Typical performance in a detection task plotting response time to detect a target as a function of target definition (conjunctive versus single feature) and display size (adapted from Treisman and Gelade, 1980).

letter task, but these were not random errors; rather they were "illusory conjunctions". Subjects reported letters and colours which had been present in the display, but assigned the wrong letters to the wrong colours. This seems to provide evidence that when focal attention cannot be directed to the locations occupied by the coloured letters, the features detected are combined in some arbitrary way.

Treisman (1986) examined the effect of pre-cueing target location. She argued that if attention is necessary for detecting a conjunction, then a pre-cue that tells attention where to go first, should have eliminated the need for serial search of any other display locations. In contrast, as feature search does not require serial search by location, a location cue should provide no benefit. Cue validity was manipulated with the expectation that invalid cues would lead to response time costs, while valid cues would be beneficial. We have already looked at similar experimental manipulations by Posner and Snyder (1975) and Eriksen and Murphy (1986). Results showed that for conjunction targets there was a substantial benefit of a valid cue but feature targets were hardly affected. This supports the idea that search for a conjunction uses attention directed to locations in the display. There was, however, a much smaller difference between the costs of an invalid cue on the two search conditions.

In the cueing experiment just described, Treisman used a similar technique to that used by Posner and his associates, but as the tasks used were rather different it could be that they were tapping different varieties of attention. Recall, from Chapter 3, the suggestion by Kahneman and Treisman (1984) that there is an important difference between selective set and selective filtering experiments. The kind of task typically used by the Posner group, in which there is usually only one target and does not involve selection of a target from distractors, is more like a selective set task. Search for a conjunction target in Treisman's experiments is a selective filtering task. Kahneman and Treisman (1984, p.33) suggest that "different processes and mechanisms may be involved in these simple tasks and in the more complex filtering tasks". This suggestion is supported by experiments reported by Lavie (1995) discussed in Chapter 3.

Briand and Klein (1987) wanted to test whether the kind of attention that Posner describes as a "beam" is the same as focal attention, described as "glue" by Treisman. They used a "Posner" spatial cueing task to orient the subject's attention to a "Treisman" type task. When the cue was an arrow at fixation (that is, a central cue requiring endogenous attentional orienting by the subject), Briand and Klein found no costs or benefits associated with valid or invalid cueing on either a feature detection or on a conjunction task. However, when the cue was a peripheral cue to the location of the targets, a valid cue improved performance for conjunctions. Briand and Klein suggest that exogenous attention is important for conjoining features and that endogenous attention is important for later, response selection processes.

Visual search and visual similarity: Attentional engagement theory

Duncan and Humphreys (1989, 1992) put forward a different theory of visual search and visual attention which stresses the importance of similarity not only between targets but also between non-targets. Similarity is a powerful grouping factor, and depending on how easily targets and distractors form into separate groups, visual search will be more or less efficient. Sometimes targets can be easily rejected as irrelevant, but in other displays targets may be much more difficult to reject. Part of the reason for this is that the more similar the targets are to the non-targets the more difficult it is for selective mechanisms to segregate, or group, the visual display. Experiments by Beck (1966) had shown that subjects found it easier to detect a visual texture boundary on a page printed with areas of upright letter Ts and Ts that were rotated by 45°, than to detect a boundary between Ts and Ls. The difference in orientation between the two kinds of T meant that they shared no features, whereas the letters L and T contain the same features. So, shapes which are more similar in their features are more difficult to group together. Duncan and Humphreys (1989) did a series of experiments in which subjects might, for example, have to search for a target such as an upright L amongst rotated Ts. The Ts might be homogeneous (i.e. all rotated the same way), or might be heterogeneous (i.e, all at different rotations): see Fig. 5.3. By manipulating the heterogeneity of distractors and their relation to the target, Duncan and Humphreys were able to show large variations in the efficiency of visual search which were not predicted by feature integration theory (FIT). Remember, FIT said that the elementary features are coded pre-attentively in parallel over the visual display, and conjunctions of features, presumably necessary for determining whether the features are arranged to make a T or an L, require serial search with focal attention. Duncan and Humphreys' experiments showed that although in some conditions conjunction search was

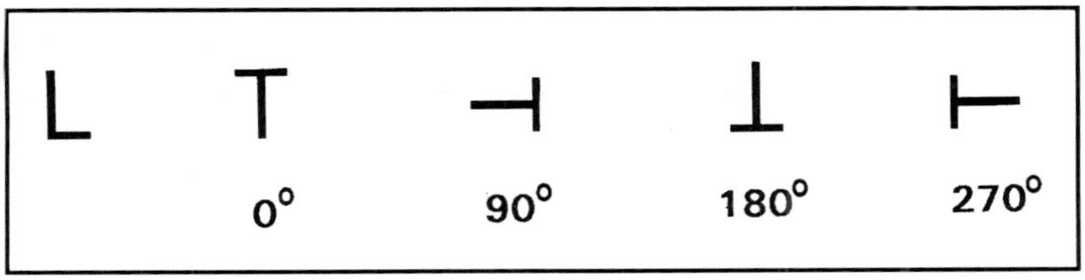

FIG. 5.3. Examples of stimuli used by Duncan and Humphreys. An upright L compared with a T at four rotations (from Duncan & Humphreys, 1989, copyright © the American Psychological Association, reprinted with permission).

affected by display size, in other conditions display size effects were reduced or absent. In fact, in conditions where all the distractors were homogeneous, absent responses could be even faster than present responses. Duncan and Humphreys (1989) called this selection at the level of the whole display and suggested that visual search for the target is, in this case, based on rapid rejection of the distractor group.

Although it might be possible to try to redefine exactly what is meant by a feature in particular discriminations—for example, the corner of an L could be a distinctive feature of an L, or the junction of the horizontal and vertical components of a T join could be a feature of a T—this is clumsy and Duncan and Humphreys have evidence to suggest that this is not the case.

Duncan and Humphreys' (1989) results led them to propose that search rate is so variable depending on tasks and conditions as to make a clear distinction between serial and parallel search tasks difficult to sustain. As the difference between targets and distractors increases, so does search efficiency. Also, as the similarity between distractors increases, search for a target becomes more efficient. These two factors— i.e. Target/non-target similarity and Non-target/non-target similarity—interact. Thus efficiency of target search depends not only on how similar or different the target is from the distractors, but also on how similar to or different from each other the distractors are. This theory is more concerned with the relationship between targets and distractors and the way in which the information in the visual field can be segregated into perceptual groups than with spatial mapping. The computer model SERR (search via recursive rejection), described a little later, models this theory.

In feature integration theory the spatial mapping of attributes is very important. Van der Heijden (1993) reviews theories of attention with respect to whether they propose that position is special or not. Van der Heijden classes Duncan and Humphreys' theory as a "position not special" theory along with that of Bundesen (1990) and Kahneman (1973), but classes FIT as a "position special" theory. According to van der Heijden (1993) position *is* special and he has his own theory in which he sees spatial position as very closely related to attention, as, he claims, there is so much evidence in favour of position information both facilitating selective attention and being involved in the breakdown of attention—for example, in visual neglect.

Filtering and movement

Driver and McLeod (1992) provide evidence that is inconsistent with a purely spatial account of perceptual integration. In their experiment they tested the ability of normal subjects to perform selective filtering tasks on the basis of conjunction of form and movement. They argued that, as cells which are sensitive to movement are less sensitive to form and vice versa, there should be an interaction between the difficulty of form discrimination (a difference in line orientation) and whether the target was moving or not. Driver and McLeod discovered that search for a moving target was easier than for a stationary target provided the discrimination of the form of targets from non-targets was easy. However, when form discrimination was difficult, search was easier for a stationary target. McLeod and Driver (1993) argue that their data establish an important link between predictions based on our knowledge of physiology and observable behaviour. Their results show that subjects can selectively attend to the moving objects in order to make simple form discriminations, but this ability is no help if the task requires a more difficult discrimination of form. Thus different properties represented by different cells in the visual system can help to explain our ability (or inability) to selectively attend to different stimulus attributes. Recently, however, experiments by Müller and Maxwell (1994) have failed to replicate McLeod and Driver's results. It had subsequently been found that display density influences search rate for conjunctions of orientation and movement. To follow the debate, the interested reader should see Müller and Found (1996) and Berger and McLeod (1996).

Feature integration theory: The position in 1993

In her most recent review, Treisman (1993) addresses a number of issues and updates her views. First she considers what "features" are. Behaviourally, features can be defined as any attribute which allows pop-out, mediates texture segregation, and may be recombined as illusory conjunctions. Functionally, features are properties which have specialised sets of detectors which respond in parallel across the visual display. It has now been shown that there is also a "feature hierarchy". Treisman distinguishes between surface-defining features such as colour, luminance, and relative motion, and shape-defining features such as orientation and size. Shape is defined by the spatial arrangement of one or more surface defining features. Treisman (1993) gives the example of creating a horizontal bar whose boundaries are defined by changes, or discontinuities in brightness or colour. She has shown that several shape-defining features can be detected in parallel within the surface-defining media of luminance, colour, relative motion, texture, and stereoscopic depth.

There is also evidence that some three-dimensional properties of objects pop out of displays. For example, Ramachandran (1988) showed that two-dimensional egg shapes, given shape from shading would segregate into a group which appeared convex and a group which appeared concave. Only the shading pattern defined the target. The concave/convex attribution is given to the shape because the perceptual system assumes that light always comes from above. According to the original FIT, shape and shading would need to be conjoined. Yet there is increasing evidence that not all conjunctions require focal attention. Treisman (1993) suggests a possible solution lies in the distinction between divided attention and pre-attention. In her initial statement of FIT Treisman proposed that pop-out and texture segregation was carried out pre-attentively, but now considers that pre-attentive processing is only an "inferred stage of early vision" (p.13) which cannot directly affect experience. As for conscious experience, some form of attention is required to combine information from different feature maps. Now she proposes that pop-out and texture segregation occur when attention is distributed over large parts of the visual display, with a broad window rather than a small spotlight. When the window of attention is large, feature maps are integrated at a global level; for accurate localisation and for conjoining features, the window must narrow down its focus. In an experiment like Ramachandran's with the shaded eggs, attention is divided over the whole display and can support global analyses for direction of illumination and orientation. Treisman (1993) also considers what happens to the unattended stimuli. If attention is narrowly focused on one part of the display, then stimuli in the unattended areas will not even be processed for global properties, as this occurs only under divided attention conditions.

We saw in the discussion of Duncan and Humphreys' (1989) experiments, that target detection times depend on the similarity of distractors to the target and the similarity of distractors to each other.

Original FIT could not handle this data. More recently Treisman has suggested that there are inhibitory connections from the feature maps to the master map of locations. The advantage of having inhibitory connections is that if we know we want to find a red circle, we can inhibit anything that is not red or a circle to speed search time. Also if we know the distractors are blue and square, we can inhibit blue and square. However, the more similar the targets are to the distractors and the more dissimilar the distractors are from each other, the less efficient the inhibitory strategy becomes.

Some of the increasing evidence that visual attention is object based, discussed earlier is accounted for by Treisman (1993). Briefly, she sees object perception and attention as depending on the interaction between feature maps, the location map and the object file. She claims that for object-based selection, attention is initially needed to set up the file, but once it is set up the object can maintain attention on the location that it occupies.

Another effect that FIT has to account for is negative priming (Tipper, 1985) which is evidence for a late selection account of attention. Generally FIT has been interpreted as an early selection model; however, Treisman (1993) thinks that selection will be at different levels depending on the load on perception. When perceptual load is low, selection for action, or response, is the only kind needed. So selection may be early or late depending on the circumstances: see Fig. 5.4.

Lavie (1995) reported some experiments showing that the amount of interference from irrelevant distractors in the Eriksen task is inversely proportional to the load imposed by target processing. So, now Treisman allows for four levels or kinds of attentional selection on the basis of location, features, object-defined locations, and a late-selection stage where attention determines which identified object file should control response. It is now evident that selectivity may operate at a number of levels depending on task demands. A strict bottleneck is therefore ruled out. There is increasing support from neurophysiology, experimental psychology, and cognitive neuropsychology for parallel processing of many stimulus attributes and attention seems to be concerned with integrating the right attributes together and mapping them onto the right representations for the coherent control of goal-directed behaviour. This is known as the *binding problem.*

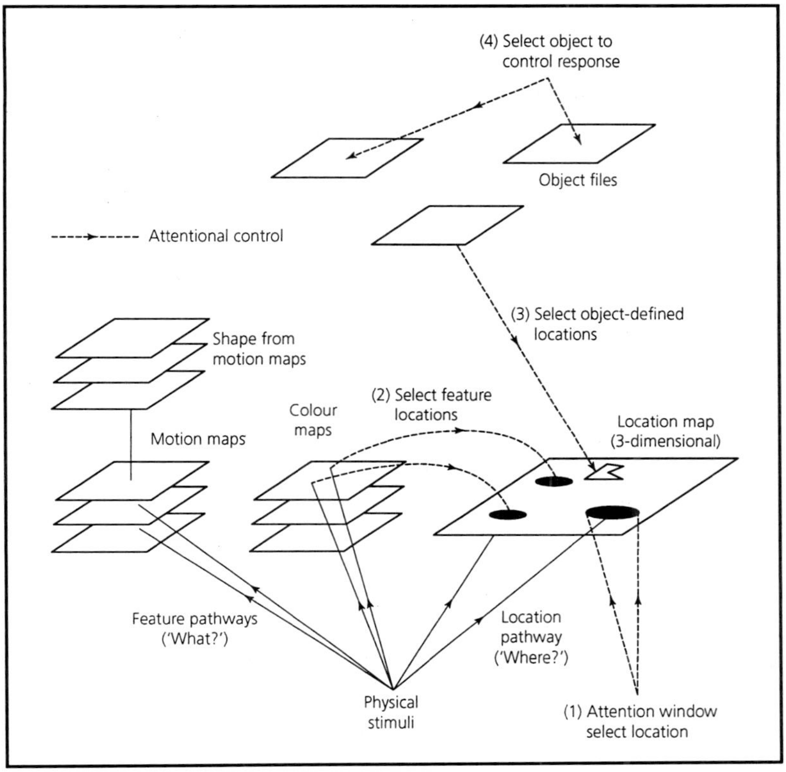

FIG. 5.4. Figure illustrating the four different forms of attentional selection, mediated by interactions between the location map, the feature maps, an object file, and a late-selection stage determining which objects file should control the response (reprinted by permission of Oxford University Press, from Treisman, 1993).

A neurophysiological explanation of the binding problem

Singer (1994) considers the binding problem in neurophysiological terms. He suggests that any representation of a sensory pattern or motor programme needs a mechanism which can bind the individual components together while preserving the integrity of the relationship between the components. The simplest way to do this would be to have a hierarchy in which neurons responsive to specific components of a pattern are mapped onto neurons responsive to specific patterns which in turn are mapped onto a single higher order neuron.

From what we have seen about the specificity of coding within the visual system this idea may seem promising. However, although at low levels of analysis we have evidence for colour, orientation, movement etc. being uniquely coded by neurons, at higher levels cells tend to become less specialised. Apart from a few exceptions, such as face-sensitive cells found by Rolls and Baylis (1986), there is little evidence for specific higher order neurons which are sensitive to complex patterns. It is implausible that we could have a neuron for every pattern we might experience and unlikely that responses to novel stimuli could proceed effectively in such a system. Instead, Singer believes that cell assemblies must be involved.

It was Hebb (1949) who first suggested the idea of cell assemblies. This idea has grown in popularity recently (for example, Grossberg, 1980; Crick, 1984; von der Malsburg, 1985; Singer, 1994). The advantage of coding information in assemblies is that individual cells contribute at different times to different representations, so sometimes a cell will be part of one assembly of concurrently active neurons and sometimes part of another assembly of coactive neurons. Thus the significance of any individual neuronal response will depend on the context within which it is active. Singer (1994) sets three basic requirements for representing objects in assemblies. First, the responses of the individual cells must be probed for meaningful relations; second, cells that can be related must be organised into an assembly; and third, once the assembly is formed, the members within it must remain distinguishable from members of other assemblies. Most suggestions for how this is achieved assume that the likelihood of cells being recruited to an assembly depends on connections between potential members, and that there are reciprocal excitatory connections which prolong and enhance the activation of cells that get organised into the assembly. One way in which neurons could be formed into assemblies would be by a temporal code. Von der Malsburg (1985) suggested that distributed circuits which represent a set of facts are bound together by their simultaneous activation. If discharges of neurons within an assembly are synchronised, their responses would be distinguishable as coming from the same assembly. Assemblies coding different information would have different rhythms, allowing different assemblies to be distinguished. Evidence has been found for the synchronised firing of neurons. Gray and Singer (1989) showed that neurons in cat cortex produce synchronous discharges when presented with a preferred stimulus. Singer (1994, p.99) says that activity of distributed neurons has to be synchronised in order to become influential, because "only coherent activity has a chance of being relayed over successive processing stages". This notion of binding by synchronous discharge has been proposed as a possible mechanism for integration over modalities (Damasio, 1990), attention (Crick, 1984), and consciousness (Crick & Koch 1990).

Singer (1994) examines the consequences of the synchronised activity of distributed neurons for attention and performance. For example, the attentional pop-out effect, in which a single odd feature draws attention to itself from amongst the rest of the field, could result from the fact that neurons responsive to the same features are mutually inhibitory, producing a relative enhancement of the activity to the odd feature (Crick & Koch, 1992), which then pops out. Singer applies the same argument to assemblies. He says that assemblies which are effective in attracting attention are those whose discharges are highly coherent. This is because, the tight synchrony allows the information of such assemblies to be relayed further in the information processing system than other less well synchronised assemblies, so influencing shifts of attention. Of course pop-out is mainly a bottom-up effect, but Singer proposes a similar effect could occur top-down if it were assumed that feedback connections from higher to lower levels could bias the probability of assemblies becoming synchronised. Shifts of attention between modalities could be achieved by selectively favouring synchronisation in one sensory area rather than another. Following Crick and Koch, he conjectures that only those patterns of activation that are sufficiently coherent reach a level of conscious awareness.

Singer's ideas are highly theoretical and may offer a promising explanation for code coordination. They are at present somewhat unclear on the nature of the top-down attentional biasing or how higher levels might bias the probability of cell assemblies becoming synchronised.

Some connectionist models of visual search and visual attention

If we want to produce realistic models of human behaviour we would ideally have a computer which was very like the brain itself. This is the attraction of a variety of systems called connectionist networks, artificial neural networks or parallel distributed processing (PDP) models. Connectionist networks have characteristics which are close to those of the brain in that they are composed of a large number of processing elements, called nodes or units, which are connected together by inhibitory or excitatory links. Each unit produces a single output if its activity exceeds a threshold, and its own activity will depend on the weighted sum of connections onto it. Representations are held in the strength of the connections between units and the same units may be involved at different times in different representations. Quite clearly this is very similar to what we know of the structure and activity of the brain. Another interesting property is that these systems learn to associate different inputs with different outputs by altering the strength of their interconnections. This way, the system learns and begins to exhibit rule-governed behaviour without having had any rules given to it.

McClelland, Rumelhart, and Hinton (1986) point out that people are good at tasks in which numerous sources of information and multiple constraints must be considered simultaneously. PDP offers a computational framework within which simultaneous constraint satisfaction can be accommodated. Because all units influence all other units, either directly or indirectly, numerous sources of information, together with what the system already knows, contribute to the pattern of activity in the system. All the local computations contribute to the global pattern which emerges after all the interactive activation and inhibition has resolved. In this way a best fit solution is arrived at which takes into account all the information and constraints on the system. Connectionist models have layers of units—for example, input units and output units—between which are, depending on the type of model, hidden units which are important for computational reasons. They may also have units dedicated to coding particular features or properties of the input; for example, colour and position (we know the brain does) and map this information onto higher order units of the network; for example, object recognition units or a motor programme. A good introduction to connectionist modelling in psychology can be found in Quinlan (1991) and Bechtel and Abrahamsen (1991).

SLAM (SeLective Attention Model)

SLAM was devised by Phaf, van der Heijden, and Hudson (1990) to perform visual selective attention tasks. Their definition of attention is as follows: "Attention is the process whereby an abundance of stimuli is ordered and integrated within the framework of current tasks and activities; it integrates ongoing activity and newly arriving information. This integration results in the apparent selection of information" (p.275). According to their analysis two processes are required in order to model attention: first, attribute selection and second, object selection. Their model is based on the interactive activation model of letter identification by McClelland and Rumelhart (1981), in which processing is hierarchical but parallel at all levels in the hierarchy with both top-down and bottom-up interactions. Within each level, there is mutual inhibition between nodes. This means that at any given level the most active node will inhibit all others and there can only be one winner. Nodes from different levels whose representations are compatible have excitatory interconnections, whereas those representations which are incompatible have inhibitory interconnections. Rather than using letters and words, SLAM is designed to process position (left and right), colour (red and blue), and form (square and circle), which we know are coded separately by the brain but need coordinating if a target is to be accurately selected. SLAM is particulary concerned with modelling the way in which these codes are coordinated in selective attention tasks.

At the first level in the model, representations consist of three modules which code combinations of the features. These are a form–position module (e.g. square in the left position), a colour–position module (e.g. red in the right position), and a form–colour module (e.g. blue circle). At the next level single features are represented—colour, form, and position; and at the third level are the representations of the six possible motor responses and a biasing mechanism called the pre-trial residual activity: see Fig. 5.5.

Phaf et al. (1990) ran numerous simulations of selective filtering tasks through the model. Of course, human subjects can be given an instruction, such as "Name the colour" or "Name the position". In the model, an instruction is set up by activating an *attribute set*, either colour or position at the first level. This has the effect of priming either all positions or all colours. However, if the instruction is "Name the colour on the left", priming a single attribute set will not allow selection as both attributes of the object are required to determine response. Phaf et al. assumed that this task requires activation at the second layer of the system and changed the weights in the model accordingly. The selection cue enhances one of the objects and the attribute set selects the response to the stimulus. Response times from the simulations were taken as measures of how long the system took to relax, where relaxation is considered to be the outcome of a multiple constraint satisfaction process. Presenting different stimuli and giving different instructions perturbs the stability of the system resulting in different relaxation patterns which, essentially, provide the answer or response to a particular task. Further, according to the task, relaxation may take more or less time, so increasing or decreasing reaction time.

FIG. 5.5. Schematic view of the SLAM model for filtering tasks (reprinted by permission of Academic Press from Phaf, van der Heijden, & Hudson, 1990).

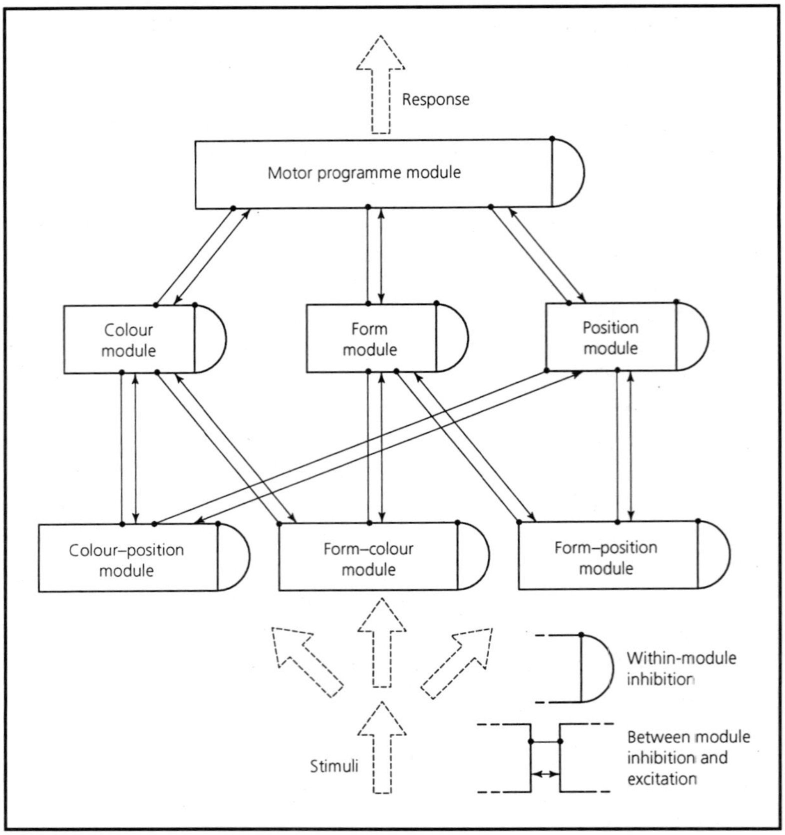

The authors claim that SLAM behaves very much like a human subject, in that it needs only a stimulus and an instruction to reach a decision. The initial simple model was extended to examine Stroop performance by adding word colour and word form modules for some simulations. The results of their simulations are impressive in that there is a high correlation between experimental and simulation data for both selective filtering and Stroop tasks.

SERR (SEarch via Recursive Rejection)

Humphreys and Müller (1993) developed SERR which is a connectionist model of visual search. Their model is based on the attentional engagement theory proposed by Duncan and Humphreys (1989) and Duncan and Humphreys (1992), discussed in the previous section. Remember, according to Duncan and Humphreys, search efficiency is affected by the strength of grouping effects between distractors compared with the strength of grouping effects between the target and distractors. Grouping can be based on the similarity of simple conjunctions and search will be parallel when the target and distractors form separate groups. As the strength of grouping that differentiates the target from distractors reduces, so does the efficiency of visual search. One particularly crucial finding is that, with homogeneous displays, target-absent responses can be faster than target-present responses. This led to the suggestion that the ease with which perceptual groups could be rapidly rejected was important for visual search efficiency.

SERR is explicitly designed to model attentional processing. It, too, is a hierarchical connectionist network similar to the interactive activation model by McClelland and Rumelhart (1981). In SERR the units at the first level are responsive to simple line segments at a particular orientation. These units feed onto units at the next level which correspond to simple form conjunctions of line segments such as L or T conjunctions. Units are organised into maps arranged topographically, so that multiple items can be processed in parallel. Figure 5.6 shows the basic architecture of the model.

Compare this to Fig. 5.4 which represents FIT. Superficially these figures look quite similar in conception. Both involve a number of interconnected maps which compute different properties of the stimuli, including features and locations. SERR is concerned only with simple lines and conjunctions of lines whereas FIT also has motion and colour maps and an attention window. In SERR motion and colour are not included, although presumably it could be modified to do this. However, although SERR does not have an attention window in the diagram, Humphreys and Müller (1993, p.102) suggest this window is rather like the spatial area over which grouping takes place: "When distractors group separately from targets ... selection operates across a broad area; when there is competition for grouping between different distractors and targets ... selection operates over increasingly small perceptual groups".

There are other differences. SERR encodes simple conjunctions of form over spatially parallel units, whereas FIT does not. In SERR distractor locations are rapidly rejected before the target reaches threshold and the area rejected varies according to the number of competing groups. Of course, a major difference between these figures is that one, FIT, represents a theoretical model whilst the other, SERR, is implemented in a working computer simulation.

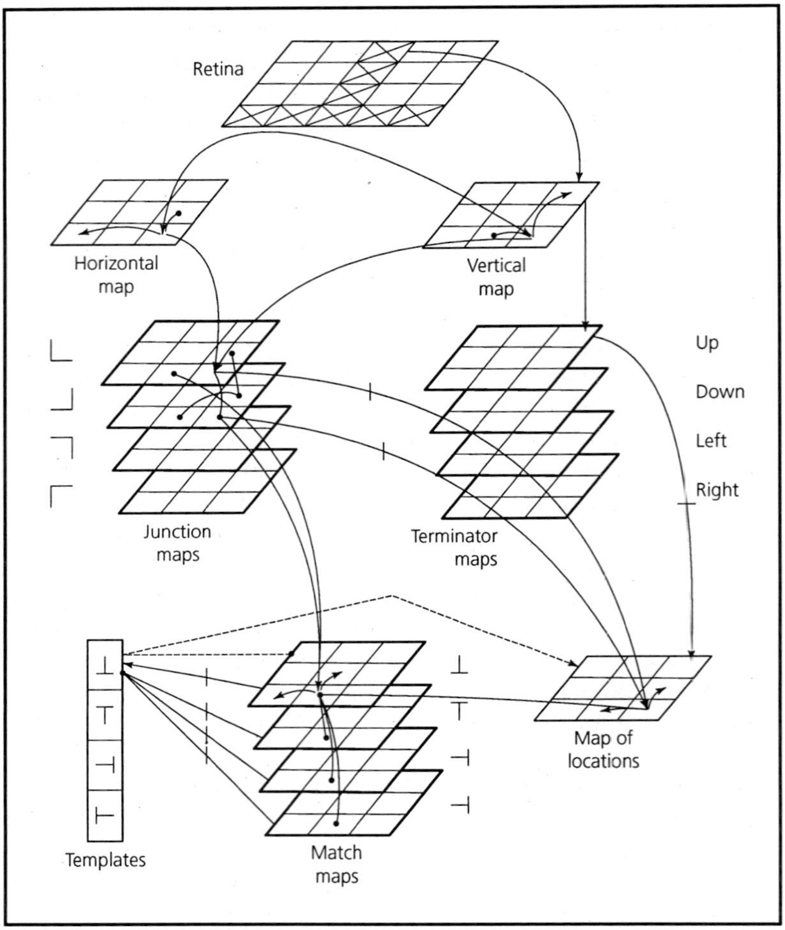

FIG. 5.6. The basic architecture of SERR. Major connections are shown for units activated by an inverted T on the model's retina: ⟶ indicates an excitatory two-way connection; —• indicates an inhibitory two-way connection; —+→ indicates an excitatory one-way connection; - - → indicates a fast excitatory connection used after a template's threshold is exceeded; and - - —• indicates a fast inhibitory connection used after a template's threshold is exceeded. Reprinted by permission of Academic Press from Humphreys and Müller (1993).

In SERR the retinal array codes the stimulus pattern which excites features in the vertical and horizontal single feature maps, which feed onto units in the eight combined-feature maps (four for the end terminators—up, down, left, and right—and four for each orientation of an L-junction). Each of the four match maps samples an area on the combined-feature maps for evidence for or against a particular target or distractor at that location. The match maps produce grouping by inhibiting units in other match maps that code competing stimuli at the same location. If the network is simulating search for Ts at particular orientations, the match map is tuned for T-conjunctions. There is a match unit for coding T in each orientation and each matching unit receives excitation from all junction and terminator units compatible with its orientation and inhibition from all junction and terminator units incompatible with its orientation. The map of locations is made up of units which are on if there is no bottom-up input. As input from the combined-feature maps increases, their activity decreases the activation in the map of locations so that when there is sufficient input, a location unit will go off, which has the effect of removing strong inhibition from the matching units. When a location unit is off, there is a mechanism which produces an inhibitory surround for a unit that is on.

Template units sample the whole array for evidence of a compatible match and accumulate evidence over time. Recursive rejection of non-targets is achieved by strong negative connections between the templates and the match-map units which can be rapidly deployed when a template fires. Templates have excitatory connections from their corresponding match-map units and inhibitory connections from incompatible match-map units. Once a template has accumulated enough evidence so that it fires, the model is designed to exclude all location units which contain no corresponding active match-map units from search. If a template fires, all corresponding match-map units are rapidly inhibited. At the same time, strong excitation is sent to all location units for which there are no active match-map units other than the one inhibited. This has the effect of preventing search of any location maps which do not have at least one active compatible match-map unit.

Humphreys and Müller (1993) tested SERR on a number of the search tasks used by Duncan and Humphreys (1989, 1992). For example, to find an inverted T amongst homogeneous or heterogeneous distractors: it produced flat search functions and faster absent than present responses with homogeneous distractors; but with heterogeneous distractors it was not so good, producing many more misses than did humans in heterogeneous displays. A checking process was introduced, essentially by rerunning the network on a number of target-absent trials, as human subjects might well be expected to include checking before making a target absent decision. With the checking mechanism in place, SERR's performance was much closer to that of human subjects with heterogeneous displays. SERR also has an impressive ability to predict some human search data. In this model, attentional behaviour emerges as a consequence of the search operations.

Search in SERR is based on objects rather than space, as it can select groups which are in different areas of the visual field. Selection is not restricted to one part of SERR's retina. The experiments by Duncan

(1984) and Driver and Baylis (1989), discussed earlier in this chapter, showed the importance of perceptual groups for selection. SERR is clearly compatible with these results and with the notion of object-based attention and not with the fixed size spatial spotlight metaphor of attention.

A connectionist model incorporating attention: MORSEL

Mozer (1987) developed a connectionist net to model word processing. MORSEL has three components: first BLIRNET, which is the central component, whose function in the model is to Build Location Independent Representations of multiple words in a NETwork; second the pull-out net (PO) and third an attentional mechanism (AM). Although specifically designed for reading, the inclusion of an attentional mechanism means it is of relevance to theories of attention. BLIRNET is an artificial retina with six independent layers of units, the first of which codes letter strokes; the next layer "coarse codes" (roughly codes) the information from level 1; the third layer coarse codes the information from level 2, etc. By layer 6, letter clusters are represented. There were a number of severe problems with the model's capability for dealing with more than one word at a time, which resulted in the addition of the second and third components: the pull-out net which acts to clean up the perceptual input using top-down knowledge of words, and the attentional mechanism which is another layer of units isomorphic with those in layer 1. This layer of attentional mechanism units was set up to bias the probability that activations in layer 1 would reach layer 2. In essence, the AM units act as an attentional spotlight of the sort proposed by Posner (1980) and Treisman and Gelade (1980) whereby attention has the effect of enhancing the activation of the information under the beam or increasing the probability that it will be selected. Following current evidence, Mozer allowed the spotlight to be focused on just one retinal location at a time. In BLIRNET attention can be captured by stimulus attributes or controlled by higher level cognitive processes. As the AM unit receives input from both the retina and higher level processes, there will sometimes be conflict which is resolved by constraint satisfaction. This means that, theoretically at least, attentional processing could be affected by both current goals and perceptual input; i.e. endogenous and exogenous attention could emerge.

MORSEL has been used to model neglect dyslexia by Behrman (1996). Kinsbourne and Warrington (1962) report a study of six patients who neglected the left half of visual space and also neglected the left-hand side of words. This neglect would occur even when the whole of the word was presented in the good field. It appears as if neglect dyslexia is based on the object of the word rather than environmental space. Ellis, Flude, and Young (1987) report another patient V.B. When reading she would read only the right half of each line of print and made errors on some words in the line. With single words she tended to misread "RIVER" as "liver" or "LOG" as "dog". Interestingly, although V.B. did not read the initial letter of words (sometimes she gave responses which reflected a simple deletion of the first letter, for example, reading "CAGE" as "age") there were a number of occasions on which she was clearly reacting to the presence of the neglected letter. Given words like "ELATE" or "PEACH" she produced "plate" and "beach". If she had no knowledge of a letter being present in the neglected area, a response of "late" or "each" would have been expected. V.B. also tended to substitute the same number of letters as she had neglected. At some level of representation, then, it seems that the reading system had knowledge about, at least, the number of letters being neglected. Ellis et al. (1987) suggest that V.B.'s performance reflects a greater deficit in the encoding of letter identity than in the encoding of letter position: she seems to know that positions are there which need to be filled but not what those letters are.

Caramazza and Hillis (1990) studied patient N.G. who also suffered unilateral neglect. In contrast to V.B., whose errors were made on the left part of the word, errors made by N.G. were independent of the orientation of the word. That is to say, whether the word was horizontal, vertical or mirror reversed, errors were made at the same relative position in the word. Caramazza and Hillis suggest that these two forms of neglect dyslexia provide evidence for a dissociation between two different levels of visual word recognition. At the level disrupted in V.B. the representation is viewer-centred, whereas in N.G. the word-centred level of representation is disrupted. These two cases are good evidence for different levels of representation at which attention can be neglectful.

Neglect dyslexia can also be material specific: for example, Patterson and Wilson (1990) report a patient who was able to name the left-hand side of an array of geometric figures, but was unable to name the left-hand side of a string of alphanumeric characters. Behrmann (1994) reviews neglect dyslexia and highlights the difficulty faced by theories of attention when trying to explain the variety of symptoms displayed by patients. Attentional neglect appears to occur in a variety of spatial frames and representational levels. MORSEL has been used by Behrmann (1994) to simulate neglect dyslexia. Three properties of AM are essential for explaining the variety of symptoms in neglect patients. First, attention selection is by location and takes place early in processing. Second, attention tries to select a single item using early segmentation of the display without higher order knowledge. Third, attention regulates the flow of activity through BLIRNET.

MORSEL also employs a top-down system called the pull-out (PO) net which cleans up degraded or noisy input using word knowledge. For the simulation, damage to AM was arranged in such a way that the bottom-up connections from the input feature map was graded so that the probability of a feature being transmitted was 90% at the right edge and only 48% at the left edge. This attentional gradient also had the effect of reducing the probability that AM will focus attention at the location of an undetected feature, as, unless a feature is detected, AM will not focus on that location.

When the lesioned model was presented with a pair of words, selection was strongly biased toward the word on the right; although the region occupied by the word on the left was also active, this activation was much weaker, or attenuated. The lesion also affected the distribution of attention over the word, so that the left side of each word was weaker than the right. This simulation shows how lesions to bottom-up connections affect the direction of AM not only over the whole retina, but also within a word. The lesion also produced higher order effects. When two words, such as COW and BOY were presented, the word BOY, on the right, was usually selected, but because BLIRNET has some ambiguity over precise letter position information, clusters representing slight re-ordering of the letters are weakly activated. In the example of COW and BOY there could, therefore, be complete activation of the word COWBOY. Now, if both BOY and COWBOY are active, the pull-out mechanism can read out either BOY or COWBOY. In contrast, if the two words did not form another word, for example SUN and FLY, FLY extinguishes SUN. This pattern of results mimics that found in patients and shows how top-down processing interacts with bottom-up processing to produce neglect at a different, higher order of representation. Evidence from the simulation suggests that neglect dyslexia is determined by the interaction between degraded input and top-down processes. Although the input is degraded, the complete input can be recovered by top-down activation. Once the complete input has been recovered, neglect may operate within the word frame, at a higher order of representation. In this way, damage at a low, perceptual level, can give rise to higher order neglect within an object-centred reference frame. Examples such as this demonstrate the power of models in clarifying mechanisms of attention.

A model for attention?

Although this chapter contains several theories and models of attention, not one of them provides a general theory. Each model or theory is concerned with explaining or modelling only a small part of the data. There is so much to explain that it seems unlikely that there could ever be a single unified theory. Not only is there a huge amount of data but also the data are concerned with attention at different levels. Some theories consider attention at a neurophysiological level, others at a cognitive level and, as we shall see in a moment, at a mathematical level. Computational models are also confined to simulating specific problems or behaviours. Recently, however, there have been attempts to provide wider ranging theories. For example, Schneider (1995) proposed a neuro-cognitive model for visual attention, VAM, and there is the following mathematical theory by Logan (1996).

Formal mathematical models

Both Bundersen (1990) and Logan (1996) have developed formal mathematical theories of visual attention. We mentioned Bundersen (1990) with respect to pigeon-holing and categorisation, in Chapter 2. Here we shall briefly consider Logan's (1996) CODE theory of visual attention (CTVA) which integrates van Oeffelen and Vos's (1982, 1983) COntour DEtector (CODE) theory for perceptual grouping with Bundersen's (1990) theory of visual attention (TVA). Logan attempts to integrate theories of space-based attention with theories of object-based attention.

Five questions to be answered

At the beginning of his paper, Logan focuses on what he considers to be the five key questions that must be addressed by any theory of visual attention. These questions will allow us to reflect on some of the theories we have already met in this chapter. The first question that any theory must consider is: how is space represented?

Space-based theories such as FIT assume that space is represented by a map of locations, with objects represented as points in space. Further, the Euclidean distances between objects is important for space-based attention; for example, Eriksen and Eriksen (1974). On the other hand, object-based theories, are, according to Logan, unclear about the way in which space is represented. When grouping factors counteract Euclidean distances (for example, Driver & Baylis, 1989), the theory is object based. Logan argues that as grouping factors such as proximity are very important for object-based theories, abandoning Euclidean space seems an odd thing for object-based theorists to do.

Logan's next important question is: what is an object? This question has no agreed answer. However, although theorists disagree, there is some consensus that objects are hierarchical and can be decomposed into component parts. Remember the example of the tree, the branch, or the leaf, when we looked at local and global processing in the last chapter. The next question is: what determines the shape of the spotlight? Logan says that theorists are generally vague on this matter and must be explicit about what determines spotlight shape, as this "leaves less work for the omnipotent homunculus to do" (1996, p.604).

The remaining two questions are: how does selection occur within the focus of attention; and how does selection between objects occur? In space-based and object-based theories of selection everything within the focus of attention is assumed to be processed. Yet the well-known Stroop effect demonstrates that selection can operate within a spatial location. (We shall discuss the Stroop effect in Chapter 9.) The classic Stroop task requires the subject to name the colour of the ink in which a colour name is written. Although there is interference between the two representations of colour, in that the ink interferes with the colour word, selection is possible. So, some other intentional selective mechanism must exist which is not based on spatial representations. Phaf et al. (1990) modelled this in SLAM discussed earlier. The question of how selection between objects occurs is important because theories must explain how attention knows which object or spatial location to choose next. Although a cue may indicate a likely target location—for example, in Posner's (1980) experiments or bar-probe tasks such as Eriksen and Yeh (1985)—attention has still to go from the cue to the target. Logan (1995) suggested that one way of doing this conceptually guided selection is to use a linguistic code. This theory is explained in Chapter 9, when we consider the intentional control of behaviour.

CTVA theory is mathematically complex and we shall not go into the maths here. However, in essence CTVA incorporates CODE theory (van Oeffelen & Vos, 1982, 1983; Compton & Logan, 1993) and TVA (Bundersen, 1990). CODE provides two representations of space: an analogue representation of the locations of items and another quasi-analogue representation of objects and groups of objects. The analogue representation is computed from bottom-up processes that depend entirely on the proximity of items in the display. The representation of objects and groups is arrived at from the interaction between top-down and bottom-up processes. In CODE, locations are not points in space, but distributions. The sum of the distributions of different items produces what is called the CODE surface and this represents the spatial array. Top-down processes can alter the threshold applied to the CODE surface. Activations above any given threshold belong to a perceptual group. We have said that within objects grouping is hierarchical: CODE can change levels in the hierarchy by changing the threshold; the lower the threshold, the larger the perceptual group. This changing of the threshold can explain why sometimes items are processed in parallel and at other times not. Logan explains the way in which CODE can account for a variety of data, including the Eriksen effect, but in order to achieve within-object or within-region selection another selective mechanism is required. This is where TVA comes in. Essentially, TVA selects between categorisations of perceptual inputs and assumes two levels of representation. At the perceptual level representations are of the features of items in the display. At the conceptual level the representation is of the categorisations of features and items. These two representations are linked by a parameter which represents the amount of evidence that a particular item belongs to a particular category. In TVA location is not special; it is just another categorisable feature of an item like shape or colour. Selection is achieved by TVA choosing a particular category or categorisations for a particular item or items. There then ensues a race, and the first item or set of items to finish wins the race. At the end of the race both an item and a category have been selected simultaneously, so this theory is both early and late at the same time.

Does CTVA answer the questions that Logan identified as essential to any theory of visual attention? First, is there explicit detail on the representation of space? In the theory, space is represented in two ways: bottom-up on the CODE surface and top-down by the imposition of the thresholds that result in perceptual groups. Second, what is an object? According to CTVA an object is a perceptual group defined by whatever threshold is set by the top-down mechanism. Thus an object may be defined by changing the threshold, at different hierarchical levels. Third, how is the shape of the spotlight determined? The spotlight is the above-threshold region of the CODE surface, which depends on both the perceptual input and the threshold set. Fourth, how does selection occur within the area of the spotlight or focus of attention? This is achieved by TVA biasing the categorisation parameter which makes the selection of some categories more likely than others. Lastly, how does selection between objects happen? This is controlled by top-down language processes and will be discussed further in the chapter on the intentional control of behaviour, Chapter 9.

While there are some limitations of CTVA, such as its inability to group by movement, or deal with overlapping objects, theories of this kind, although extremely abstract, offer a promising look into the future of cognitive modelling

Summary

For objects to be formed the attributes that make them up must be accurately combined. Treisman and Gelade (1980) put forward feature integration theory (FIT) in which they proposed that focal attention provided the "glue" that integrated the features of objects. When a conjunction of features is needed to select a target from distractors, search is serial using focal attention, but if a target can be selected on the basis of a single feature, search is parallel and does not need focal attention. Initially the theory suggested that all conjunctions of features needed to be integrated if selection were to be possible, but as time has passed Treisman has accommodated a variety of data by modifying the theory to include a feature hierarchy and defining features behaviourally as any attribute which allows pop-out. Thus features may include some three-dimensional properties of objects, movement etc. In FIT information about separable attributes are coded onto their own maps, and then are related together via a master map of locations on which focal attention acts. Selected objects also map onto object files which accumulate information about an object and allow access to semantics. Duncan and Humphreys (1989, 1992) suggested that, rather than serial or parallel processing depending on whether features need to be combined or not, serial or parallel search will be necessary depending on the ease with which targets and distractors can be segregated, which in turn depends on target/non-target homogeneity and the homogeneity of the distractors. Humphreys and Müller's (1993) model of visual search SERR is based on the rejection of perceptually segregated groups in the visual display. In this model it is objects rather than space which mediates search. FIT can now accommodate perceptual grouping effects with the notion of inhibitory connections from feature maps to the master map of locations, but it is still essentially a space-based theory. FIT is more directly concerned with the *binding* problem than is Duncan and Humphrey's theory. The binding problem could be explained neurophysiologically by the synchronisation of activity over concurrently active neurons, as suggested by Crick and Koch (1990) and Singer (1994). The idea here is that the brain knows what belongs together because of what is concurrently active and this coherent activity could then give rise to conscious experience of the object. Other approaches to understanding visual attention are via formal mathematical theory, such as CTVA, which is an attempt to combine both space-based and object-based visual attention within one theory.

Further reading

Allport, (D.)A. (1989). Visual attention. In M.I. Posner (Ed.), *Foundations of cognitive science.* Cambridge, MA: MIT Press. A detailed review of the biological, neuropsychological, and experimental evidence.

Bundesen, C., & Shibuya, H. (Eds.) (1995). *Visual selective attention: A special issue of Visual Cognition.* Hove, UK: Lawrence Erlbaum Associates Ltd.

Humphreys, G.W., & Bruce, V. (1989). *Visual cognition: Computational, experimental, and neuropsychological perspectives.* Hove, UK: Lawrence Erlbaum Associates Ltd. Chapter 5 on visual attention reviews theories of visual attention and provides a detailed criticism of FIT as it stood in 1989.

Treisman, A. (1993). The perception of features and objects. In A.D. Baddeley & L. Weiskrantz (Eds.), *Attention: Awareness, selection, and control.* Oxford: Oxford University Press. This gives a clear review of the history and development of feature integration theory.

Selection for action 6

Asking the right questions

So far, we have seen how different selective attention experiments, by virtue of their design, might be considered to be measuring, manipulating, or observing different varieties of attention. On the small scale some answers may have been found: for example, the minimum width of the spotlight (in certain conditions); stimulus dimensions which facilitate selectivity (in certain conditions); how the perceptual display is segregated (in particular conditions) and so on. In later chapters, the difficulty of combining tasks or dividing attention will be discussed and again some answers will be offered.

Psychologists have collected an enormous amount of data, on normal subjects and neuropsychological patients, driven by particular questions about selectivity, task combination, consciousness and control. All of these questions are, of course, important and there are chapters in this book with such titles. However, at this point, having spent four chapters on selective attention, perhaps we should just stop to consider what we have been looking at. Generally, as was evident at the end of the last chapter, most studies, theories and models address issues about how selection operates and at what level of representation. Are we any nearer discovering the nature of human performance in specific experimental tasks concerned with attention? Possibly, but are we any nearer discovering the general nature of attention? Will we ever? Well, Marr (1982) explained that to find the right answers in psychology we must ask the right questions. In formulating the right questions we need to reconsider some fundamental assumptions and take into account what is known about the neurophysiology and neuropsychology of the brain. We have seen that this is important and that, more recently, these types of evidence are being used. However, according to Marr, the most basic questions we should ask are What is attention for and what design considerations might have been selected by evolutionary forces as important for the effective use of a complex brain? Of course, the questions we ask will be modified by our conception of what the brain is like, our "metaphor of mind", together with our interpretation of available data. In the beginning, Broadbent (1958) thought that attention served to protect the hypothetical limited capacity processing system from information overload, and hence had considered what attention was for. However, the conception of the mind was different then, so although the question was asked, the answer was different. Clearly it is not simply a case of asking the right question, but also of having the right metaphor of mind.

A paradox

One of the most obvious behavioural properties of the human information processing system is that there seems to be a fundamental limit on our ability to do a number of things at once. A classic experiment by Hick (1952) showed that choice reaction time, to a single stimulus, increases with the number of possible alternatives (Hick's law). Simply preparing to respond to signals is costly. Also, evidence of the psychological refractory period (PRP), discussed in Chapters 2 and 7, shows that when two stimuli are presented in rapid succession, so that the first stimulus has not been responded to when the second stimulus arrives, response to the second stimulus is slowed (Welford, 1952; Fagot & Pashler, 1992). This suggests that the response to the second stimulus must wait until the response to the first stimulus has been selected and provides clear indications of such a limit. At the same time there is now clear evidence that the brain can process an enormous amount of information simultaneously in parallel over a variety of modality specific subsystems. In fact Neisser (1976) said there was no physiologically established limit on the amount of information that can be picked up at once. Here we have a paradox. The brain is apparently unlimited in its ability to process information, yet human performance is severely limited even when asked to do two very simple tasks at once.

Metaphors of mind

For early workers (e.g. Broadbent, 1958, 1971; Treisman, 1960), this bottleneck suggested a limited capacity system and psychologists were interested to find out where the bottleneck was located. The concept of a bottleneck necessarily implies one place where processing can proceed only at a limited rate, or a limit in capacity to process information. A bottleneck implies a point where parallel processing becomes serial and was originally couched in the metaphor of likening the mind to the old digital computer, which had "buffer storage" and "limited capacity" processing components, and whose programmes were written as flow charts in which different "stages" had to be completed before others could begin. Of course these psychologists knew that the brain was not actually like a digital computer and it is still accepted that writing flowcharts is a good way to conceptualise the component processes needed to achieve a processing goal. Indeed such flowchart models are still used, but as a description at what Marr (1982) called the computational level of explanation. At the computational level of description it does not matter about the rules or algorithms used, or the neuronal hardware which implements the rules. Although Deutsch and Deutsch (1963) is often interpreted as a late bottleneck model and simply tagged on the end of a list of theories which proposed a structural limit on parallel processing somewhere between sensory coding and response, in some ways their ideas are quite modern. Rather than a model, their paper puts forward a set of considerations, some of which we looked at in Chapter 2. There I explained that a set of multiple comparison processes, which Deutsch and Deutsch proposed could assess the most highly activated signal from amongst others, seemed computationally impossible in 1963, and led to many people dismissing this view. Deutsch and Deutsch thought that a neuropsychological mechanism involved in selective attention might be found which had connections to and from "all discriminatory and perceptual systems" (1963, p.88). This idea of a highly connected system did not fit well with a serial computing metaphor.

Over the last 10 to 15 years, however, there has been an explosion in the use and development of computers which can process information in parallel over multiple processing units, pioneered by Hinton and Anderson (1981), McClelland and Rumelhart (1986), and Rumelhart and McClelland (1986). This "new connectionism", otherwise known as parallel distributed processing (PDP), or artificial neural network approach, has had profound influence on current metaphors of mind. It would be fair to say that the new metaphor for the mind most currently in favour is that the brain is like (in fact, is) a neural network. The principal impact of PDP has been on modelling learning and memory, and such models very successfully solve all sorts of previously intractable modelling difficulties. More recently PDP has been successfully applied to show how, by damaging a normal system, a neuropsychological deficit can arise (e.g. Hinton & Shallice, 1989; Farah, 1988) and is beginning to be applied to modelling attention, as we saw in the last chapter. So, we now know from neurophysiological studies that the brain is a massively parallel, highly interconnected and interactive computing device, with different specialised subsystems designed to respond selectively to particular perceptual events and compute specialised information processing operations, (e.g. van Essen & Maunsell, 1983). These processing events do not proceed in a stage-like serial fashion but happen simultaneously in parallel. Although we may draw flowcharts of information processing, where the boxes represent theoretical computational stages or specific modules for processing specific information, we need to remember that the brain is, in fact, a simultaneous parallel processing device with many neurons and pathways. It is also important to know that there are neurons and pathways and brain regions selectively responsive to particular types of information.

If the brain is concurrently processing vast amounts of information in parallel perhaps there is a problem to be solved. That problem is how to allow behaviour to be controlled by the right information at the right time to the right objects in the right order. Perhaps the bottleneck, or change from parallel to serial, happens just before response. The brain processes all information as far as it can in parallel; but at the moment of response we are limited. This is certainly what the most recent evidence on the psychological refractory period suggests. We shall discuss this recent evidence in more detail when we consider dual-task performance in the following chapter.

Possible functions of attention

Schneider (1993) considers what functions we might attribute to (visual) attention. He identifies three broad classes of theory. First, "selection-for-object-recognition", concerned with the computation of visual descriptions; e.g. Marr (1982). Second, "selection-for-feature-integration"; e.g. Treisman's feature integration theory; Treisman and Gelade (1980); Treisman (1993). Third, there is the class of theories that Schneider says are in some ways more fundamental than the others: these he calls "selection-for-action" after Allport's (1987) phraseology. It is to that class of theory that we now turn.

Selection for action

Workers in the field of attention are making increasing use of real-world examples to characterise the kinds of problems faced by a complex brain when interacting with the environment. In 1987 both Allport and Neuman wrote influential papers considering the functional and neurophysiological bases of attentional behaviour.

Both propose that the question of what attentional behaviour is for, or why it appears the way it does must motivate its explanation. Consider some of Allport's (1987, p.396) examples:

> Many fruit are within reach, and clearly visible, yet for each individual reach of the hand, for each act of plucking, information about just one of them must govern the particular pattern and direction of movements. The disposition of the other apples, already encoded by the brain, must be in some way temporarily decoupled from the direct control of reaching, though it may of course still influence the action, for example as representing an obstacle to be reached around, not to be dislodged and so on. A predator (a sparrow hawk, say) encounters a pack of similar prey animals, but she must direct her attack selectively towards just one of them; the fleeing prey must, with equal speed, select just one among the possible routes of escape.

As Allport (1987) points out, although the senses are capable of encoding information about many objects simultaneously, there is a strict limit on action, in that we can usually make only one action at a time with any effector. Basically we can direct our eyes only to one place at a time, we can reach for only one apple at a time, we can run only one way or the other. Allport (1987, p.397) argues that there is a biological necessity for "selection for action", and that there must be:

> A mechanism of fundamental importance for the sensory control of action ... that can selectively designate a subset of the available and potentially relevant information to have control over a given effector system, and can selectively decouple the remainder from such control. This need ... arises directly from the many-to-many possible mappings between domains of sensory input and of motor output within the very highly parallel distributed organisation of the nervous system.

How are actions controlled?

Neuman (1987) considers this problem. If all potential actions were simultaneously trying to control action, there would be behavioural chaos. In order to prevent such disorganisation of behaviour there must be selection and, Neuman argues, it is this need for selection which produces the limit on human performance. The psychological refractory period, which arises when two successive stimuli require rapid response, suggests that the response to the second stimulus must wait until the response to the first stimulus has, at least, been selected and may be a functional way of preventing two responses becoming available at once. However, Neuman (p.374) suggests that there are a variety of selectional problems and consequently a variety of selectional mechanisms are needed: "Hence, 'attention', in this view, does not denote a single type of phenomenon. Rather it should be viewed as the generic term for a number of phenomena each of which is related to a different selection mechanism."

To specify how actions are controlled we need to establish what an action is and whether there are different kinds of actions. Neuman (p.375) defines an action as a "sequence of movements that is controlled by the same internal control structure and that is not a reflex". Actions can be adjusted to prevailing conditions, such as opening or closing the grip according to the size of the apple you want to grasp; reflexes cannot. To simplify Neuman's argument, he says that actions are controlled by skills which are stored as nested schemata in long-term memory and skills are used to attain goals. (See Chapter 9 on the intentional control of behaviour and goal-directed action.) To attain a goal, either one or a combination of skills have to be selected and made available to control the motor apparatus, or effector. Neuman states there are two immediate problems to be overcome. The first is to recruit the right effector (e.g. for speaking a response the vocal apparatus must be recruited; for a button press response, the correct finger of the correct hand must be recruited). The problem of effector recruitment is a major limit on performance as we have only one pair of hands, only one voice. Skills control the effectors, but different skills do not have different dedicated effectors as the hand or the mouth can be used for a variety of skills. Skills do not provide all the parameters needed to carry out an action. Other parameters are provided by the environment. We shall consider Neuman's (1984) arguments on skills, dual-task performance, automaticity and control in Chapter 7.

Neuman (1987) says that the problem of selecting the right effector at the right time, so that only one action is attempted, is rather like preventing train crashes on a busy railway network. One way to avoid crashes would be to have a central station monitoring the trains on the tracks, the other would be to have a system where the network was divided into sections and when one train was on a track within the section it automatically set the signals to prevent other trains coming along. He argues that the brain uses the blocking method. This results in a capacity limit, as one ongoing action inhibits all other possible actions. Of course, it would be dangerous to have a blocking mechanism that could not be interrupted by a change in environmental circumstances. Orienting responses to unexpected events which have been processed pre-attentively, will break through the block.

Overall Neuman views attention as an "ensemble of mechanisms" which allow the brain to cope with the problem of selecting appropriate information to control action. The apparent limitation on our abilities is not a result of a limited processing capacity but has evolved to ensure coherent behaviour.

The importance of perceptual integration

In order to achieve efficient selection for action, Allport (1987) stressed the importance of perceptual integration. The attributes of all the possible objects available for action must be properly combined; in the example of picking apples, colour and size will be important for our choice. (We have discussed perceptual integration in Chapter 5.) Provided the attributes belonging together are integrated, the next problem is for the processing system to ensure that all the possible actions are prevented from interfering with each other. This, suggested Neuman, was achieved by blocking. Exactly how selective coupling, decoupling, or blocking are achieved is not made entirely clear in Allport's or Neuman's arguments. The psychological refractory period (PRP) might be an important reflection of fundamental response limitation, and we shall discuss some underlying reasons for PRP in Chapter 7. We also know from work by Tipper (1985), Driver and Baylis (1989) (see Chapter 4) that objects which are not selected to control a response are inhibited. This inhibition manifests itself as *negative priming*, or a slowing of response relative to the control condition, when the previously ignored object is presented as a target on the next trial. More recently Tipper, Brehaut, and Driver (1990) have shown that negative priming can be produced by moving objects, when subjects have to respond by indicating where an identified object is in a moving display. In the picking apples example described above, we assume that the picker and the apple are stationary. Tipper et al. (1990) stress that predators must be able to track the movement of an identified object, using the example of a pike trying to catch a stickleback: there are many sticklebacks present, but one must be selected as the object for action by its relative position within a group. Tipper et al. (1990) show that stimulus identity can control spatially directed action and inhibition can be directed to irrelevant object locations. The phenomenon of negative priming suggests that one way of decoupling potentially relevant objects from the immediate control of action is to inhibit their representations or response mappings.

Levels of representation in selection for action

Tipper, Weaver, and Houghton (1994) have shown that inhibitory mechanisms are goal dependent and that inhibition is directed to different properties of a stimulus depending on which properties of the stimulus are required to control response and how difficult the selection task is. They propose that selection is "dynamic and sensitive to task demands" (p.836). As selection and inhibition can be shown to operate at a number of levels, it seems likely; and Tipper et al. argue that distracting objects are represented at multiple levels, some representations are inhibited while others remain active, and the complex effects of distractor information can be explained only if this is the case.

Further support for selection operating at different levels and inhibition applying to different features of an object, depending on goals or task demands, comes from both neurological and normal data. Patients with visual neglect and extinction were discussed in Chapter 4. Neglect is usually considered to be an attentional problem. These patients can name a single object, even if presented to the side of visual space contralateral to their lesion, but when two objects are presented simultaneously, only the object in the good side is reportable; the other object is neglected.

Baylis, Driver, and Rafal (1993) examined patients who exhibited visual extinction following unilateral parietal damage. Patients were presented with two coloured letters, one either side of fixation, or with a single letter. Their task was to report the colour or the letter. Baylis et al. found that when two objects were presented simultaneously, and either the colours or the letters were the same, extinction was more severe. However, performance appeared to be unaffected by unattended dimensions. When presented with a red O and a green O the patient would report each colour correct in its position; however, when asked to report the letter, they reported only one O in the good side, and said there was nothing else there. Likewise if colour was repeated over the two stimuli, extinction occurred for the colour. Baylis et al. argued that their patients were exhibiting an exaggerated form of an effect observed in neurologically normal people, called repetition blindness (RB). This effect refers to a reduction in accuracy of report when two identical stimuli are presented (e.g. Kanwisher, 1987; Hochaus & Moran, 1991). Kanwisher (1991) found that subjects asked to attend to coloured letters presented in a rapid sequence showed RB for letters of repeated colour, but if the second presentation of letter had been preceded by a white (i.e. unattended) letter there was no RB. Kanwisher et al. (1995) suggest that RB results from difficulty in combining two identical *types* to their own episodic records (*tokens*). We have already suggested that linking or integrating semantic (type) and episodic (token) information is necessary for conscious report in Chapter 3 (e.g. Allport, 1977; Coltheart, 1980). Although there is one problem integrating, for example, the identity and location of an object, and this may be necessary for selection for action or conscious report, the type–token problem seems to be particulary troublesome in the case where there are two identical examples of the same type that can only be differentiated by another source of information. Kanwisher et al. (1995) argue that, if there is an attentional system responsible for integrating information of type and token, it may be unable to link repeated types to different tokens. They report a series of experiments to see if the extinction effects discovered in patients by Baylis et al. (1993) can be mimicked in neurologically normal people. Subjects were presented with pairs of brief, pattern-masked, coloured letters. The letters could be the same (repeated) or different (non-repeated) and the colours of the letters could also be repeated or not. Subjects were asked to respond first to the left-hand stimulus and then to the right-hand stimulus. Results showed that, as in the experiment by Baylis et al., repetition of the reported dimension reduced performance on the second report but repetition of the unreported dimension did not. According to Fagot and Pashler (1994) RB may arise because subjects are unwilling or reluctant to repeat a response when they are uncertain whether it is correct. If this is the case, then RB is a result of a response strategy. In order to rule this out Kanwisher et al. (1995) introduced conditions in which subjects had to switch the basis for their response between the first and second stimulus and obtained confidence ratings from subjects about their certainty of the responses they chose. In sum, RB appears to be produced by the repetition of attended dimensions.

When different dimensions are relevant for the two responses in the switching attention condition, both attended dimensions affect RB. These results, they argue, rule out a response strategy explanation. The most important implication here, is that the goal of the task influences what is attended and attentional demands will be different in different situations. Both Tipper et al. (1994) and Kanwisher et al. (1995) suggest that, although unattended dimensions can be excluded from the processes underlying performance of a task, if the previously excluded dimension is subsequently selected for another object, those dimensions can still be accessed and influence later performance. So, the level at which selection takes place for a given task does not necessarily mean that the unselected information is entirely lost to the processing system. It seems then that behavioural goals determine the nature of selectivity; appropriate information is selected or not depending on the task.

Listening and looking

Quite obviously we usually need to draw on multiple sources of information in order to achieve goals. In the examples above, we were concerned entirely with responses to visual stimuli. Real-world behaviour involves integrating information across modalities; for example, between sights and sounds—when a number of people are speaking at once, we are able to attribute a voice to a speaker. Driver and Spence (1994) investigated the way in which visual and auditory attention work together by manipulating the spatial relationship between the words we see and the words we hear. When a subject attends to one ear in a dichotic listening task, attention must be directed at the will of the subject, or endogenously, to the relevant location in auditory space. Similarly, if you want to attend to one side of visual space, attention is endogenously directed to the intended location. (See Chapter 4 for a discussion of endogenous and exogenous orienting.) Driver and Spence designed a technique in which they were able to present subjects with visual and auditory information to either side of their midline. In their experiments they could make the attended side either the same or different for the two modalities; i.e. subjects might need to attend to the left for the visual task and to the right for the auditory task. Using this method it is possible to see whether endogenous attentional orienting can be controlled independently for the two modalities.

Two monitors, one to the left and one to the right, displayed visual information while two loudspeakers, immediately below the monitors, were used to present auditory information. A third loudspeaker was positioned in the centre in front of the subject and could be used to present continuous white noise. The monitor could show someone speaking a list of words that were accurately synchronised with an audiotape of the same words on the same side of space, or with the same words coming from the loudspeaker on the opposite side of space. Alternatively, the monitor could show a person who was not speaking, but chewing, so that the lip movements did not provide the opportunity for any lip-reading. Subjects had either to name the words coming from a loudspeaker that was on the same side as the monitor they fixated (Same, speaking lips), or name the words coming from the loudspeaker on the opposite side to the monitor they were fixating, so that now the words they were attending to were on the opposite side to the words they were looking at (Opposite, speaking lips). Similar conditions for Same, chewing lips and Opposite, chewing lips were included. Eye movements were monitored to check where the subject was looking. Results showed that when the lip-read and auditory words matched in location (Same, speaking lips) performance was better than when the visual and auditory information came from opposite sides (Opposite, speaking lips). There was, however some benefit for speaking lips in the Opposite condition, when compared to the chewing lips condition. Driver and Spence suggested a spatial synergy between visual and auditory attention. To check the result was not due to a special case where speech sounds and movements were integrated, the experiment was repeated using a visual monitoring task instead of the faces. The spatial synergy remained, suggesting to Driver and Spence (1994), that endogenous attention does not operate independently in the two modalities tested. That is to say, if you orient attention to a location, selection of information about both modalities is enhanced. As attentional mechanisms must have evolved to help us interact with the environment, such an arrangement is obviously sensible, as stimuli at the same spatial location are usually concerned with the same object. They suggest that one way of solving the problem of coordinating information across modalities might be via the spatial attention links.

More recently, Spence and Driver (1996) have tested for cross-modal links between hearing and vision in endogenous orienting. Using a variety of spatial cueing tasks, in which visual and auditory attention were centrally cued to the same or opposite side of space, they found that it was possible for subjects to split auditory and visual attention under certain conditions, but when targets were expected on the same side in both modalities, the covert orienting effects were greater. They concluded (p.1005) that "although endogenous covert orienting does not operate exclusively within a supra-modal system, there are strong spatial links between auditory and visual attention".

Reaching and grasping

In addition to knowing which attributes of an object belong together, whether within or between modalities, unless we are going to be content with just reporting the presence of those objects we need to be able to move to, reach and grasp, or perhaps run away from, those objects. Let's go back to picking apples. Not only do you have to extend your arm the correct distance in the right direction so that it arrives at the selected apple, but at the same time your grasp must be adapted to fit the shape of an apple. Think about the difference in grasp needed for an apple as opposed to a blackberry. Of course the blackberry is smaller and you would need finer control of the fingers to reach it, but once the fruit is reached, still more planning is required. While the apple is hard and heavy, the blackberry is soft and light. If you were to use the same pressure of grip on the blackberry as the apple, the blackberry would be squashed. Quite clearly many sources of information need to be integrated not only visual and spatial information from the environment about the colour, shape and distance, but also semantic information from memory, about the sensory properties, hard/soft, heavy/light etc. While we do know a little about the planning and control of reaching and grasping in response to visuo-spatial information from the environment, we know rather less about the way in which other properties are involved in the control of action. Jeannerod (1984) analysed videos of subjects reaching for objects and decided that movements could be analysed into two components, the reach and the grasp. Reaching involves aiming the hand in the right direction and moving it the right distance, the grasp phase begins during the reaching movement and the shape of the grasp depends on the target object. During the grasp phase, the fingers and thumb first open out and then three-quarters of the way through the reaching movement, the grasp begins to close up to fit the object. Smyth, Collins, Morris, and Levy (1994) provide an accessible review of planning and controlling movements.

Controlling actions is specified by so many possible combinations of sizes, distances and object properties that there are an enormous number of possible movements that might be required. This is called the " degrees of freedom problem" which is discussed by Jordan and Rosenbaum (1989). They suggest that one way of reducing the number of degrees of freedom is to have connections between potentially independent systems, so that they work in synergy. In the experiments described earlier, Driver and Spence (1994) suggested that the attentional system might rely on spatial synergy. Spatial maps are important for integrating visual features (Treisman, 1993), but "space" is not easy to define according to Rizzolati, Riggio, and Sheliga (1994). There is evidence from studies on monkeys that space can be sub-divided. Rizzolati and colleagues (Rizzolati, Gentilucci, & Matelli, 1985; Rizzolati & Carmarda, 1987; Rizzolati & Gallese, 1988) have demonstrated that lesions in different pre-motor areas can produce different kinds of visual neglect, either to "reaching" space, "oculomotor" space, or "orofacial" space. In the first case the animal makes no attempt to reach for an object, in the second case the animal will not make eye movements toward objects, and in the third case it will, for example, not lick juice from around the mouth. Clearly "space", and hence spatial attention, needs to be considered in terms of the kinds of actions which are appropriate at different distances. Further, "consciousness" must also be considered to break down within the same frames.

We have already seen that in monkeys with visual neglect, space can dissociate into that around the mouth, that within grasping distance, and that to which eye movements can be made, and (in Chapter 3) that the brain has distinct systems for coding *what* and *where* in vision. From studies of monkeys, it is known that the cortical system that knows where objects are connects from the visual cortex to the inferior parietal lobule, which is itself made up of a number of distinct anatomical and functional areas. Rizzolati et al. (1994) review the neuronal properties of the frontoparietal circuits and conclude that different spatial representations are computed in parallel in different cortical circuits. Further, space representation is linked to movement organisation and the "mechanisms for representing space are different in different circuits and most likely are related to and depend on the motor requirements of the effectors controlled by a given circuit" (p.235).

Neurons have been found which seem to compute the reaching and grasping components identified in Jeannerod's analysis. Gentilucci and Rizzolati (1990) identified a brain area which codes the spatial relationship between the target of action and the body and translates it into a pattern of movements. Other areas seem to be selective for different types of grip, (Rizzolati et al., 1988) and other neurons fire to objects of expected size even in the absence of any movement. Interestingly, neurons which code grasping do not code space, so in a sense , while they know what the object is in terms of specifying the grasp, they do not know where the object is: a somewhat analogous case to the what/where problem in vision (Chapter 3).

Experimental evidence on the selective spatial control of arm movements is sparse, but studies are beginning. Tipper, Lortie, and Baylis (1992) looked at selective reaching to see if there was evidence for "action-centred attention". Their subjects' task was to press a button if a red light came on next to it. On some trials a yellow distractor light would come on and the interference effects of this light were studied. The subject's hand was either at the top or the bottom of the board at the start of a trial. If the yellow distractor light came on at the top when the subject's hand was at the top there was greater interference than if the subject's hand was at the bottom. Similar results were found for left and right. When subjects were to respond with the right hand and the distractor came on the right-hand side, interference was greater than if it was on the left. Likewise if the left hand was used for response, a distractor on the left had more effect than one on the right. Taking this together with other evidence, Rizzolati et al. (1994, p.256) argue that programming arm movements produces a spatial attentional field that is not dependent on eye movements and "that the same system that controls action is the same system that controls spatial attention". This pre-motor theory of attention proposes that spatial selective attention results from activation of neurons in "spatial pragmatic maps" and the activation of those neurons starts at the same time as the preparation for goal-directed, spatial movements. According to the task, different spatial pragmatic maps may be required and spatial attention can originate in any of the maps. Lastly, in humans and other primates the fovea is highly developed and so the oculomotor spatial pragmatic map is usually most important.

This evidence tells us something about spatially directed movements, but the question of how other information—for example, semantics—is involved in controlling action is as yet little explored.

Attention for memory

In early experiments, Moray (1959) showed that a word presented more than 30 times to the unattended ear in a dichotic listening experiment was recognised at chance levels. In contrast, a word presented only once to the attended ear was easily recognised. This result among others, suggests that attended words are remembered but unattended words are not. Hasher and Zacks (1979) proposed that memory-encoding operations vary in their attentional requirements and suggested that automatic encoding requires minimal attention but intentional encoding into memory needs attentional effort of the kind proposed by Kahneman (1973).

Fisk and Schneider (1984) examined the memorial consequences of controlled and automatic processing on word frequency judgements. They showed that subjects trained to do automatic categorisation using a constant mapping task had very poor recognition memory for the words and showed no frequency learning. Other subjects who had been forced to use controlled processing in a varied mapping task with different semantic orienting conditions showed much better long-term learning. This result was taken to demonstrate that controlled processing requiring attention and long-term learning are closely related and that accurate automatic processing can take place without long-term storage. We shall consider the difference between constant and varied mapping conditions with respect to Shiffrin and Schneider's (1977) theory of attention in the next chapter.

One major difference between the cognitive operations necessary to allow a stimulus to control response in a varied mapping task, as opposed to a constant mapping task, is that varied mapping requires information from conceptual and perceptual domains to be combined (at least temporarily) in order for the object meeting the target criteria to be differentiated from other objects. In varied mapping all stimuli are possible targets, and selection of the stimulus that meets the target criteria depends not only on what the stimulus is but also on some physical information such as where or what colour the stimulus is. In constant mapping, detection of a target may be possible on the basis of its being the most active member of a primed target set. Therefore, in a constant mapping task, perceptual integration is necessary before the target can be found. Allport (1988) and Styles and Allport (1986) proposed that this perceptual integration necessary for selecting the target for action could provide the basis for a new longer-lasting, episodic memory and also allow confident report. When we were discussing report from brief visual displays in Chapter 3, we noted that both Allport (1977) and Coltheart (1980) suggested that identity codes need to be linked or "stabilised" with appropriate physical codes if they were to be reported, and that unstabilised semantic activation, although not reported, could underlie semantic activation without conscious awareness (Marcel, 1983). Masking of brief pattern-masked displays disrupts the physical information that is needed for perceptual integration leaving semantic activation in an unreportable form. This activation may modify memory and be inaccessible by voluntary recall, but recognition time may show a priming effect due to residual semantic activation. Patients with amnesia show better recognition than recall and may exhibit a "feeling of knowing" (Huppert & Piercy, 1976; Schacter & Tulving, 1983). Stern (1981) suggests this effect arises from a failure to integrate contextual or physical information with an object or event. Unless there is integration there may be no episodic trace to allow subsequent recall. These studies are relevant to discussions on the nature and function of consciousness which are the subject of Chapter 10.

Some studies have tried to manipulate the availability of attention in memory tasks by dividing the subject's attention while learning. Johnson and Heinz (1978) used a dichotic listening task in which their subjects either shadowed a message which moved from ear to ear on the basis of meaning or voice. At the same time, if a light came on, the subject was to press a button as fast as possible. The rationale was that the RT to the light would indicate the amount of processing dedicated to the shadowing task. Results showed that when shadowing was by voice, RT to the light was faster than when shadowing was by semantics. So, the argument was, shadowing by semantics needed more attention and so RT performance on the light detection task suffered. An unexpected recall test at the end of the experiment showed that memory was best for words which had been shadowed in the semantic condition, providing further evidence for attentional involvement in memory. Craik (1983) reported an experiment in which subjects were presented with lists of unrelated nouns to learn under conditions of full attention, or in a condition where attention was divided between learning and a card sorting task. Later tests of recall and recognition showed that subjects in the divided attention condition remembered significantly less than controls. It has been argued (e.g. Eich, 1984) that attention to an event is necessary for later intentional use of memory, but not for automatic or unconscious memory. According to Jacoby (1994) the trouble with divided attention experiments is that even if it can be shown that dividing attention reduces memory performance it is not easy to say whether the effect of dividing attention was on intentional or automatic uses of memory. Jacoby, Woloshyn, and Kelley (1989) set unconscious (automatic) and conscious (intentional) influences on memory in opposition. Their experiments examined what they called "false fame". Subjects read a list of names, which they were told belonged to people who were not famous, in either full attention or divided attention conditions. When attention was divided, subjects were to concurrently monitor a list of digits for a run of three odd numbers. In the second half of the experiment subjects were given another list in which some of the names from the first list were mixed with other non-famous names and some famous names. As subjects had been told that no name in the first list was famous, they should know, if they consciously recalled one of those names, that it belonged to a non-famous person. If they recalled a name and said it was famous (when consciously they should have known it was not) then the mistake must be due to unconscious processing. So, old non-famous names would be mistakenly recalled as famous only if the name was familiar, but not recollected as being in the first list. Dividing attention was expected to reduce the probability of recollection and therefore increase the chance of a name being judged on familiarity alone. In the divided attention condition the old non-famous names were more likely to be mistaken as famous, showing that, when attention was divided, subjects were less able to use conscious recollection to oppose the familiarity produced by reading the names earlier. This "false fame" effect is also shown by the elderly and amnesic patients. Impressively, it is also found when the names are presented to patients under a general anaesthetic: Jelicic et al., cited in Jacoby (1994). These results support the suggestion that conscious intentional memory is affected by attentional processing, but feelings of familiarity are served by automatic unconscious processing.

Memory for intention: Short-term plans

Most studies of memory are retrospective: they involve the subject in recalling what has already happened or retrieving facts. However, in daily life memory is often prospective in that it involves remembering to do something in the future, or to perform a series of actions in an intentional sequence. Cohen (1989) points out that these two types of memory must interact. First the plan, or intention, must be encoded into retrospective memory, it must be retrieved at the appropriate moment, then checked off to avoid repetition. The fact that the plan has been executed must be encoded in retrospective memory so that you remember you have done it, and we must then be able to distinguish the plan, or intention to do the action from the actual implementation of the plan. When we look at voluntary control in Chapter 9, we shall meet some tasks in which subjects have to alternately respond with different responses to ambiguous stimuli; for example, Allport, Styles, and Hseih (1994); Rogers and Monsell (1995). Whilst these experiments were concerned with shifting mental set and the intentional executive attentional processes underlying performance, these tasks also involve intention memory. When a stimulus does not cue the action to be made to it, the subject has to remember what task they just did and what task they have to do next. Certainly in our own experiments subjects often self-instructed themselves, "Colour, Word, Colour, Word ..." when alternating between these tasks. In the same way that Logan (1995), as we shall see in Chapter 9, has suggested that language might aid selection in visual space, it is possible that as subjects talked to themselves they were providing an additional cue to activate the appropriate task set. Alternatively, the echoic trace provided a supplement to an overloaded executive system by utilising the articulatory loop of working memory. One of the main purposes of the articulatory loop is to maintain order in short-term memory. This is essential for comprehension, reasoning, and span tasks. Burgess and Hitch (1992) have developed a network model of the articulatory loop, in which phonemic output for one item feeds back to excite the phonemic input for the next item. This feedback maintains ordered relations between items in short-term working memory. Such feedback could help maintain order when task sets need sequencing. However, Allport and Styles (1990) found that task switching costs for subjects who are concurrently maintaining a span size memory load show no interaction with the number of tasks to be switched between, so in this case memory for intention must be maintained in some other, non-articulatory form. Gillie and Broadbent (1989) studied the effects of interruptions on subjects doing a computer game which involved remembering where they were in a sequence; for example, moving round getting shopping. They concluded, amongst other things that subjects remembered what they should be doing, when they resumed the task after being interrupted to do, say, mental arithmetic, which would involve the articulatory loop, by using some form of non-articulatory memory which was not affected by the length of the interruption. Clearly intention can be represented outside the articulatory loop.

Long-term plans

Of course, many intentional or prospective memory tasks, like remembering to return a library book, are for the future and not continuously represented in short-term working memory. Often we need to retrieve an intention at the appropriate time from long-term memory. We may do this by providing ourselves with an external reminder like tying a knot in our handkerchief, writing a list etc. Alternatively we may just intend to remember. The interested reader is referred to Harris and Morris (1984) which offers a collection of work on everyday memory, actions, and absent mindedness. Sinnott (1989, p.352) suggests that prospective/intentional memory reflects the "action-oriented function of memory, one that is adaptive in a world where there is some stability and where taking action is often useful". Sinnott categorises component processes involved in prospective memory into two types: firstly, monitoring and control processes; and secondly lower-level processes. The monitoring level controls attention shifts, as he suggests; conscious attentional processing is essential for intentional memory. Outside attention action slips will occur. Other processes at the monitoring/control level involve setting goals, appraising current information as relevant to ongoing plans and goals, interrupting habitual behaviour, monitoring time, deciding to act etc. To a large extent the functions of the monitoring/control processes proposed by Sinnott are similar to the conditions in which Norman and Shallice (1986) say the Supervisory Attentional System is required for the willed control of action; see Chapter 9. Sinnott approaches the issue from the perspective of prospective memory within which our goals are represented and interact with states of the world. Norman and Shallice approach from the angle of will and conscious control over schemata in long-term memory. What is clear is that problems of attention are also problems of memory: to separate the two produces a false dichotomy. Attentional processing acts upon and interacts with the same system that represents our knowledge of the world, i.e. memory. As we shall see in the next chapter, attention may emerge from the interaction between all the different processes involved in performing a particular task. Sejnowski (1986) comments that as information processing and memory share the same circuitry in the brain, the two must necessarily be very closely related.

Summary

People have begun to consider the question of what attention is for. The brain is known to be a massively parallel computational device in which many varieties of information are concurrently available from different parts of the system. In order to maintain coherent behaviour, some of this information needs to be combined for response while other subsets need to be ignored to allow selection for action. Two influential papers, Allport (1987) and Neuman (1987) put forward the ideas behind "selection for action". The idea is that we must consider the functional and neuropsychological bases of attentional behaviour. For example, when picking apples, what is demanded of the system and how might attention guide behaviour? Allport proposed that the control of action necessitated a fundamentally important mechanism which could allow relevant information to control behaviour and decouple irrelevant information from interfering. In Neuman's view attention is an "ensemble of mechanisms"which allows the brain to cope with the problem of selection for action and that the apparent limit on attention has evolved to allow coherent behaviour. Numerous studies have shown the negative priming effect: Tipper et al. (1990, 1994), have shown that stimuli which are not to control behaviour are inhibited and that this inhibition can be at different levels of representation depending on the task being performed. In everyday life, information needs to be coordinated across different modalities. Driver and Spence (1994) demonstrated synergy between visual and auditory stimuli, suggesting that spatial attention does not operate independently for the different modalities, which would help us to interact effectively with the environment. Attention also seems important in motor movements like reaching and grasping, remembering and planning.

Further reading

Allport, (D.)A. (1993). Attention and control: Have we been asking the right questions? A critical review of twenty five years. In D.E. Meyer & S. Kornblum (Eds.), *Attention and performance XIV: Synergies in experimental psychology, artificial intelligence, and cognitive neuroscience.* Cambridge, MA: MIT Press. This chapter critically reviews the literature and asks "What is attention for?"

Heuer, H., & Sanders, A.F. (Eds.) (1987). *Perspectives on perception and action*. Hillsdale, NJ: Lawrence Erlbaum Associates Inc. This book contains a selection of papers which have the "selection for action" theme, in particular the chapters by Allport and by Neuman.

Jeannerod, M. (1997). *The cognitive neuroscience of action*. Oxford: Blackwell.

Task combination and divided attention 7

Introduction

Just as there is controversy over the nature of attentional processing in selective attention tasks, psychologists hold a variety of views about the best explanation for human performance in divided attention conditions. When two tasks need to be done at the same time, is attention shared? Are there different attentional mechanisms responsible for different tasks? Different modalities? But what, exactly, is it that we do "at the same time"? The classic psychological refractory period (PRP) studies by Welford (1952) looked at overlapping tasks in which one and then another simple stimulus was presented for speeded response. Other tasks, some of which we shall meet here, require subjects to do two tasks at the same time, but on a trial by trial basis; e.g. Posner and Boies (1971). Sometimes, experiments involve the continuous performance of two, quite lengthy, ongoing tasks; e.g. Allport, Antonis, and Reynolds (1972). It is possible that these different tasks make quite different demands on the attentional system. Pashler (1993) reviewed dual-task performance and examined dual-task interference over a wide variety of experimental paradigms.

According to original filter theory, there was just one processing channel and therefore task combination could be achieved only by rapid switching of the filter and multiplexing, or time-sharing tasks. If it could be demonstrated that two complex tasks which should require continuous attentional processing could be combined without loss of speed or accuracy, then the argument that there was only a single processing channel would have to be abandoned. Allport, Antonis, and Reynolds (1972) asked competent keyboard players to play the piano, sight-reading examination pieces that they had not seen before, at the same time as shadowing prose at a rate of 150 words per minute. With only a little practice, Allport et al.'s subjects were able to perform both tasks in combination as fast and as accurately as they could when they performed them separately. This result was interpreted as evidence against a single channel for attentional processing. Experiments like that of Allport, Antonis, and Reynolds (1972) are not without their critics. Broadbent (1982) points out that it is possible to detect decrements in the performance data when the two tasks are combined. Furthermore, it is extremely difficult to determine whether or not each individual task requires absolutely continuous attentional processing. Broadbent would argue that both shadowing prose and sight-reading music, are tasks involving stimuli that have a certain amount of redundancy in them. *Redundancy* is a concept from information theory, explained in Chapter 2: it means that the prose and music contain information which allows the subjects to predict what letter or note is likely to come next. If the subject can predict with some certainty what is likely to come next in either task, then, at those moments when predictability of the next word or note is high, attention can be rapidly switched, allowing time-sharing between the tasks rather than simultaneous combination. To be certain that there was no time-sharing, both tasks would have to be absolutely continuous and include no redundancy whatsoever. We would also have to be certain that each individual task was being performed at the limit of attentional resources. Only if these conditions were fulfilled for the separate tasks, and we could be certain that there were absolutely no decrements in either task when they were performed together, could we say that there was no limit to dual-task combination.

Single channel or general purpose processing capacity?

Both Welford (1952) and Broadbent (1958) suggested that there was a central bottleneck in processing which limited dual-task performance. Other theorists argued that the bottleneck was not due to the structure of the human information processing system, but rather reflected a limited amount of processing capacity which could be allocated to a single task or shared between a number of tasks according to priorities. We shall examine some of these theories in a moment. We can see here that while we have one metaphor that likens attention to a resource or capacity or "amount of something", we have the other metaphor in which attention is like a bottleneck where selection has to take place owing to the fact that parallel processing must change to serial processing to protect the limited capacity component of the processing system. Although these metaphors are rather different they are related. If either the attentional resource, or capacity that limits the system is of a "general purpose" type, then all tasks which require attention will draw upon the same resource or compete at the same bottleneck. This is the concept of a single, general purpose, limited capacity central processor (GPLCP). According to this conception, if the GPLPC is engaged in one mental operation, such as shadowing, then it is not available for another operation, such as sight reading. If one response is being selected, then another response will have to wait until the GPLPC is free.

However, if there are different varieties of resources, or different capacities that are dedicated to processing different kinds of information, then although there may be specific limits on each variety of resource, there need not be a general limit on task combination. Provided two tasks do not compete at the same time for the same resource there is no reason why they should interfere, unless there is competition at some other common level, such as data extraction. (See Allport, 1980b, for a critical review.)

Capacity theories and the human operator

A selective bottleneck in processing is a structural limitation and many of the experiments on selective attention discussed in the previous chapters were concerned with discovering the location of that bottleneck. Although we have seen evidence for selective attention operating at different levels dependent on the task demand, the idea of selection at some point in processing remains. However, the amount of information processing that an organism can do at any one time might alternatively be conceived of as being limited by the amount of processing capacity, or processing resources available to the organism. Human factors research—which is concerned with measuring work-load, stress, noise etc. and human performance—clearly suggests that the human information processor is limited in the number and complexity of operations that can be concurrently performed, and that in different circumstances task combination is more or less difficult. This difficulty might be moderated by other variables external to the operator, such as heat or noise, or by variables internal to the operator such as personality, lack of sleep, or fear. Revelle (1993) provides a useful review of non-cognitive factors that can affect an individual's ability to perform attentionally demanding tasks: most of these effects are to do with personality and levels of arousal.

Knowles (1963) proposed that the "human operator" could be thought of as having a "pool" of processing resources, and that this pool was of limited capacity. If one task demands more of the resources, then there will be less of the pool available to another task. As the first task becomes more and more difficult, more and more resources will be drawn from the pool, resulting in poorer and poorer performance of the secondary task. Note here an important difference from the structural view of attention. Rather than attention being directed to one task at a time, resource, or capacity theory allows for attention to be shared between tasks in a graded manner. Moray (1967) pointed out that the adoption of a capacity view of attention did away with the need to assume a bottleneck. Interference between tasks simply arose out of the capacity demands of the tasks and this could appear at any stage in processing.

Kahneman's theory of attention and effort

Kahneman (1973) put forward a theory that likens attention to a limited resource which can be flexibly allocated as the human operator changes their allocation policy from moment to moment. Attention can be focused on one particular activity, or can be divided between a number of activities. When tasks are more difficult, more attention is needed. Unlike Broadbent's flowchart of information through a structural system (see Fig. 2.1, Chapter 2), Kahneman's model is a model of mind. It includes enduring dispositions, momentary intentions and an evaluative decision process that determines the current demand on capacity. Attention here is rather like a limited power supply: if you turn on the rings of a gas cooker, and the central heating boiler fires up, the height of the gas jets in the cooker rings goes down. There is only a limited supply of gas to these two appliances, and the demand from the boiler reduces the amount of fuel available to the cooker. However, in Kahneman's theory, if we put more effort into a task we can do better—for example, during increased demand the gas company might raise the gas pressure in the main supply. So, the amount of attentional capacity can vary according to motivation. The amount of effort available is also related to overall arousal level: as arousal increases or decreases, so does attentional capacity.

Whilst there are some attractive properties in this model, such as the move away from structural limitations to processing limitations, there are some serious problems with the theory. Firstly, it is known that at low levels of arousal, performance is poor; according to Kahneman this would be because the attentional capacity is low when arousal is low. As arousal increases, so does performance, up to an optimum level, beyond which further increases in arousal, rather than improving performance, produce decrements. This is known as Yerkes-Dodson's law (Yerkes & Dodson, 1908). We have probably all experienced situations, where, for example, a little background noise helps to keep us alert, and improves performance, but if the noise becomes extremely loud, we find it impossible to do anything else. If attentional effort were directly related to the arousing effect of the noise, task performance should improve monotonically with the increase in the noise. Secondly, defining arousal is very problematic (Revelle, 1993). Thirdly, and possibly this is the most serious problem: how can task difficulty be measured independently (Allport, 1980b)? Kahneman put forward the idea that task difficulty could be determined by the amount of interference on a concurrent task. However, if task difficulty is measured by interference, and interference is an index of difficulty, we have no independent measure. Another problem is that interference between concurrent tasks is said to be non-specific. As capacity is "general purpose", any combination of tasks will result in some decrement in one or other or both tasks. We shall see a little later that there is now ample evidence to suggest that interference between tasks is task-specific; see for example, Posner and Boies (1971) and McLeod and Posner (1984). For the moment we shall continue our discussion of capacity theories.

Measuring resource allocation

Limitations: Data-limited and resource-limited processing

Wickens (1984) prefers the word "resources" to other terms such as "attention", "effort" and "capacity": attention, he feels, has so many ambiguous meanings as to be meaningless; effort suggests a motivational variable that does not necessarily have to correlate with performance; and capacity suggests some kind of limit rather than a variable amount. Wickens' paper is a useful review of ideas concerning processing resources in attention.

Perhaps the first, best developed theory of resources in attention came from Norman and Bobrow (1975). Norman and Bobrow introduced the idea of a performance–resource function (PRF): see

Fig. 7.1. For a single task, resources can be invested up to a point where, no matter how much more resource is invested, performance will not improve. At this point, performance is said to be *data limited*. There will be a data limitation if the data input is of poor quality—for example, when conversations are noisy, or print is smudged. Data limitations could also arise in memory. A data limitation cannot be overcome no matter how much we try. However, if more resources are invested or withdrawn and performance changes accordingly, performance is said to be *resource limited*.

When two tasks are combined, resources must be allocated between both tasks. Depending on the priorities we set, more or less resource can be allocated to one or other of the tasks. If performance on one task is plotted against performance on the other task, a Performance Operating Characteristic (POC) is obtained. Using POCs it is possible to try to capture resource allocation to each task. The curve of a POC represents the change in level of performance on one task when the level of performance on another concurrently performed task is changed. If the two tasks are resource limited, then there will be a complementary relationship between the two tasks, so that as performance on one task improves there will be a corresponding decline in performance on the other task. Figure 7.2 shows two possible POCs. Curve A shows the case when both tasks share a particular resource. Here diverting resources from the secondary task results in a corresponding improvement in the primary task. The other POC, curve B, shows a case where this complementary relationship

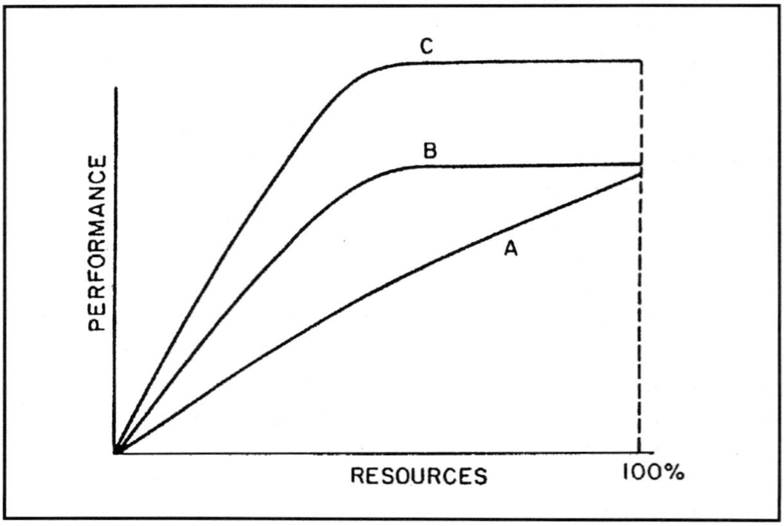

FIG. 7.1. Performance–resource functions for tasks differing in practice or difficulty. A = difficult; B = easier, or practised; C = higher data-limited asymptote (reprinted by permission of Academic Press from Wickens, 1984).

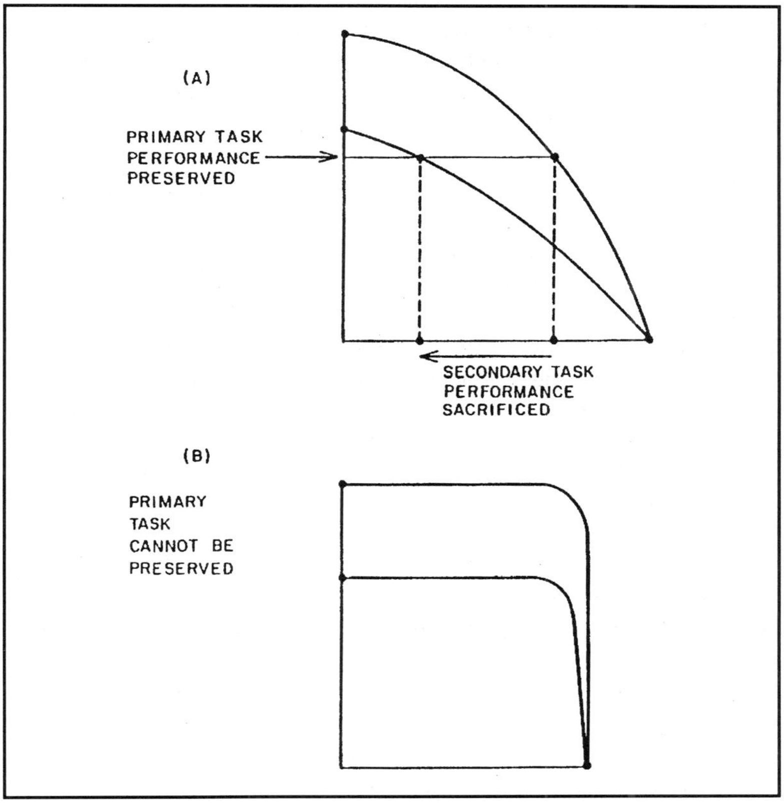

FIG. 7.2. Performance Operating Characteristic representation of (A) a case in which resources from a secondary task on the abscissa can compensate for difficulty changes in primary task on the ordinate: and (B) a case in which this reallocation is not possible (reprinted by permission of Academic Press from Wickens, 1984).

does not hold. This can be interpreted as showing that either the tasks do not share resources, or that the tasks are data limited.

Norman and Bobrow (1975, p.45) believed that there were a variety of resources such as "processing effort, the various forms of memory capacity and communication channels". This means that each kind of resource would have to be investigated separately to determine whether or not two tasks were competing for them. Allport (1980b) provides an in-depth analysis and critical review of Norman and Bobrow's (1975) theory. He claims that this theory ends up being as circular as that of Kahneman (1973). One problem is that, again, there is no independent way of measuring the resource demands made by tasks and whether these resources are from the same or different pools. If two tasks interfere, they are said to be competing for the same resource; if they don't interfere, they are using separate resources or are data limited.

Hirst (1986), too, points out that until resources are better specified, it will be difficult to come up with a good theory of divided attention. He remarks that psychologists are not even clear about whether there is one central resource on which all tasks draw, or whether there are multiple resources drawn on by different tasks—for example, a "visual pool" drawn on by visual tasks and a "verbal pool" drawn on by verbal tasks—or, possibly, whether there is a combination of specific multiple resources and a central resource!

Dual-task performance: How many resources?

Let's look at some of the evidence that has led psychologists to think that resources are shared between tasks or are specific to different kinds of task. Posner and Boies (1971) asked their subjects to do two things at once. One task involved letter matching, in which a warning signal was followed by a letter (e.g. A). After half a second, another letter was presented, and the subject had to judge whether or not the letters were the same. While responding to the letter-matching task with their right hand by pressing a key, subjects were also monitoring for the presentation of an auditory tone. When they detected the tone they were to press the left-hand key. The auditory signal could be presented at varying times during the presentation sequence of the visual task. Posner and Boies (1971) showed that reaction time to the tones was more or less equal during the parts of the visual task in which the warning signal was presented and during the waiting time before the first letter. This was taken to show that processing the warning signal takes little attention. However, if the tone was presented at the same time as either of the letters, response was slower; but not as slow as when the tone was presented during the interval between letter presentation—that is, when the subject was attending to the first letter in preparation for response to the second. This experiment could be taken as evidence for a general limit on attentional processing. During the easy part of the visual task, attention is free to support the tone detection task; but in the difficult part of the visual task, which demands attention, there is less available for tone detection, or response. There is, of course an alternative explanation.

In a clever experimental manipulation, McLeod (1977, 1978) altered just one aspect of Posner and Boies' (1971) task. Rather than responding to the auditory tone by pressing a key, McLeod asked his subjects to say "bip", a response completely different from the key-press required in the visual matching task. Using these response arrangements, there was no interference between the letter-matching task and tone detection, irrespective of whereabouts in the letter-matching task the tone was presented. So, if the response systems for the two tasks are separated, interference disappears. The result of McLeod's experiment is clearly contrary to a general resource limitation on attentional processing, as the limit here is specific to the type of response required. There appears to be no attentional limit on the subject's ability to perform the letter-matching task and concurrently monitor for a tone, which are in different domains, one visual and one auditory. Taken in conjunction with the Posner and Boies study, this suggests that we are limited in making two similar responses to two different tasks.

More effects of stimulus response compatibility

McLeod and Posner (1984) carried out further experiments on stimulus response compatibility. They suggested that there is a special class of translations between input and output (that is, relations between stimuli and responses) in their dual-task conditions. They tested the effects of different auditory/vocal transformations by combining a number of auditory/vocal tasks with visual/manual pattern matching. The basic method involved two tasks. The first task was a version of the visual letter-matching task used by Posner and Boies (1971) and McLeod (1977). This task was then combined with an auditory task that varied in the nature of the transformation between stimulus and response. We shall look at this experiment in some detail as it is rather interesting.

There were four groups of subjects. Three groups made a vocal response to the auditory task, and moved a lever to the left or right depending on whether the letters in the visual task were the same or different. The fourth group, called the modality cross-over group, responded manually to the auditory task and made a vocal response "same" or "different" to the visual task. Each group did a different auditory task. Subjects in group 1 were to shadow the auditory stimulus: they heard "up" or "down" and repeated the word. The second group of subjects also heard "up" or "down" but responded by saying a semantic associate, i.e. "high" or "low". The subjects in group 3 heard the word "high" to which they responded "up", or a

400Hz tone to which they responded "low". The fourth cross-modality group, heard "up" or "down" and responded by moving a lever up or down; remember that this group was making a vocal response to the visual task. Presentation of the auditory stimulus, or probe, was given at 6 different stages during the visual task. The probe could be given as follows:

1. 700ms before letter 1;
2. 100ms before letter 1;
3. 100ms after the onset of letter 1;
4. 100ms before letter 2;
5. 100ms after the onset of letter 2;
6. 1000ms after the onset of letter 2.

These 6 probe positions give three different kinds of dual-task trials. For the probe positions 1 and 6, there was no temporal overlap between the two responses. However, when the probe was presented at positions 2 and 3, a response was required for the auditory stimulus during the time in which the first letter was being encoded. If the auditory probe was presented at positions 4 or 5, a response was needed for both tasks simultaneously.

Two main results were clear. First, when the processing demands of the two tasks overlapped in positions 2, 3, 4 and 5, there was interference between tasks. The group doing the semantic auditory task, saying "high" to "up", showed more interference than the shadowing group, but the modality cross-over group showed far more interference than the other groups at positions 3 and 4—that is, in the condition when they had to give a verbal response to the visual task at the same time as giving a manual response to the auditory task. The mixed word-tone group showed more interference when response was to a tone than to a word. Clearly performance is very good when the subject simply shadows, or repeats the auditory probe, but is very poor in the modality cross-over condition. The shadowing task is "ideomotor compatible" in that the response resembles the stimulus, but McLeod and Posner suggest a different reason for the difference between shadowing and the cross-modality task. They suggest, on the basis of neuropsychological evidence, that there is a "privileged loop" which allows the articulatory programme involved in word production to be retrieved by hearing a word. This loop is separate from the rest of the processing system and allows spoken repetition of heard words to proceed without interference from other tasks.

In the modality cross-over condition, the subject is prepared, or primed, to make a vocal response to the visual stimulus. However, if the auditory probe arrives while the subject is waiting to do this, the articulatory response to the word is activated via the privileged loop. This then causes interference with the word that the subject is trying to produce in response to the visual task. McLeod and Posner suggest that there is an automatic linking between an auditory input and a vocal response that is always active. If there are other privileged loops between particular inputs and outputs such as the one proposed here, then it begins to look as if the human information processing system may have multiple channels which relate particular input patterns to overt actions. Interference will be observed only when there is specific competition, within channels. This interference will always appear and make some tasks impossible to combine without cost. Shaffer (1975) found that typists could copy-type and simultaneously do a shadowing task, but could not audio-type and read aloud. The difficulty here is that, when people listen to the auditory message, the privileged loop from those heard words tends to activate the motor programmes for their pronunciation. If at the same time other words that the subject is trying to read are also activating their motor programmes there will be interference. However, copy-typing can be easily combined with shadowing because there is a direct route from the shadowed input to speech output, which is quite independent of the mapping between the seen words and manual response of copy-typing. In Chapter 8 we shall look more closely at skills like typing, the effects of practice and automaticity, and the differences between the performance of experts and novices.

The psychological refractory period (PRP)

The psychological refractory period (PRP) has already been put forward as evidence for a central processing bottleneck. When two signals requiring two responses are presented in rapid succession, so that the second stimulus is presented before response has been made to the first, the second response tends to be delayed. As the onset of the two signals gets closer, so the delay in the response to the second tends to increase.

This delay became known as the psychological refractory period. Welford (1952) suggested that this effect was evidence for a limited capacity mechanism that could process only one response decision at

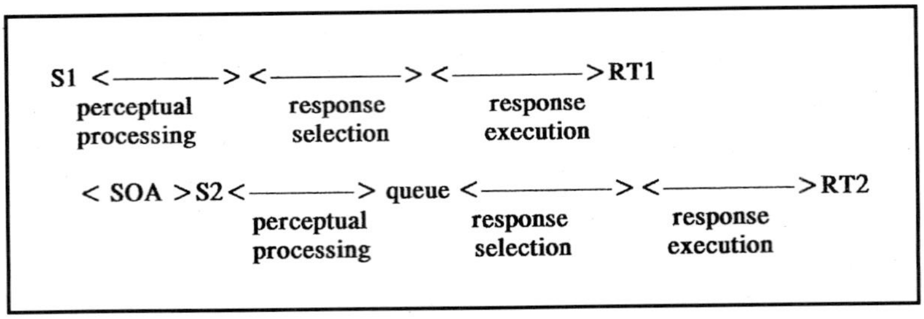

FIG. 7.3. A typical PRP procedure. Stimulus 2 (S2) follows stimulus 1 (S1) after a stimulus onset asynchrony (SOA). According to a response queueing account of PRP, selection of response to second stimulus (RT2) must wait until response to first stimulus (RT1) has been selected.

a time and was part of the initial evidence for a single channel theory of attention. It was reasoned that a bottleneck at the response decision stage meant that the second response had to "queue" until the first response has been selected; see Fig. 7.3.

Research has shown that one particularly important factor influencing PRP is the compatibility between the stimulus and the response to be made to it. (Welford, 1967, provides a review of PRP research up to that date.) In the Posner and Boies (1971) study, the key-press response to the auditory tone was not very compatible, and would have required a translation from the auditory input to a manual response. McLeod (1978) asked his subjects to say "bip" in response to hearing a "bip", a more compatible response, and the interference disappeared. Greenwald and Schulman (1973) experimented with stimulus response compatibility and PRP. Two signals were presented in rapid succession. The first task was to push a switch in the direction of an arrow, the second task had either a compatible or incompatible response with its stimulus. In the compatible condition, subjects were to say "one" in response to hearing "one"; in the incompatible condition, they were to say "A" when they heard "one". When the stimulus and response were highly compatible there was no refractoriness, but when the response to the second stimulus was incompatible (saying "A" to hearing "one") there was evidence for a refractory period. Thus refractoriness in Posner and Boies' experiment may be contributing to the observed interference between letter matching and tone detection because the auditory signal has to be translated to a keypress. In McLeod's experiment, hearing a "bip" and saying "bip" is similar to hearing "one" and saying "one" in the Greenwald and Schulman study; i.e. no psychological refractory period is found because there is a more direct matching between stimulus and response. Greenwald and Schulman (1973) suggested that, when the response to a stimulus was "ideomotor compatible", the feedback from the response resembled the stimulus to which the response was made, and tasks of this kind could be combined with other tasks without cost. Pashler (1984) has extended and refined work on PRP, providing strong evidence for a central bottleneck in overlapping tasks.

More recently, Pashler (1990) investigated refractoriness in an experiment in which subjects were, as is usual in PRP experiments, given two successive stimuli to which they had to respond as fast as possible. However, in one experiment Pashler (1990) manipulated the similarity between the two stimuli and their responses. The stimuli were an auditorily presented tone requiring a spoken response and a visually presented word requiring a key-press response. Thus, the stimulus response mapping was very similar to the experiment by McLeod (1978) in which no dual-task interference was found. Of course the dual-task technique used by Posner and Boies (1975) and McLeod (1978) gives less accurate measures of the relation between the two tasks, than can be obtained in a PRP experiment. One of the questions Pashler asked, was: does the PRP arise because of a central processing bottleneck or because the stimuli and responses are similar? If the bottleneck account is correct, there will be refractoriness even if the stimuli and their associated responses are quite different. On the other hand, if similarity is the cause, there should be no PRP when the stimuli and responses for them are different. Pashler found that even when the stimuli and responses were dissimilar (i.e. the spoken response to the tone and the key-press response to the visual word) there was still a psychological refractory period. Furthermore, in a condition where the subjects did not know the order in which the stimuli would be presented, response to the first stimulus was slower than it was when subjects knew which task would come first. It looks as if the subjects were not able to prepare in advance for both possible stimulus response pairs. Knowing the order of tasks allowed the subjects to get ready for the expected stimulus and its response. The results therefore supported the existence of a processing bottleneck, even when tasks are quite different.

Fagot and Pashler (1992) considered the possibility that the problem people have in making two responses to two stimuli in quick succession might be due to the difficulty of making responses to two different objects. We have seen already in the chapter on visual attention that there is evidence for attention being allocated to objects. For example, Duncan (1984) showed that two judgements could be made about two attributes of a single object as easily as one. We also saw that attention is allocated to items that form a perceptual group—see, for example, the experiment by Driver and Baylis (1989) who showed that interference in the Eriksen and Eriksen (1974) task was not necessarily spatially based, as letters which moved together (hence forming a perceptual group, or object) exhibited the flanker compatibility effect. These results, together with others from Treisman (e.g. Treisman & Gelade, 1980; Treisman, Kahneman, & Burkell, 1983), suggest that focal attention is directed to one object at a time and the features of that object are then integrated: we have examined this kind of evidence in Chapter 5. Applying these findings to the PRP experiment, Fagot and Pashler (1992) hypothesised that there were two ways of explaining the occurrence of the bottleneck in processing. One model could be that after an object is identified, focal attention is used to send information about the object to the response decision stage where a response decision mechanism selects all the possible responses for that single object. An alternative model is that the bottleneck can select only one response, but the number of objects is irrelevant. In a series of experiments Fagot and Pashler asked their subjects to make two separate responses to the attributes of a single object. The results showed that even when the two different responses are to the same object (e.g. name the letter; press a button for the colour) only one response can be selected at a time. However, when asked to make two responses to the same attribute of an object (e.g. name the colour; press a button for the colour) this can be done with only one response selection. Based on other manipulations of stimulus response compatibility, using Stroop stimuli and the Simon effect (e.g. pressing the left button to a stimulus on the right), Fagot and Pashler (1992) concluded that only one response selection operation occurs when subjects make two responses to the same attribute of an object. So the response selection mechanism which was hypothesised to be the location of the bottleneck can select two responses at once, provided certain conditions are met.

A tentative model for the bottleneck in PRP

Fagot and Pashler (1992) suggest a straightforward model, based on a production system framework. Anderson's (1983) ACT* is a production system used by computer scientists and is described in Chapter 8. Fagot and Pashler (1992) propose that the model to explain the bottleneck in production system terms would have these properties:

1. Prior to the task being performed, a number of response selection rules are activated. The more rules that are activated the less the individual activation for each rule.
2. Each rule has a condition and an action. When the condition for the action is met, the rule applies and the action is carried out. The higher the activation of the rule, the faster it will be applied.
3. Only one rule can be applied at once.
4. A rule can specify multiple motor responses in its action statement.

In order to find the right action, given a particular condition specified by the perceptual input, a code must be generated or retrieved from memory. Fagot and Pashler say the code can be considered as a specification of where to find a description of how to make the response which, their experiments have shown, can be multiple motor actions. They suggest that the bottleneck is at the point of generating the code and only one response can be retrieved at a time. Later mechanisms which look up response specifications and translate them into action are not limited. Overall, Fagot and Pashler believe the evidence is consistent with a bottleneck in processing at the stage where action codes are retrieved and generated. They do, however, point out some problems for the model. In Chapter 3 we looked at the question of early and late selection in visual attention and found evidence in the experiment by Eriksen and Eriksen (1974) for irrelevant letters which flank a target causing interference. This interference was interpreted as evidence for response activation from the distractors conflicting with the response to the target letter. This effect should not happen if only one response can be retrieved from memory at a time as the model above has just suggested. Fagot and Pashler (1992) suggest a way round this paradox. If the system was incapable of implementing two rules at a time because the neural mechanisms which implement the rules cannot settle into two different patterns of activity at the same time, then, although two responses could not be made at once, the pattern of activity from redundant inputs could still interfere with the process of settling into one pattern, hence slowing response and producing the Eriksen effect. The idea that the brain has to resolve conflict to "settle" to a steady state is a consequence of viewing information processing within the new connectionist framework mentioned in Chapter 5 which we shall discuss again in Chapter 10. Recently, Carrier and Pashler (1995, p.1339) have done experiments which provide evidence that "memory retrieval is delayed by central processes in the choice task, arguing that the central bottleneck responsible for dual-task interference encompasses memory retrieval as well as response selection".

The bottleneck lives on?

The experiments on the psychological refractory period seem to indicate that there really is a fundamental limit on the performance of concurrent tasks. When two tasks overlap in time both the first and the second task need to use the same mechanism that retrieves the code for response. If this central mechanism is busy processing the information from the first task, the second task simply has to wait. This wait causes PRP, or refractoriness. De Jong (1995) examined how the performance of two overlapping tasks is organised and controlled. In De Jong's experiments, subjects were presented with stimuli in unpredictable order. It was found that expected order rather then actual presentation order affected performance; that there was facilitation when task order was repeated on the next trial; and that it was the performance of the second task which benefitted most when task order was held constant over a number of trials. These effects were greatest at short intertrial intervals. De Jong (1995, p.21) suggests that the results support the notion that overlapping task performance is controlled by a "multi-level control structure that prepares the processing system not only for the immediate processing of the first task but also for a timely and rapid switch to the second task". Although there is evidence that preparation and response selection limit performance in overlapping PRP tasks, De Jong points out that we need to know the relative importance of the limitations on response preparation and the limitations on response selection. Although there is no clear evidence on this as yet, task similarity effects such as those we discussed in the dual-task experiments of McLeod and Posner (1984), and Greenwald and Shulman (1973) suggest that when tasks are highly ideomotor compatible, the limitation on response preparation may be reduced. However, De Jong suggests that this compatibility may equally well demand less of the central channel.

De Jong (1995) considers the question of how the switch to the second task is accomplished. The voluntary control of task switching is a topic considered in Chapter 9, but here let us note that De Jong suggests that there may be two components of the control operation. Picking up on suggestions by Allport and Styles (1990), he suggests that one part of the operation might be the retrieval of the rules from memory, followed by a second operation which implements these rules. As De Jong (1995) points out, either of these control components could benefit from advance preparation; but the answers await further research.

Summary

Rather than there being a central bottleneck in information processing, some psychologists proposed that the human operator had a pool of processing resources available, which could be allocated according to task demand (e.g. Kahneman, 1973; Wickens, 1984). Tasks are data limited if, no matter how much resource we apply to the task, we cannot improve. Resource-limited tasks are those in which, as resources are invested or withdrawn, performance changes accordingly (Norman & Bobrow, 1975). Initial research suggested that there was a general limit on task combination (e.g. Posner & Boies, 1971), but manipulations of the input and output for the two tasks showed that in some cases tasks could be combined without cost (e.g. McLeod, 1977). Other experiments seemed to indicate that complex tasks such as sight reading for piano playing and shadowing could be combined with no apparent decrement in either task (e.g. Allport et al., 1972). These results suggested that, rather than a single general purpose channel or general purpose resource, there are a variety of resources, or capacities, which are task specific, and provided that the tasks to be combined are not competing for the same resource or capacity, there will be no dual-task interference (McLeod & Posner, 1984). It might be that in dual-task combination—for example, piano playing and shadowing—measurements are not precise enough to detect a performance decrement. Recent results from experiments on refractoriness by Pashler and colleagues, (Pashler, 1990; Fagot & Pashler, 1992; Carrier & Pashler, 1995) suggest there are attentional limits in memory retrieval, which limits task performance even when tasks are dissimilar. As a response needs to have a code retrieved from memory and only one retrieval can happen at once, response to more than one object is limited. However, objects specify all the responses that can be made to them and so two responses can be made to one object, but when two objects need two responses this is limited. De Jong (1995) suggests that overlapping tasks are controlled by a multi-level control structure involved not only in the preparation of tasks, but also in switching between them.

Further reading

Most introductory texts have something on dual-task performance. Here are some examples:

Hirst, W. (1986). The psychology of attention. In J.E. Le Doux & W. Hirst (Eds.), *Mind and brain: Dialogues in cognitive neuroscience*. Cambridge: Cambridge University Press.

Smyth, M.M., Collins, A.F., Morris, P.E., & Levy, P. (1994). *Cognition in action* (2nd ed., Chapter 5). Hove, UK: Lawrence Erlbaum Associates Ltd.

Pashler, H. (1993). Dual task performance and elementary mental mechanisms. In D.E. Meyer & S. Kornblum (Eds.), *Attention and performance XIV: A Silver Jubilee*. London: MIT Press. This is not an introductory text, but is a useful review of dual task and PRP work over its history.

Automaticity, skill, and expertise 8

Introduction

When we first start learning a complex task such as driving a car, there seem to be too many component tasks involved. We are overwhelmed by the combination of steering, operating the clutch, monitoring the road, and changing gears. With practice, less and less conscious effort is necessary: steering round a corner while operating the clutch and changing gear is accomplished in one operation, often while we converse with the passenger. Clearly, something changes with practice; driving the car seems to be controlled in a very different way by the experienced driver than the learner. The expert can drive while talking, the novice cannot; the expert can control two tasks yet the novice has difficulty with even one. What has been learned by the expert? When driving a new car, the expert may initially switch on the windscreen wipers every time they intend to indicate. It can take many hours of driving the new car before the new configuration of controls is learned. The expert has become able to make many actions, such as moving the indicator lever automatically, but when one of these actions needs modifying, time and practice is needed all over again. The automatic response has to be deliberately modified; i.e. control has to be wrested from the automatic mode by conscious control. So, what is learnt with practice and what can this tell us about the nature of the systems that control information processing?

It looks as if there are two different modes of controlling information processing, "automatic" control and "controlled" control. Automatic control has at least four meanings (Norman & Shallice, 1986). First, it refers to the way that some actions are carried out without awareness; for example, walking on an even surface. Second, it refers to the way that some actions are initiated without any conscious deliberation, such as sipping a drink while talking. Third, attention may be automatically drawn to a stimulus, as in the orienting response to a sudden onset of a visual signal in the periphery (Posner, 1978). Last, automatic control is used to refer to the cases where tasks can be combined without any apparent interference or competition for processing resources. Controlled processing is deliberate and conscious and can deal with only a limited amount of information at once. When tasks interfere this is usually taken to indicate competition for limited attentional processing resources. Conscious control requires attention; automatic control does not.

In Chapter 7, we looked at some of the difficulties people have when they try to combine two tasks. We saw that while some tasks could be combined without much difficulty, other tasks were impossible to do together. One explanation for this is that tasks can be combined provided that the mappings between the input and output systems of one task are independent of the mappings between input and output of the other task. If there is crossover between input and output systems required for both tasks, there will be interference. Examples like this were evident in the studies by McLeod and Posner (1984) and Shaffer (1975). When tasks can be combined successfully, they seem to be controlled automatically and independently; that is, each task shows no evidence of being interfered with by the other and is performed as well in combination as it is alone. However, when the mappings between the stimuli and their responses are not direct, the tasks interfere with each other and a different kind of control is required, one which requires conscious attention and appears to be of limited capacity. Some tasks which interfere when first combined, become independent with enough practice. Why is this so?

Learning to do two things at once

Spelke, Hirst, and Neisser (1976) examined the effect of extended practice on peoples' ability to combine tasks. They gave two students 85 hours of practice spread over 17 weeks and monitored the ways in which dual-task performance changed over that period. To begin with, when the students were asked to read stories at the same time as writing to dictation, they found the task combination extremely difficult. Reading rate was very slow and their handwriting was poorly formed. Initially, Spelke et al.'s students showed extremely poor performance, but after 6 weeks of extended practice their reading rate had increased; they could comprehend the text; and their handwriting of the dictated words had improved. Tests of memory for the dictated words showed that the students were rarely able to recall any of the words they had written down. (Note here that this suggests attention is necessary for remembering. In Chapter 2, we discovered that words presented on the unattended channel in a dichotic listening task were not remembered even after repeated presentations; Moray, 1959.) In Spelke et al.'s experiment, after even more practice, the students were able to detect rhymes and semantically related words within the dictated lists and finally they were able to write down the category to which the dictated word belonged rather than the word itself at the same time as reading the text at normal speed and fully comprehending it! This dramatic improvement in performance clearly needs an explanation. It looks as if, although both tasks needed attention to start with, they did not need it later. Did the tasks become increasingly automatic or could attentional capacity have increased with practice? How could we tell how much attention is needed for a task, or whether the amount of attention has increased with practice? Many theories of attention assume that capacity is general purpose and limited. (We discussed this issue in Chapter 2.) If attentional resources are assumed to be of fixed capacity and general purpose, then certain further assumptions can be made—for example, that if two tasks interfere they are drawing on the same attentional resource. On the other hand, if tasks do not interfere, it must be that one or both do not require attention. However, in Chapter 7, we have already seen that tasks which do not interfere in one combination, may interfere in another combination. So tasks that appear not to require attention in one case, do seem to require it in another case. We have already analysed these problems, but for the moment we must step back in time to examine some influential theories that did assume general purpose limited capacity attentional resources, which were amenable to strategic control by the subject.

Two-process theory of attention: Automatic and controlled processing

According to the two-process approach, mental processing can operate in two different modes. In *automatic* mode, processing is a passive outcome of stimulation; it is parallel and does not draw on attentional capacity. In *conscious control* mode, mental processing is consciously controlled by intentions and does draw on attentional capacity. Some of the first people to explicitly involve control processes in their theorising were Atkinson and Shiffrin (1968) in their model of memory. Previously, control processes were simply assumed. For example, when we looked at Broadbent's filter model in Chapter 2, did you ask yourself: who sets the filter? Atkinson and Shiffrin pointed out the importance of understanding not only the structure of the information processing system, but also how it was controlled. Whilst their model was one of memory, it is in fact quite similar to Broadbent's model. Information entered the system in parallel, residing in a sensory buffer from which some information was selected for entry into short-term memory. In Atkinson and Shiffrin's model, the selection, rehearsal and recoding of information in short-term memory all required control processes. Short-term memory was seen as a *working memory* in which both storage and processing took place. The more demanding the processing was, the less capacity would be available for storage and vice versa. We have all experienced the difficulty of trying to solve a mental problem, where, as soon as the products of part of the computation become available, we forget what the question was! We just don't seem able to keep all the information in mind at the same time as consciously manipulating it. In this example we can see the close relationship between working memory and conscious attentional control. Later modifications of the working memory concept have all included both storage and control aspects; e.g. Baddeley (1986); Broadbent (1984). For information in working memory to be "working" it needs manipulation by "the subject" and what the subject does is "control". Atkinson and Shiffrin tell us nothing about this control except that it is something that the subject does. If we are to avoid the homunculus, or little-man-in-the-head, we must try to explain the difference between these two kinds of processing in terms of well-defined psychological mechanisms. This, as we shall see, is extremely difficult to do. Leaving aside for a moment the problem of determining how control processes operate or are instigated (the subject of the next chapter), let us look at some of the proposed differences between tasks that do or do not require the subject or homunculus to take control.

Posner and Snyder (1975)

Posner and Snyder (1975, p.81–82) drew the distinction between "… automatic activation processes which are solely the result of past learning and processes that are under current conscious control":

> Automatic activation processes are those which may occur without intention, without any conscious awareness and without interference with other mental activity. They are

> distinguished from operations that are performed by the conscious processing system since the latter system is of limited capacity and thus its commitments to any operation reduces its availability to perform any other operation.

Posner and Snyder were interested in the extent to which our conscious intentions and strategies are in control of the way information is processed in our minds. We can see from the above quotation that they thought the conscious processing system was a general purpose limited capacity system because they say that any attention demand of one task would reduce the amount of attention available for another attention demanding task. Let's look at some of the reasons behind Posner and Snyder's ideas.

One of the most widely investigated effects in cognitive psychology, is the Stroop Effect (Stroop, 1935). Imagine you are presented with the word BLUE written in red ink. If our task is to read the word as quickly as possible there is no problem. The word is available immediately and without any apparent effort, it seems to pop into our mind automatically. However, if our task is to produce the name of the ink colour (red, in this case), response is much slower; subjectively we feel as if more conscious effort is needed to overcome the tendency to produce the incongruent written word which seems to interfere with naming the ink. This slowing is not simply because colour naming is always slower than word reading; naming a colour patch is much faster than naming the ink in an incongruent Stroop stimulus. What seems to be happening here is that our ability to respond selectively to one aspect of the Stroop stimulus is interfered with by the other. No matter what our conscious intentions are, the written word cannot be completely ignored. The Stroop effect can be found with other kinds of stimuli in which there are (usually) two responses available from the same stimulus. Another example is having to count the number of characters present in a display, when the characters themselves are digits. Usually the Stroop effect is asymmetrical: in the case of colour words written in an incongruent ink colour, the word interferes with the ink naming, but not vice versa. It seems that the word automatically activates its response and although conscious control can prevent the response from being made overtly, there is a time cost while the intended response, ink naming, gains control of overt action. The asymmetry arises because the ink naming is less strongly mapped onto a response and is easily overcome by the stronger mapping of the word to its response. Word reading in adults is an extremely well-learned skill, but in early readers, the effect is not present, or may even be reversed. On the other hand, the direction of interference may depend on task demands: when the task involves deciding whether stimuli match physically, judgements are made more quickly for colours than words, and in this case, experiments show that there is more interference from colours on words (Murray, Mastroddi, & Duncan, 1972). However, if the ink colour and word are congruent the word may facilitate vocal colour naming (Hintzman et al., 1972).

Posner and Snyder (1975) suggest that there is automatic parallel processing of both features of the stimulus until close to output. Automatic processing cannot be prevented, but conscious attention can be used flexibly. So, while some cognitive operations proceed automatically, others take place under strategic, conscious, attentional control which is deployed according to the subject's intentions.

To test their theory Posner and Snyder (1975) conducted a series of experiments using a letter-matching task. On each trial the subject was presented with a priming stimulus, either a letter or a plus sign. The prime was followed by a pair of letters and the task was to decide, as quickly as possible, whether the letters were the same or different. There were two basic predictions. First, the prime would automatically activate its representation in memory, so that if the prime was A and the pair of letters to be matched were AA, response would be facilitated because the activation in memory was confirmed. According to their view, if the prime was different from the target, there would be no inhibition produced by this automatic memory activation on other responses. Second, Posner and Snyder predicted that once the subject "invests his conscious attention in the processing of a stimulus" the benefit of pathway activation would be accompanied by a widespread cost, or inhibition on other signals. This would account for the fact that subjects do well when they receive an expected stimulus, but perform poorly when an unexpected stimulus arrives. They applied a cost–benefit analysis to their data, measuring how much better or worse subjects perform in the experimental conditions relative to a neutral control.

The basic design of the experiment is to precede the target stimulus by either a neutral warning signal, in this case the plus sign, or a non-neutral prime which should, if attended, bias target processing. The probability that the prime would be a valid cue for the target was manipulated, as it was assumed that the subject would adopt a strategy whereby they invested more or less attention in the prime depending on whether or not they thought it would be a valid predictor of the target. According to the theory, when the subject pays little processing capacity to the prime, a valid cue will automatically produce facilitation but no costs. However, when the subject "actively attends" to the prime there will be facilitatory benefits from both automatic activation and from conscious attention if the prime is valid, but when the prime is not valid there will be inhibitory costs due to strategic processing.

Results showed that when the prime was a poor predictor of the target there was benefit but no cost. When the prime was of high validity the benefit accrues more rapidly than the cost. This effect was interpreted as showing that the allocation of conscious attention takes more time than automatic activation. The differential time course of facilitatory and inhibitory effects suggested a real difference between the two kinds of processing.

Shiffrin and Schneider's (1977) theory

A general theory involving controlled and automatic processing was proposed by Shiffrin and Schneider (1977) who carried out a series of experiments on visual search and attention. Schneider and Shiffrin (1977) report a series of experiments on visual search using a multiple-frame visual search paradigm. They gave their subjects one, two, or four letters as the memory set, presented in advance of each search trial. Then a fixation dot appeared for 500ms, followed by a series of 20 frames presented for a fixed time. On each frame there would be either none or one member of the memory set. In different experiments they manipulated frame time, memory set size, and frame size. This same paradigm was also used in the companion paper by Shiffrin and Schneider (1977). In one experiment performance was tested when subjects had to search for a member of the memory set in visual displays containing one, two, or four items. Their task was to decide as rapidly as possible whether any of the letters from the memory set were present in the display. The crucial experimental manipulation was the mapping between stimuli and responses. For the *consistent mapping* condition, targets were always consonants and distractors were always digits; i.e. there was a consistent mapping of target and distractors onto their responses. In this case, whenever the subject detected a member of the memory set in the display, it had to be a target. Performance in the consistent mapping condition was contrasted with that in the *varied mapping* condition. In this condition both the memory set and the distractors were a mixture of letters and digits. Schneider and Shiffrin found a clear difference between performance in the two conditions. With consistent mapping, search is virtually independent of both the number of items in the memory set and the number of items in the display, as if search is taking place in parallel. Shiffrin and Schneider (1977) said this type of performance reflected "automatic processing". However, with varied mapping where the target and distractor set changed from trial to trial, subjects were slower to detect the target and their response times increased with the number of distractors in the display. Search seemed to remain serial. This type of performance was said to be indicative of "controlled processing".

Of course letters and digits have well-learned responses associated with them, learnt over years of practice. Shiffrin and Schneider were interested to see whether, given enough practice, subjects would develop automatic processing of items divided by a novel, arbitrary distinction. To do this they divided consonants into two sets, B to L and Q to Z. In consistent mapping, only one set of consonants was used to make up the memory set and distractors were always selected from the other set. After over 2100 trials performance began to resemble that of subjects in the letter/digit experiment. Search became fast and independent of the number of items in the memory set, or the number of items in the display. Having had all this practice with one response mapping, subjects were given another 2400 trials in which the mapping between sets was reversed; i.e. letters that were once targets were now distractors and vice versa. There was a dramatic change in performance. In the early stages subjects were unable to "change set" and performance was very poor: slow and limited by both the memory set size and number of distractors, subjects gave many false alarms. Very gradually subjects began to improve their hit rate and after 2400 trials of reversal training, subjects were performing at the same level as they were after 1500 trials of the original training. It was as if the subjects either had to "unlearn" an automatic attentional response to the previous memory set or overcome some kind of learnt inhibition to the previous distractor set, or both, before the reversed set could become automatic.

It appears, then, that after extended practice with one consistent mapping between stimulus and response, subjects find it extremely difficult to change to a different stimulus response mapping. However, Shiffrin and Schneider showed that varied mappings, despite extended practice, could easily be altered according to instructions, so the difficulties that subjects experienced in the consistent mapping condition were not simply due to changing from one set to another. From the results of these experiments it appears that there are indeed two different processes involved in attention: one type of processing which can be quickly adapted by the subject's conscious intentions and another kind of process which runs off automatically beyond conscious control. This distinction is supported by the results of another experiment by Shiffrin and Schneider. Subjects were asked to attend to some display locations and to ignore others. When a target that had been a member of the consistent mapping set appeared in an irrelevant location subjects were unable to ignore it; there was an attentional pop-out effect rather like those we looked at in the chapter on visual search. This intrusion of information from the irrelevant location suggests that automatic processes are operating in parallel over the display, taking in information from both relevant and irrelevant display locations, rather like the parallel feature search in Treisman's feature integration theory. Irrelevant targets from previous varied mapping, control search conditions, did not pop-out, subjects were unaware of them, and they did not interfere with target processing. These results were taken as evidence that even under controlled search conditions subjects are not always successful in controlling their attention if an automatic detection is made.

Neuman's critique of two-process theory

Neuman (1984) summarises the "primary criteria" of automaticity on which most two-process theories agree, under three headings:

1. Mode of operation: Automatic processes operate without capacity and they neither suffer nor cause interference.
2. Mode of control: Automatic processes are under the control of stimulation rather than under the control of the intentions (strategies, expectancies, plans) of the person.
3. Mode of representation: Automatic processes do not necessarily give rise to conscious awareness.

Some "secondary criteria"—which do not necessarily define automaticity but which are suggested or implied by some theories—are that automatic processes are determined by connections that are either wired in or are learned through practice; and that this kind of processing is relatively simple, rapid, and inflexible in that it can be modified only by extended practice.

Neuman then goes on to evaluate the data to try to determine whether these criteria are correct and then to specify the functional properties of automatic and non-automatic processes. He argues that it is extremely difficult to demonstrate that a task which appears to be "automatic" does not require attentional capacity. While a task may be "interference free" in one task combination, in a different combination, interference may well be found—hence, the task now appears to require attention while before it did not. The experiment by Spelke et al. (1976) which we looked at earlier, is one in which there was a constant rule between input and output. Subjects always wrote what they heard and read what they saw. Thus the stimuli were presented in different modalities and one task, the reading, did not require overt response. In this situation, practice can lead to apparent automaticity. However, when both tasks involve similar stimuli—as for example, in some of Shiffrin and Schneider's experiments—even well-practised tasks cannot be carried out simultaneously. We saw a similar effect in McLeod's (1978) experiment where changing the response mode affected whether or not there was task interference. Neuman (1984, p.269) suggests that practice leads to the development of a skill, which "includes a sensory and, at least during practice, a motor response. After practice the response may remain covert, but is still ... as Schneider and Shiffrin's term correctly suggests ... an attentional response connected to the particular target stimuli." However, even well-practised tasks will display interference if the responses are similar. Tasks may also interfere, according to Neuman, if the initiation of a new response is required; only when there is a continuous stream of information guiding action, as in the Spelke et al. study, can apparent automaticity be found. It would seem then that Neuman's analysis throws doubt over the lack of interference criterion.

What about the criterion concerning mode of control? Automatic processes are, according to two-process theory, unavoidable: they run off as a consequence of stimuli in the environment, rather than as a consequence of intentions. Evidence from studies of the Stroop effect have been interpreted as demonstrating obligatory processing of the unwanted word name even when the subject was intending to name the ink colour. This is the case when the colour and the word occupy the same stimulus location; i.e. when the word is itself written in a colour. However, Kahneman and Henik (1971) have shown that when the word and incongruent colour are separated, interference is reduced. In Chapters 3, 4, and 5, we discussed some examples from the literature on visual attention which demonstrated that both grouping factors and spatial separation are involved in the efficiency of selection. Processing of the unwanted stimulus dimension will be "automatic" only within a constrained set of circumstances when the subject's ability to focus attention breaks down. Neuman suggests that distractors produce interference not simply because they are present in the stimulus environment, but because they are related to the intended action. So, Stroop interference may arise because both the ink and the word are related to the currently active task set. We have already seen that the direction of interference may depend on task demands. Stroop interference depends very much upon where attention is directed, the task to be performed, and what strategies are used. If this is so, then it is the strategic, controlled attention allocation deployed to set up the cognitive system to "respond to colours", which results in the production of interference. Normally this interference is defined as a result of automatic processes, but we can see here that there is an involvement of intention in automatic processing. Automatic processing is not, therefore, an "invariant consequence of stimulation, independent of a subject's intentions" (p.270). Despite this evidence, Neuman admits that there probably are situations in which stimulus processing may be unavoidable, and outside the control of current intentions.

Neuman believes that automatic processing is not uncontrolled, but rather is controlled below the level of conscious awareness. Awareness is one of the key properties of conscious control. But what do we mean by awareness? Or consciousness, for that matter? Later, in Chapter 10, we shall look in detail at some definitions of consciousness and some criteria for deciding when people are conscious. In Neuman's analysis there are three kinds of unawareness. He says there are three questions we can ask. First, whether brain processes not directly related to ongoing activity are "unaware"; second, whether there are some processes within the execution of a task that may escape awareness; and third, whether an action as a whole can proceed without awareness. Certainly the answer to the first question is *Yes*. Neuman says, for example, that we are unaware of the contents of long-term memory, and the changes that take place during forgetting. We can also answer *Yes* to the second question. Again Neuman takes an example from memory, the "tip-of-the-tongue phenomenon". When people are given a definition like " a far-eastern trade vessel", they may be unable to recall the word "sampan" immediately although they feel it is on the "tip-of-the-tongue"; they may come up with some candidate answers that they know are wrong, but sound like what they are looking for. After abandoning memory search, the answer suddenly springs to mind, clearly as a result of some ongoing processing activity that has been working below the level of awareness. It is probably the case that the lion's share of information processing takes place at a level below conscious awareness. We are not, for example, able to introspect on the processes which underlie the production of words in sentences we produce, although when the sentence is articulated it appears, making perfect sense. For the main part we are aware only of the outcome of processing not the working of the underlying processes themselves.

The answer to the third question is also *Yes*; whole actions can be carried out without a person being aware. For example, you arrive home having driven along a familiar route, but cannot recall passing the traffic lights. You know you intended to lock the back door but cannot remember doing it; on checking you find that you have. Whether you were unaware of carrying out the action at the time, or simply forgot that you had done it is difficult to determine, but these "slips of action" (Reason, 1979; Norman, 1981) suggest some failure of whatever system controls and monitors ongoing activity.

Slips of action usually happen during the execution of frequently performed routine activities that have become "automatic" in Neuman's (1984) third use of the term. There is little experimental data on whole tasks proceeding outside awareness; however, Neuman cites an experiment similar to that of Spelke et al. (1976), reported by Hirst et al. (1980), in which highly practised subjects became able to read for comprehension at the same time as writing down and understanding dictated sentences of which they had little or no awareness.

The first type of processes really do happen outside awareness but account for only a small proportion of tasks that are usually considered to be automatic according to two-process theory. The second type of processes occur in the context of some ongoing activity and must therefore depend to some extent on intention although many of them may take place with little or no awareness. The third case, where a whole action may happen without awareness, will happen only in particular circumstances, which Neuman likens to the conditions that are a prerequisite for interference free dual-task performance.

Neuman proposes a different conception of automaticity: he suggests that the difference between automatic and controlled processing is the level of control required. Actions can be performed only if all the parameters for that action are specified as, for example, naming the ink colour of an incongruent Stroop stimulus. To do the action as planned we must select one aspect, the colour not the word, of a particular object. Also we must retrieve specific information, the colour's name rather than its category "colour"; then we must carry out a movement sequence to pronounce the response as quickly as possible. Some parameter specifications are stored in long-term memory; Neuman terms these "skills". Other specifications come from the stimulus itself, but the remaining specifications must come from an attentional mechanism, whose function is "to provide the specifications that cannot be obtained by linking input information to skills" (p.281). These three sources of constraint work together to guide our actions.

According to Neuman, skills have two functions. First, they specify actions and secondly they help pick up information from the environment. Skilled typists produce very even, predictable finger movements (Rumelhart & Norman, 1982); novices do not. Thus the actions of a skilled typist are strongly constrained by their skill. Skilled chess players can encode the arrangement of a chess game very much more quickly than novices (Chase & Simon, 1973). For an expert chess player, the game in progress matches and activates existing schemata in long-term memory, enabling the information to be picked up more quickly. Novices do not have these pre-existing schemata to aid them. When parameters are left unspecified, the action cannot be successfully performed, and it is in this case that the attentional mode of parameter specification is needed. Thus, according to Neuman (1984, p.282), "a process is automatic if its parameters are specified by a skill in conjunction with input information. If this is not possible, one or several attentional mechanisms for parameter specification must come into play. They are responsible for interference and give rise to conscious awareness." It is clear from Neuman's argument that automaticity is not some kind of process, but something that seems to emerge when conditions are right. The right conditions depend not only on the processing system but also on the situation.

Modelling the Stroop task

Cohen, Dunbar, and McClelland (1990) and Cohen and Huston (1994) produced a connectionist model of Stroop performance. In the model there are two processing pathways, one for word reading and one for colour naming. The model is trained more on the word reading than colour naming and this results in greater increases in the strength of the connections within the word reading pathway; i.e. there is an asymmetry in connection strength. As a result, when the network is presented with a word, such as "red" written in green ink, it responds more quickly and strongly to red than green, just as humans do. However, humans are able to produce the weaker response, albeit more slowly. To model this, the network needs to be able in some sense to inhibit or modulate the strongest response in order to output the weaker one. This is achieved by including a set of input units which are responsive to task demands and represent intended behaviour: see Fig. 8.1.

Activation of a task demand unit "sensitises" the appropriate processing pathway and "desensitises" the task irrelevant pathway. This modulation allows the weaker response to ink colour to control output even though the connection strengths are strongest in the word reading pathway. We have already met Singer's (1994) idea that intentional behaviour might be achieved by modulation of activity in cortical areas by the thalamus in Chapter 5. So it would seem plausible that the intentional selection of a weak response over a strong one could be achieved the same way in humans.

Phaf, van der Heijden, and Hudson's (1990) model SLAM, mentioned at the end of Chapter 5, also models Stroop performance. Phaf et al. argue that Cohen et al.'s (1990) model has a problem, because if Stroop interference were a result of differential learning or practice, then we should, by practice, be able to reverse the Stroop

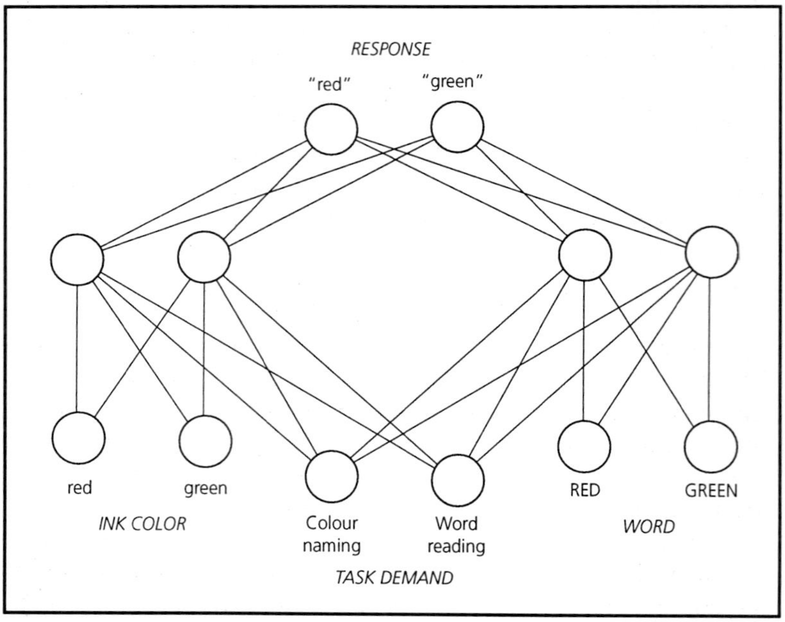

FIG. 8.1. Network architecture for the model of the Stroop task. Units at bottom are input units; units at top are output (response) units (reprinted from Cohen & Huston, 1994, copyright © MIT Press).

effect. In fact, there is some evidence for reduction of Stroop interference with practice (Neill, 1977), and presumably reading is such an overlearnt skill acquired over years, that it would take as many years of practice to remove the asymmetry.

MacLeod and Dunbar (1988) directly studied the effect of practice on Stroop interference. They trained subjects to call each of four different shapes by the name of a colour (green, pink, orange, or blue). These shapes could then be presented in a neutral colour, the congruent colour, or the incongruent colour and the subjects asked to name either the shape or the colour of the ink. MacLeod and Dunbar discovered that, when subjects had been given only a little shape-naming practice, ink colour interfered with shape naming, but not the reverse. At moderate levels of practice in shape naming, interference was equal in each task. After extended practice, shape names interfered with ink-colour naming, but not the reverse. Thus, increased practice with shape naming systematically increased interference on the naming of ink colour. This is particularly interesting because there was no competing "colour word" as there is in conventional Stroop tasks, and because shape naming never became faster than ink-colour naming, so ruling out a "race" model of interference.

In his review of the Stroop effect, MacLeod (1991, p.182) concluded that, in general, the "degree of practice in processing each of the dimensions of a multidimensional stimulus is influential in determining the extent of interference from one dimension to another. The greater the practice in processing a dimension, the more capable that dimension is of influencing the processing of another dimension." Therefore the reason why one task appears automatic is the relative strength of the pathways of the two tasks, exactly as modelled by Cohen, Dunbar, and McClelland (1990) and Cohen and Huston (1994).

Attentional control as a skill

We have spent some time examining the criteria for automaticity and discovered that there are a number of problems with the two-process theory. The distinction between automaticity and control is not as clear cut as once thought. Over the years it has proved notoriously difficult to make a clear empirical distinction between these two modes of processing. A more promising approach seems to be to accept ideas like Neuman's, in which there is no clear distinction but a gradation.

Neuman (1984) suggested that practice can produce skills which constrain the parameters of actions. When skills do not provide enough specification, attention is needed. Presumably more or less attention will be needed depending on how well or how many parameters are specified by pre-existing skills. Hirst (1986) discusses a rather different kind of skill, that of allocating attention itself, and Gopher (1993) also investigates whether there are skills involved in attentional control. In his paper, Gopher seeks evidence to support the idea that attention management is a skill and that it can be learnt through training. He argues that we would need to show: first, that subjects do actually have the potential to control their allocation of attention; second, that this potential is not always fulfilled, in so far as subjects may fail to maintain control; and last, that with appropriate training, difficulties of control can be overcome. In everyday life we are continually having to perform complex tasks. These require the division, allocation and re-allocation of attention, depending on task demands and our currently active goals and intentions. A good example of this is driving. The driver must divide attention between controlling the car, monitoring the behaviour of other vehicles, watching for traffic signals, following the route, and possibly listening to the radio or having a conversation. If an emergency arises the driver may stop talking while avoiding an obstruction. Driver behaviour suggests that there is moment by moment priority setting and attentional trade-offs involved in complex task performance. Gopher suggests that we employ strategies to allow us to cope as best as we can with competing task demands within the boundaries of our processing and response limitations. Given that we are able to adopt and execute attentional strategies, Gopher asks two further questions about control. First, to what extent are we consciously aware of the strategies we use and their efficiency? Second, how do we do it? How are changes in attentional strategy implemented? So far we have mentioned many theories and models that have appealed to some kind of control or controlled processing, but the best explanation of how control works is almost invariably to say "that the subject does it". This, of course, is no explanation at all.

While as yet we have not been provided with an explanation for how subjects in experiments actually operate or implement control, we have seen many examples where control is said to be operating. In focused attention experiments, subjects do focus attention as far as they are able within the context of the experiment. In divided attention experiments subjects are able to divide attention, and can do so according to priorities. If you ask subjects to give 70% attention to one task and 30% to another task, they can usually become able to do this. We have looked at performance operating characteristics (POC) in

Chapter 7 when we considered resource theories of attention. In tasks like these, subjects allocate more or less attention according to instructions, and the trade-off between tasks is studied. This is a clear example of the manipulation of strategic control. Subjects can also alternately respond to different dimensions of a stimulus. Allport, Styles, and Hseih (1994) showed that subjects can alternately switch attention between the conflicting responses of a Stroop stimulus. In this example the stimulus provides no clues as to which response the subjects must make. All shifts of attention must be executed by intentional control, and although there may be a time cost of shifting, subjects can do this task successfully. We shall examine these experiments in more detail later.

Although we are usually successful in controlling attention, there are plenty of examples of situations where control fails. In the experiments combining writing to dictation while reading, Spelke et al.'s subjects were unable to divide their attention, at least in the beginning. In Shiffrin and Schneider's experiments, letters that were from the overlearned constant mapping condition could not be ignored: attention was automatically "captured" despite the subjects' intentions of control. So, we have, as Gopher required, evidence that control is possible, but that it can also fail. In the rest of his paper Gopher looks at how people can learn to improve their attentional skills by training. One of the tasks used for this training is called the Space Fortress which was designed to present the subject with a complex, dynamic environment within the confines of a well-specified (as far as the experimenters were concerned) computer game. The game involved the player in controlling the movements of a space ship as if they were flying it, at the same time as firing missiles, to try to destroy the fortress. While doing this they must avoid being destroyed themselves. The rules of the game are quite complex and the main aim is to score points.

When players first tried the game their first response was usually panic. They felt that the demands of the situation were too high: everything happened too fast; too much happened at once; and the situation seemed to be out of control. This sounds very like our feeling when we first attempt any complex skill, like driving a car. After considerable practice the players began to work out a strategy and performance improved. Without specific training, people would not necessarily work out or adopt an optimal strategy, but Gopher found that if subjects were led through a sequence of emphasis changes for sub-components of the game, similar to the variable priority method used in POC studies, performance could be improved. Subjects were advised to concentrate on one sub-component at a time, and respond to the other components only if they could do so without neglecting the component they were to concentrate on. The game remained exactly the same, apart from the introduction of a reward element in that the selected game component received more points. (This was to give subjects positive feedback on their success.) Otherwise, only the allocation of attentional priorities was altered. Four groups of subjects were studied. The control group were given practice but no specific emphasis training; two groups were given emphasis training on just one task component, mine handling or ship control; and the fourth group of subjects were given emphasis training on both, in alternation. The results showed that the group who had received the double manipulation outperformed all other groups which did not differ from each other. An interesting finding was that although special training finished after six sessions, the improvement in performance continued over the next four sessions to the end of the experiment. This result suggests, as Gopher (1993, p.315) reports, that after six sessions the double manipulation group "had already internalised their specialised knowledge and gained sufficient control to continue to improve on their own".

The application of this kind of training is demonstrated in another study reported by Gopher in which Israeli airforce cadets were given training on a modification of the *Space Fortress* game. Cadets who drop out often do so because they have difficulty coping with the load of a flight task, dividing and controlling attention. In comparison to a control group who were given no training on the game, the experimental cadets who were given double emphasis training, showed a 30% increase in their actual flight performance. The advantage was largest in the manoeuvres requiring integration of several elements. After 18 months there were twice as many graduates in the experimental group as the control group. Gopher points out that the advantage of game training is not because it is similar to actual flying, because real flying is very much more demanding than the game, and the game is not very realistic. What the game does is train people in the kinds of attentional skills needed in complex situations. Given direct experience with different attentional strategies, performance improves and these skills transfer to new situations and different task demands. The skill of attentional control appears to be learned. Gopher suggests that there is a move from controlled application of attentional strategies to automated schemata, where response schemata that have become associated with proficient behaviour become hard-wired. With learning, the attentional strategies that once needed control become automatic.

But what about the question of how control processing is actually done? Who or what does the controlling? What changes with practice? Gopher's review has demonstrated that people can operate attentional control and improve with training, but it still seems that it is always "the subject" that is in control, rather than a well-specified cognitive mechanism. How do people do it?

Production systems

One theoretical option is that skills, including attentional skills, result from the operation of *procedures*. The basic principle underlying production systems is that human cognition can be conceived of as a set of condition–action pairs called productions. The condition specifies a set of data patterns, and if elements matching these patterns are in working memory then the production can apply. So a procedure is a condition–action link between a set of conditions in working memory and data, or knowledge stored as schemata in long-term memory. Production systems are widely used in artificial intelligence and can be extremely powerful computational devices. They are expressed as IF ... THEN correspondence rules, so that IF a condition, or set of conditions are active in the working memory part of the system, and there is rule or schema in long-term memory corresponding to the IF conditions, the THEN part of the rule will be executed. New information resulting from the computation is then deposited in working memory leading to a new data pattern and the sequence of IF ... THEN matching can start again. In his 1984 Maltese Cross model of memory Broadbent tries to avoid the homunculus problem of attentional control by proposing a production system architecture rather like ACT*. Rather than the little-man-in-the-head, control emerges from the correspondence between input patterns, long-term knowledge and the contents of working memory.

ACT* cognitive architecture

Anderson (1983) provides a theory of cognition based on a production system called ACT*. In ACT* there are three memories, working, procedural and declarative: see Fig. 8.2. Working memory contains the information to which the system currently has access. This comprises information that has been retrieved from long-term memory together with the temporary structures that have arisen from

FIG. 8.2. Overview of the ACT* cognitive architecture (reprinted from Anderson, 1983, by permission of the author).

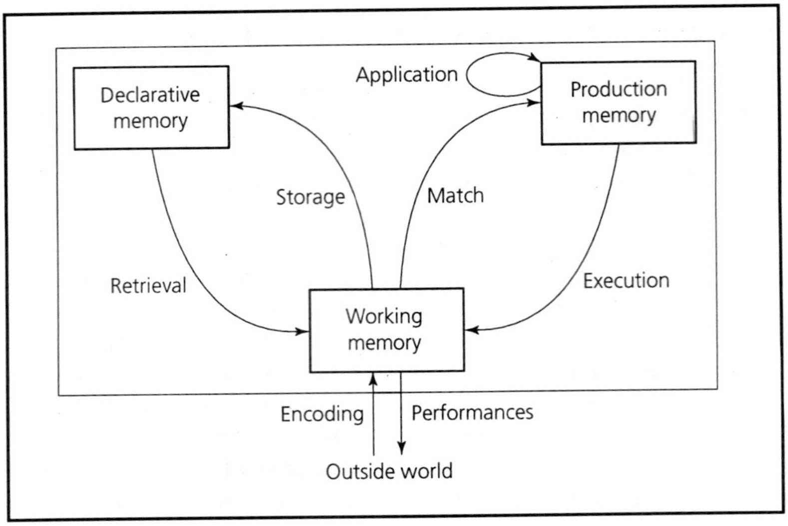

encoding processes and the action of productions. Working memory is, therefore, declarative knowledge, either permanent or temporary, that is currently active. (In the human processor, this would be equivalent to the consciously available contents of short-term working memory.) An important distinction made by memory theorists is between declarative knowledge, to which we have conscious access, and procedural knowledge, to which we have no conscious access. This distinction between procedural and declarative knowledge is fundamental to ACT*. Working memory is severely limited in the amount of information that can be concurrently represented in it. If all the computational steps involved in human information processing had to be represented in declarative form in working memory, the system would be in danger of overload. However, if only a small amount of task-relevant information needed to be represented in declarative form, the system could run much more efficiently. Provided the declarative system has access to the outputs from productions, there is no need for the productions themselves to be open to conscious inspection. Allport (1980a, 1988), like Neuman (1984), suggests that only a very small amount of information processing is available to consciousness and that unconscious processing is the rule rather than the exception. Productions in Anderson's ACT* model run off automatically as a result of pattern matching, and only the products of their execution enter working memory.

Learning in production systems

In the initial stages of learning a new task or skill, such as playing chess, peoples' performance is usually slow and full of mistakes. Novices repeat the rules to themselves and have to work out the implications of each move one at a time. An expert on the other hand, can rapidly sum up the state of the game and make a good move without seeming to have had a problem to solve at all. On interrogation the expert may have difficulty in explaining exactly why they made one move rather than another. In contrast to the novice, the expert seems to have poor access to declarative knowledge for the reasons underlying their decision although the expert's performance is much better than that of the novice. According to Anderson's theory, there are three successive stages of learning involved in the acquisition of cognitive skills. In the beginning, learning involves the collection of relevant facts. So, for example, when learning to play chess, we need to know which moves are legal and which pieces move which way. The novice then applies previous experience in problem solving, to work out which is the best move. However, performance is slow and error prone because of the need to activate and retrieve all relevant knowledge into the working memory. When working memory is overloaded relevant information may be lost and an error result. With more practice, the rules of chess begin to become proceduralised. New productions are formed from the declarative knowledge gained in the initial stages of learning. This proceduralisation frees space in working memory as the knowledge that was once declarative becomes embedded in procedures which do not need to be retrieved in declarative form to be used by the information processing system. So, for example, the rules governing legal moves by different chess pieces are just "known" by the system; the player does not have to keep on retrieving that knowledge into active working memory. The player will also begin to learn that, if a particular configuration of pieces is on the board, making a particular move is likely to produce a good outcome. In the final stages of learning, new procedures are formed from existing productions. This composition of procedures allows complex patterns of IF … THEN rules to be compiled, so that the IF side of the production can be made up of several clauses, which will THEN produce one or a series of actions. Production rules become strengthened with use, and may become so "automatic" that the information within them is no longer available in declarative form. Experts just "know" the answer to problems and may find it extremely difficult to explain why they come to decisions.

Anderson (1983) uses bridge as an example of procedural learning in ACT*; however, the same kind of learning could be equally well applied to chess. Here are two cases taken from Anderson (1983, p.242–244) where generalisation takes place in a player who is assumed to already have some procedures which have been compiled by experience. P1, P2 etc. refer to production 1, production 2 etc.

P1 IF I am playing no trump
    and my dummy has a long suit
  THEN try to establish that suit
    and then run that suit.

P2 IF I am playing spades
    and my dummy has a long suit
  THEN try to establish that suit
    and then run that suit.

These two productions, P1 and P2 will be generalised by ACT* into a different production P3 by the deletion of a condition clause which was different in each production:

P3 IF my dummy has a long suit
  THEN try to establish that suit
    and run that suit.

More complex generalisation can occur when, rather than deletions, constants are replaced by variables (LVs). Anderson gives another example from bridge:

P4 IF I am playing no trump
    and I have a king in a suit
    and I have the queen in that suit
    and my opponent leads a lower card in that suit
  THEN I can play the queen.

P5 IF I am playing no trump
    and I have a queen in a suit
    and I have a jack in that suit
    and my opponent leads a lower card in that suit
  THEN I can play the jack.

By substituting constants for variables, the generalisation of these two procedures becomes:

P6 IF I am playing no trump
and I have LV card 1 in a suit
and I have LV card 2 in the suit
and my opponent leads a lower card in that suit
THEN play LV card 2.

However, an important fact has been lost by this generalisation. Additional constraints need to be added to capture the fact that the cards are honours and they follow each other. Adding these constraints gives rise to the following production:

P7 IF I am playing no trump
and I have LV card 1 in a suit
and LV card 1 is an honour
and I have LV card 2 in the suit
and LV card 2 is an honour
and LV card 1 follows LVcard 2
and my opponent leads a lower card
THEN I can play LV card 2.

This is the rule for playing touching honours in bridge. Once a rule is proceduralised it can be easily applied to novel situations.

Chase and Simon (1973) carried out a classic study of chess players. They showed that Master chess players could memorise the positions of pieces on a chess board far more quickly than novices, but only when the pieces formed part of a valid game. If the pieces were placed at random, the novices and experts were just the same. It appears that experts perceive board positions in much larger "chunks" than novices. An expert sees the pieces in relational groups whereas the novice sees each piece individually. In terms of production systems like ACT* the expert has acquired a whole set of productions in which patterns of pieces on the board specify the conditions for making particular moves, which allows information that matches previous experience to be grouped into a coherent whole. Random patterns of pieces do not fit with previous experience and are no easier for the expert than the novice.

Gopher's (1993) experiments on training attentional strategies, he suggests, could be considered in terms of production rules which have aggregated into complex "macro-operators". Because productions run off automatically, skill learning can be viewed as procedure learning. As more and more declarative knowledge becomes proceduralised there is less and less demand on the conscious, strategic processing that is said to be attention demanding.

Long-term working memory and skill

Although productions are stored in long-term memory, and, as we have already explained, can be run off automatically without any demand on working memory, Ericsson and Kintsch (1995) have recently argued that the traditional view of the use of memory in skilled activity needs to include a long-term working memory. They say that current models of memory (e.g. Anderson's, 1983, ACT*; Baddeley's working memory model, 1986) cannot account for the massively increased demand for information required by skilled task performance. They outline a theory of long-term working memory (LT-WM) which is an extension of skilled memory theory (Chase & Ericsson, 1982). The proposal is that in skilled performance, say of chess players, what is needed is rapid access to relevant information in long-term memory. This is achieved by the use of LT-WM in addition to short-term working memory (ST-WM). They suggest that learned memory skills allow experts to use LTM as an extension of ST-WM in areas where they are well practised. LT-WM is basically a set of retrieval structures in LTM. A retrieval structure is a stable organisation made up of many retrieval cues. Load on ST-WM is reduced because rather than all the retrieval cues having to be held there, only the node allowing access to the whole structure need to be available in ST-WM. Thus in skilled performance, all the relevant information stored in LTM is rapidly accessible through the retrieval cue in ST-WM. Indirect evidence for LT-WM was found in a series of experiments by Ericsson and Kintsch, in that a concurrent memory task produced virtually no interference on the working memory of experts.

Ericsson and Oliver (1984) and Ericsson and Staszewski (1989) studied the ability of expert chess players to mentally represent a chess game without the presence of a chess board. Over 40 moves were presented and the chess player's representation of the resulting game position was tested in a form of cued recall task. It was found that his responses were fast and accurate, suggesting a very efficient and accurate memory representation despite the number of moves made, which far exceed the capacity of ST-WM. The results suggest that the expert chess player is using this additional LT-WM to maintain and access chess positions. The ability to perform tasks automatically, therefore, depends on a variety of factors and as we become more expert what we have learnt modifies the way tasks are controlled.

Summary

Tasks which start off being very difficult to combine may be combined successfully after extended practice. Initially both tasks seem to require attention but later seem to proceed quite effectively without it. Posner and Snyder (1975) distinguished automatic processes which occur without intention and controlled processes which are performed by the conscious, limited capacity processing system and are open to strategic attentional control. The question of what happened with practice was addressed in two papers by Shiffrin and Schneider (1977) and Schneider and Shiffrin (1977) who proposed a general theory of automatic and controlled processing. After extensive practice in constant mapping conditions where targets were always targets and distractors were always distractors, target processing could become automatic. However, in varied mapping conditions where the target distractor relationship changed from trial to trial, so that targets on one trial could be distractors in another, automatic processing never emerged. Neuman (1984) gave a critical appraisal of the distinction between these two hypothetical processes and searched for reliable criteria to distinguish between them. Neuman concludes that automatic processing is not "uncontrolled", but is controlled below the level of conscious awareness. In Neuman's view a process is automatic if its parameters are specified by the perceptual input and by skills, learned through practice, stored in long-term memory. When it is the case that not all the parameters to control an action are specified by these two sources, then an attentional mechanism provides the specifications which are missing. Rather than there being a clear distinction, Neuman thinks there is a gradation between so-called "automatic" and "controlled" processing. Attentional control itself has been suggested to be a skill (Hirst, 1986; Gopher, 1993). Subjects can learn to be more effective in complex task combination. Skills and expertise have been modelled in production systems, like ACT* (Anderson, 1983). In essence, a production system works using sets of IF ... THEN condition action pairs: IF the condition is met, THEN the rule applies. Through practice these procedures are entered into procedural memory, which is not open to conscious inspection and will run off automatically. Hence, experts are often unable to explicitly give the reason for their decisions. It is possible that experts also use long-term working memory in skilled performance (Ericsson & Kintch, 1995).

Further reading

Hirst, W. (1986). The psychology of attention. In J.E. Le Doux & W. Hirst (Eds.), *Mind and brain: Dialogues in cognitive neuroscience.* Cambridge: Cambridge University Press. A useful section in this chapter gives Hirst's view of attention as skill, and a critical review of practice, controlled and automatic processes.

Allport, D.A. (1980b). Attention and performance. In G. Claxton (Ed.), *Cognitive psychology: New directions.* London: Routledge & Kegan Paul. Although rather old, this chapter is one of the clearest, in-depth critical appraisals of capacity theory, automatic and controlled processing and concurrent task performance.

Newell, A., Rosenbloom, P.S., & Laird, J.E. (1989). Symbolic architectures for cognition. In M.I. Posner (Ed.), *Foundations of cognitive science.* Cambridge, MA: MIT Press. This explains production systems such as ACT* and SOAR.

Intentional control and willed behaviour 9

Control of actions

If all our actions were determined solely by condition–action links we would not be able to choose which action we wanted to make to a particular stimulus, because the strongest condition–action link would always capture the control of behaviour. We would behave like the conditioned rats of the behaviourist tradition. Clearly there is more to it. In everyday life we are continually making a series of actions to objects which are inviting, or afford a variety of appropriate responses. Usually, we make these actions, in a goal-directed sequence. For example, when making a cup of tea the sugar bowl, the milk jug and the cup are all containers into which we can pour things. In one part of the tea-making sequence we have to be sure to pour tea into the cup and milk into the jug, not vice versa. Later in the sequence it is appropriate to pour milk into the cup. When distracted, we may make a mistake such as pouring tea into the milk jug. Such "slips of action" have been studied and interpreted as failures of control (Reason, 1979; Norman, 1981). While it is well appreciated that complex behaviour requires some kind of control process to coordinate and organise it, there is to date no clear idea of exactly how this is achieved. However, if we ask an experimental subject to do one task rather than another, respond to one aspect of a stimulus and ignore all others, the subject is able to do it. Somehow the cognitive system can be configured to do one task at one time and another task at another time on the basis of intentions. Thus a major question psychologists have to address is: how is behaviour controlled by internal intentional states (endogenously) rather than by external perceptual states (exogenously)? Until recently little experimentation had been done on the internal control of tasks but this work is beginning and we shall examine some of it later in this chapter.

Much of the evidence concerning intentional behaviour has been gathered from the study of patients who show gross behavioural disorganisation following damage to their frontal lobes. Before we look at theories of control we should consider some of this evidence.

Disorders of control: Functional deficits following frontal damage in humans

At the beginning of the chapter we noted that, occasionally, we do not do exactly what we planned to do. These errors were termed by Reason (1978) "slips of action". A famous example of such a slip is reported by William James (1890) who went upstairs to change and then discovered himself in bed. We all experience "capture errors" occasionally, but for some patients these happen all the time. Classical symptoms of frontal lobe damage are deficits in planning, controlling and coordinating sequences of actions. Perhaps the first reported case of frontal lobe damage was the famous Phineas Gage (Harlow, 1868). While Gage was working on the railway, an iron rod flew up and punctured the front of his skull. He lived, and his cognitive abilities seemed well preserved, but he showed impairment in control, behaving in a generally disinhibited anti-social way. He also showed changes in mood and personality. A recent example of the effects of bilateral frontal damage is given by Eslinger and Damasio (1985) in their patient E.V.R. Before his operation E.V.R. had been an accountant, but now was extremely disabled in his day-to-day life, because he was unable to plan and make decisions. He lost a succession of jobs because he could not make financial decisions: even deciding what to buy at the shop or which restaurant to eat in was a major task involving in-depth consideration of brands and prices in the shop or menus, seating plan, and management style in the restaurant. As early as 1895, Bianchi hypothesised that the frontal lobes were the seat of coordination of information coming in and out of the sensory and motor areas of the cortex. Bianchi (1922) reports studies of monkeys with frontal lobe lesions. Typically their behaviour is characterised by disorganised fragmentary sequences which are left incomplete. They make repetitive, aimless movements, such as poking at a spot on the wall and repeatedly make actions which have failed to achieve their goal. Although one must be cautious in generalising from monkey to mankind, the similarity between these experimental monkeys and human patients is close. Luria (1966) introduced the term "frontal lobe syndrome" to describe patients who, following frontal lobe damage, showed similarly disorganised, incoherent, incomplete behaviour. Although Hécaen and Albert (1978) suggest it is premature to try to relate specific parts of the frontal lobes with specific behavioural deficits, it is possible to categorise a group of behavioural deficits which correlate with frontal damage in general.

Difficulty changing mental set

One of the most typical difficulties patients have is that of behavioural rigidity. Milner (1963) tested a variety of patients' performance on the Wisconsin card-sorting test and discovered that the group of patients with frontal lesions performed much worse than patients with lesions in other parts of the cortex. In the Wisconsin card-sorting test, the subject is given four key cards on which there are shapes, such as circles, crosses, stars, and triangles; there are different numbers of the shapes on each card and the shapes may be in four different colours. There are, then, three different dimensions which might be relevant for sorting the cards: colour, number, and shape. The experimenter has a rule "in mind" and the subject has to discover that rule by using a pack of "response" cards which also have groups of coloured shapes on them. Each time the subject places a response card on a key card, they are told whether or not they have sorted according to the rule. Whichever rule is first used by the patient is said to be correct and the patient continues to sort on that rule. After a number of trials the patient is told that the rule has now changed and they are to try to discover the change. This means, of course, that the old rule must no longer be followed and some new categorisation rules must be tried out. Patients with frontal damage were unable to change from their original rule. They showed "perseveration", in that despite being instructed to stop sorting on the old rule and look for another, they were unable to do so. Sandson and Albert (1984) have called this "stuck in set" perseveration. Milner (1963) suggested that her patients were unable to override the activation of well-learned schema. This idea is supported by the fact that naming the ink colour of a Stroop colour word may be totally impossible in patients with frontal damage. Perret (1974) found that patients with left frontal lesions were unable to inhibit word reading to name the ink colour. Further evidence for these patients being inflexible in their mental set is seen in tests of word fluency. Some of Milner's patients are asked to write down as many four-letter words as possible beginning with a particular letter. Typical, normal output is about 30 or 40 words, but frontal patients are often able to produce only 5 or 6. Not only is the output poor, but also they may repeat words or break the rule by including words of more or less than four letters. As is often the case with the Wisconsin card-sorting tasks, while patients are breaking the rule or repeating an incorrect action, they frequently comment that they are doing the wrong thing, but are unable to prevent themselves from doing it.

Distracted behaviour

Frontal lobe patients are often described as distractible (Rylander, 1939). Shallice (1988b) reviews some of the evidence and concludes that, in general, there is evidence for an increased distractibility in frontal patients, in that they seem to have difficulty in both focusing and maintaining concentration. It seems that, although they have difficulty in shifting mental set, leading to inflexible behaviour, these patients also have difficulty in maintaining mental set or inhibiting unwanted actions. This may be because the frontal lobes are large and subserve a variety of functions.

Baddeley (1986) reports a patient, R.J., with severe bilateral frontal lesions, studied by himself and Barbara Wilson. R.J. was asked to measure out a length of string so that it could be cut later, but immediately picked up the scissors and cut it. Although he knew the string was not to be cut, saying, "Yes, I know I'm not to cut it", he carried on cutting! This behaviour of R.J. is similar to "utilisation behaviour" described by Lhermitte (1983) who reports a patient who, having a glass and a jug of water placed in front of them, picks up the jug and pours water into the glass. These errors in patient behaviour are similar to "capture errors" in normals, where an unintended, familiar action, for example, going to bed when you go to the bedroom rather than implementing the intended action of fetching something from the bedroom (James, 1890).

Planning ahead and goal-directed behaviour

Another difficulty frequently found in frontal lobe syndrome is the inability to maintain goal-directed behaviour. Shallice (1982) devised a version of the Tower of Hanoi problem (a standard problem-solving task often used by cognitive psychologists) which he called the Tower of London and was suitable for testing patients as it allowed a graded score. In The Tower of London task there are three different length pegs and three different coloured balls. Initially there are two balls on the longest peg and one on the middle peg. The goal is to get all the balls in the correct colour order, onto the longest peg in a specified number of moves. Typically, neurologically intact subjects will think through the puzzle before they make their moves, to plan the best course of action. Patients with frontal damage find the Tower of London extremely difficult and Baddeley (1986) reports that R.J. was unable even to begin the task. Another planning task is Link's cube, (Luria, 1966, reporting Gadzhiev): in this task the subject is given 27 small cubes, with varying numbers of yellow sides. The goal is to construct one large yellow cube from all the small ones. Again the frontal patients find this very difficult. It appears that goal-directed behaviours which require planning or looking ahead are almost impossible for these patients.

Some neurophysiological characteristics of the frontal regions

The frontal lobes are a generally inhomogeneous area occupying all brain areas forward of the central sulcus. However, some areas can be distinguished: primary motor cortex, pre-motor cortex, Broca's area, medial cortex, and prefrontal cortex. The prefrontal cortex can be further subdivided into three regions each with their own pattern of connectivity: the frontal eye fields, the dorsal lateral cortex and the orbitofrontal cortex. Prefrontal cortex has complex connections with other cortical and subcortical regions. Inputs come from visual, somatosensory areas in parietal cortex and there are inputs from and outputs to caudate, thalamus, amygdala, and hypothalamus. It is because the frontal lobes are so complex that such a wide variety of deficits can arise when they are damaged.

Roland (1985) measured regional changes in metabolism and blood flow in human frontal cortex during a variety of tasks. He found that when behaviour was voluntarily controlled there was heightened activity in primary motor cortex just prior to the beginning of what Roland calls "brain work". The brain seems to prepare the cortical fields expected to be needed for the task. Of most interest, Roland found that superior prefrontal cortex had a number of areas which were prepared in advance of a variety of different kinds of attentional tasks, but were independent of the modality of input or output. These areas seemed to be particulary involved with preparing and recruiting cortical fields. The anterior part became active in tasks where subjects were given a prior instruction, the middle part was active when attention was being directed or switched, and the posterior part of the prefrontal cortex became active when a sequential task was performed. Roland (1985, p.155) characterises voluntary behaviour as requiring "temporal or sequential changes in motor output" and this behaviour must be preceded by a series of brain events. Reviewing a variety of work, Roland concluded that the mid-section of superior prefrontal cortex is important for selective attention and the mechanism that underlies selectivity is differential tuning, or preparation of cortical fields. Roland (p.164) has shown increased metabolism in task relevant areas with depressed metabolism in areas that might have been expected to interfere with processing: "Control of attention implies that the brain maintains a specific organisation of differentially tuned fields and areas." The mid-section of superior prefrontal cortex is most active when "the tuned subset of task-related information has to be protected from irrelevant information" as when selection from distractors is required, and when "differential tuning has to be switched from one group of cortical fields and areas to another group", as when tasks are shifted. Roland assumed that cortical tuning must also involve the basal ganglia and thalamus.

Theories of intentional control: The importance of goals

First, let us consider how control might be achieved in some cognitive models. In Chapter 8 we looked at a production system called ACT*, designed by Anderson (1983). A crucial concept in production systems is that of *goals*. Productions require not only the activation of a particular data pattern, but also the activation of a goal. So, for example, when presented with a Stroop word, where the colour of the ink is different from the colour word in which it is written, we would be unable to respond alternately to the ink or the word, unless the goal could be changed. In one case the goal is "Name the ink colour", in the other it is "Read the word". We have seen that the condition–action link between the word and its name is strongest because of the asymmetry of interference but nevertheless, it is possible to respond to the ink colour; so in some way or other the goal "Name the ink" can be set to gain control of action. Once the goal has been set, perhaps by the experimenter's instruction priming the system, the weaker production rule can apply, albeit slowly. In human performance, if we name the word in error, this could be interpreted as a failure to maintain the correct goal. Production systems include the concept of goal but do not specify how the goals are set. However as soon as we say the "subject" sets the goals, we have returned to the homunculus problem. In Cohen, Dunbar, and McClelland's (1990) connectionist model of Stroop task performance, mentioned at the end of the last chapter, the model has ways of modulating the pathways by task demand, in order for the "weaker" pathway to output a response.

Duncan (1986, 1993), stresses the importance of goals in the selection of inputs to the information processing system and in directing behaviour. When we discussed Broadbent's (1958) filter theory in Chapter 2, a question left unanswered was "Who sets the filter"? In his (1993) paper, Duncan considers this question proposing that the filter is controlled by current goals. That is, the filter will select information relevant to ongoing behaviour. He suggests that both experimental and neurophysiological evidence support the idea that control of the selective filter is achieved by a process of matching inputs against an "attentional template" which specifies what information is currently needed. This idea is similar to that of Broadbent (1971) who had, in his refinement of filter theory, proposed two mechanisms—pigeon-holing and categorisation—which were able to bias central mechanisms toward one outcome rather than another. For more discussion of this, see Chapter 2.

Duncan (1986) argued that in normal activities people set a list of "task requirements". He called this a "goal list". In everyday life goal lists originate from the environment and needs, whereas in the laboratory they may originate from the experimenter's instructions. Goal lists are used to create "action structures" which are the actions needed to achieve the goals. Duncan says that, to produce the necessary action structure from a goal list, people use "means–end analysis", which is a common heuristic useful in problem solving. Basically means–end analysis computes the difference between the current state and the desired end state and makes moves or actions that reduce the difference between where you are now (the present state) and where you would like to be (the goal state). Duncan's overall theory involves three components. First, there must be a store of actions and their consequences: these, he sees as similar to a memory of productions as in ACT* discussed earlier. Secondly, there is a process by which goals are selected to control behaviour. This proceeds by means–end analysis whereby an action is selected to minimise the difference between the current and the goal state, and this process will continue until the mismatch between the states is minimal or nil. In order to keep behaviour coherent it is important that the goal list inhibits other potential actions and allows relevant actions to continue.

Normally, the goal list is maintained until all the actions that make it up are carried out and the goal state is reached. Then, control of behaviour by the goal list is relinquished. According to Duncan, frontal patients have difficulty in setting up, maintaining, and using goal lists. This means that either they will not be able to do the task at all or they will be easily distracted if the goal list is not maintained. A goal list makes performance of goal-directed actions coherent, by inhibiting irrelevant actions. Behaviour will become incoherent if there is no goal list, as irrelevant actions will not be inhibited. Hécaen and Albert (1978) noted that when frontal patients are given instructions, they often have to be repeated several times, and the patients often stop half way into a task needing several verbal prompts before they will continue. This failure to continue a task until the goal is achieved is taken by Duncan (1986) as evidence of the patients' inability to control behaviour by matching current achievement to the goal list. Further, if a goal list has been set up and the goal reached but then the goal list does not relinquish behaviour, the same behaviour, or perseveration, will occur. Duncan's emphasis on the importance of setting and maintenance of goals in normal behaviour seems well justified and provides a parsimonious account of a variety of apparently inconsistent symptoms found in patients who have suffered frontal damage. For example, the fact that they can exhibit both perseveration and the inability to initiate spontaneous actions is easily explained by the difficulty they have with using goal structures.

Norman and Shallice's model of willed and automatic control of behaviour

Norman and Shallice (1986) propose that there are a number of different kinds of tasks that require deliberate attentional resources. These tasks, they say, correspond to what William James (1890, quoted in Norman & Shallice, 1986, p.2) called "willed" acts. A willed act involves "an additional conscious element, in the shape of a fiat, mandate or express consent". In contrast, there are other acts, which James called "ideo-motor" where we are "aware of nothing between the conception and the execution". Norman and Shallice propose that deliberate attentional resources are needed when tasks:

1. Require planning or decision making.
2. Involve components of trouble shooting.
3. Are ill-learned or contain novel sequences.
4. Are judged to be dangerous or technically difficult.
5. Require overcoming a strong habitual response.

Norman and Shallice attempt to account for a variety of phenomena concerning controlled and automatic behaviour. For example, some action sequences that normally run off automatically can be carried out under conscious control if needed, so deliberate conscious control can suppress unwanted actions and facilitate wanted actions. A classic example here would be the Stroop colour word task that we have looked at several times already. The unwanted action "Name the word" (automatic) can be suppressed (by deliberate conscious control) in order to "Name the colour". This example is one that falls into the "overcoming habitual response" category. Their theoretical framework centres around the idea that we have action schemata in long-term memory which are awaiting the appropriate set of conditions to be triggered. This idea is similar to that of the production system ACT* in that if the conditions are right then the appropriate production will run. However, here it is schemata that will be activated not productions. (For a discussion of schemata versus production systems, the interested reader should refer to Anderson, 1983, pp.36–40.)

Normally, the most strongly activated schema will take control of action. In the Stroop example, this would be the written word. However, for the colour to be named, there must be attentional biasing of the schema for naming the colour that allows the normally weaker response to become the most active schema and gain control of action. There are, then, two sources of activation, one from the stimulus environment which acts bottom-up and another which acts top-down according to the current goal. An important component of the model is a basic mechanism called "contention scheduling". This sorts out conflicting schemata by interactive inhibition and excitation. The operation of this system is similar to the interactive activation model of letter recognition proposed by McClelland and Rumelhart (1981).

Figure 9.1 shows a version of the Norman and Shallice model. Well-learned sequences of behaviour, can be represented as a horizontal thread of linear processing, where schemata are activated if they match the triggering conditions in the data base, or memory. Thus for habitual tasks there is a set of conditions, processing structures, and procedures which allow actions to be carried out without any need for deliberate conscious attentional control. However, when there is no pre-existing schema—for example, in a novel task, or when some additional control is required—top-down biasing of schemata is provided by the supervisory attentional system (SAS). This biasing operates by the application of additional excitation and inhibition to schemata which changes the probability of selection

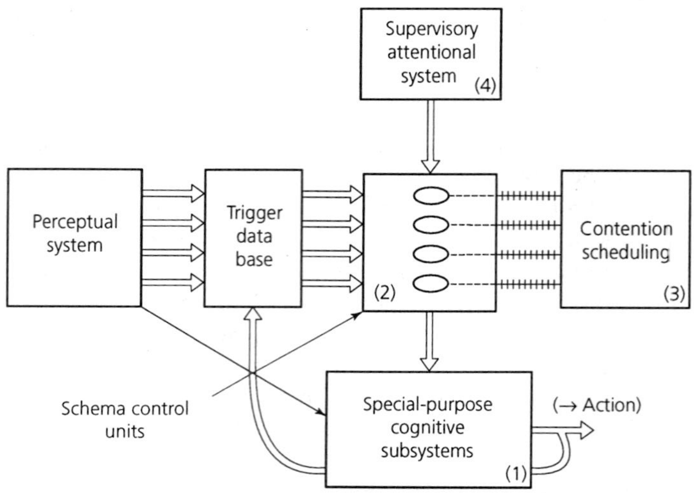

FIG. 9.1. The Norman and Shallice model (reprinted by permission of Oxford University Press from Shallice et al., 1989), see text for details.

by the contention scheduling mechanism. This top-down biasing by the SAS is called a vertical thread and comes into operation when attentional control is required. The Norman and Shallice model is discussed further by Shallice, Burgess, Schon, and Baxter (1989) and by Shallice and Burgess (1993).

Recently the SAS has been equated with the central executive in Baddeley's (1986) model of working memory. Unlike Broadbent (1984), who tried to avoid the homunculus problem in his Maltese Cross model of memory by proposing control resulted from the operation of productions, Baddeley posits control by the SAS. Is this, however, a homunculus by a different name? By giving control over to the SAS, Norman and Shallice (1986) and Baddeley (1986, 1990) seem to have done little more than re-name "the subject" in Atkinson and Shiffrin's (1968) model of short-term memory as "the supervisory attentional system". However, Baddeley (1996, p.26) believes that the homunculus can serve a useful purpose provided that we remember it is a way of labelling a problem rather than explaining it and that we continue to work at "stripping away the various functions we previously attributed to our homunculus until eventually it can be declared redundant". Baddeley points out that whether the central executive will prove to be a single unitary system or a number of autonomous control processes is yet to be discovered. Certainly there is good evidence that people act as if they have an SAS and can behave in goal-directed ways, initiating and changing behaviours, apparently at will.

The symptoms of frontal lobe patients are well explained in terms of Norman and Shallice's (1986) model. Indeed, it is patient data that has provided a large part of the data on which these authors based their ideas. If the SAS is damaged, it will be unable to bias the schemata which are intended to control action, or switch from a currently active schema (current mental-set) to a new one. The inability to change the schema which is currently controlling action would produce perseveration errors, as in the Wisconsin card-sorting test. Further, if the SAS is out of action, the schema most strongly activated by the environmental cues, will capture control of action, as in the example of R.J. cutting string, and would explain impulsive, "uncontrolled" behaviour. An interesting point to note here is, that although the patient can tell you what they should be doing (i.e. *not* cutting string) the verbal information has no impact on behaviour. So although at a conscious level the patient "knows" what to do, at another, unconscious level, the information-processing system does not "know".

Exploring the voluntary control of tasks

While there has been much research effort directed to discovering the differences between automatic and controlled processing, there has been surprisingly little work on the nature of controlled processing itself. Jersild (1927) is the first person we can find in the literature who investigated "mental set" and "mental shift". In his experiments Jersild asked his subjects to switch between different calculation tasks, not block by block, as is often the case in experiments, but between elements within the task. For example, subjects were given a list of 25 two-digit numbers and told to add 6 to the first number, subtract 3 from the second number, add 6 to the third and so on. This condition Jersild called a "shift task". When time to work through the list in the shift task is compared with the mean of both the single tasks, Jersild found a "shift loss" or reduction in efficiency reflected by longer list completion times. This "shift loss" was found to be just over a second per item, which in comparison to many psychological investigations, where every millisecond counts, represents an enormous effect. Spector and Beiderman (1976) whose paper was called "Mental set and mental shift revisited" did more experiments which replicated and extended Jersild's original work. They demonstrated that if subjects had alternately to add 3 to a number and give a verbal opposite to written words, in mixed lists of letters and numbers, there was no cost of alternation at all; that is, the mean time taken to perform the pure single tasks was just the same as in the mixed task. In this case, they argue, the stimulus acts as a retrieval cue for the task to be performed on it; you can not add 3 to a word or generate the opposite to a number. We could interpret this as showing that the operation to be performed is stimulus driven and therefore no intentional control processes are needed. However, when the stimulus did not unambiguously cue the task to be performed, in lists of all numbers or of all words, Spector and Beiderman (1976, p.669) also found large and reliable shift costs and suggested that "changes of set will have a large effect when the selection of appropriate operations requires that one keep track of previously performed operations". Spector and Beiderman are implying here, that the cost of shifting is a memory problem rather than a control problem. Clearly memory must be involved if we are to make the intended response to the correct stimulus at the appropriate time, but in addition there must also be reconfiguration of the cognitive system to change the mental set that we have remembered as appropriate.

Mental set and mental shift revisited again

Despite the discovery of such striking time costs when mental set is shifted, nothing further seems to have been done on this topic for nearly twenty years. Allport, Styles, and Hseih (1994) have reported some experiments in which subjects were asked to shift intentionally between the responses they made to ambiguous stimuli in rapid pre-instructed sequences. For example, we might ask a subject to read down a list of Stroop colour words responding alternately with the name of the word and the colour of the ink, or to give alternately the number of identical digits in a group or the numerical value of the digit. In Fig. 9.2, there are three different lists of stimuli. Using the

Uniform digit list	Mixed list	Uniform word list
2 2 2 2	8 8 8 8 8	GREEN
7	BLUE	YELLOW
4 4	1 1 1 1	BLUE
5 5 5	RED	PINK
2	3 3 3 3 3 3	RED
3 3 3 3 3 3	GREEN	BROWN
8 8	6	GREEN
6 6 6 6	YELLOW	BLUE
5 5	3 3	YELLOW

NOTE:
In the experiment, the colour words were written in an incongruent ink colour.

FIG. 9.2. Examples of uniform and mixed lists of the type used by Allport et al. (1994).

Uniform digit list in Fig. 9.2, you could try to do the task. It is surprisingly difficult, but nevertheless you can do it: try to respond as fast as possible, but slowly enough to be accurate.

If you measure the time taken to read down the list doing the same task repeatedly, digit naming is faster than group naming (the Stroop effect); but reading the list in the alternating condition is much slower than the average of both single tasks. This slowing in the alternation condition is a demonstration to what we call a "shift cost". When tasks alternate there is a time cost: what does this reflect?

Let's consider in terms of the Norman and Shallice model what is happening when you do this task alternation experiment. The stimulus is ambiguous; both the number in the group and the digit name enter the perceptual system along the horizontal threads. As digit naming is a more habitual action, the schema for digit naming is triggered. Unless top-down biasing from the vertical system, activated by the SAS is brought into play, the weaker schema for group naming could not "win" in the contention scheduling system to produce an output. If the responses are to be produced in alternation, according to the task instruction, the control system or SAS must alternately activate/inhibit the immediately relevant/irrelevant task schema. It looks as if this setting and re-setting takes time and reflects the operation of a control system. Subjectively, as well, this task feels very effortful and you may well agree with Spector and Beiderman that there is also a problem of remembering, or keeping a running record of which tasks you are supposed to be doing.

In our experiments we have found reliable shift costs using a variety of Stroop-type stimuli. One crucial factor in producing the shift cost, is that the stimulus itself must not provide an unambiguous cue as to which response is to be made.

We compared task shifting between the different dimensions of Stroop stimuli in conditions where the stimulus did or did not specify the task to be performed on it. One kind of stimuli were traditional Stroop colour words and the other stimuli were groups of numerals (as illustrated in the task you have just done) in which the subjects could respond either to the number of numerals (we call this *group*) or to the name of the numeral value (we call this *value*). Two types of list were constructed, mixed lists and uniform lists. In the uniform lists the stimuli were either all colour words, written in an incongruent ink colour, or all numeral groups, in which the numerosity and individual digit value were incongruent. In mixed lists the stimuli were alternately colour words written in an incongruent ink colour, and incongruent numeral groups.

Subjects reading down uniform lists would respond alternately to the colour word and ink colour, or to the group size and numeral value. List reading times for shifting were compared with the average of each component task alone. In these uniform lists, where the stimuli are all of the same type, there is nothing in the stimulus to provide an unambiguous external cue as to which task to perform, so this task must require controlled processing. In the mixed lists, the stimuli are alternately colour words and numeral groups, so should exogenously trigger the appropriate task without the need for control. Subjects reading the mixed lists would respond alternately with group and ink colour or value and word, and these response times were compared to the baseline average of the component tasks.

As we already know, colour naming is slower than word naming. It is also the case that group naming is slower than value naming (Fox, Shor, & Steinman, 1971); that is, in colour words the word meaning is dominant over ink colour, and in numeral groups value is dominant over group. If execution of the non-dominant task involves overcoming Stroop-type interference from the dominant task, we would expect control processing to be needed. When subjects have to alternate between the two non-dominant stimulus attributes of ink colour and group, we might therefore expect more biasing to be needed and so a greater shift cost than when alternation is between the dominant attributes of word and value. Example lists are shown in Fig. 9.2.

The results of this experiment are shown in Fig. 9.3. In uniform lists there is a large shift cost and the response to coloured words is slower than to the numeral groups. However, the shift cost is the same for

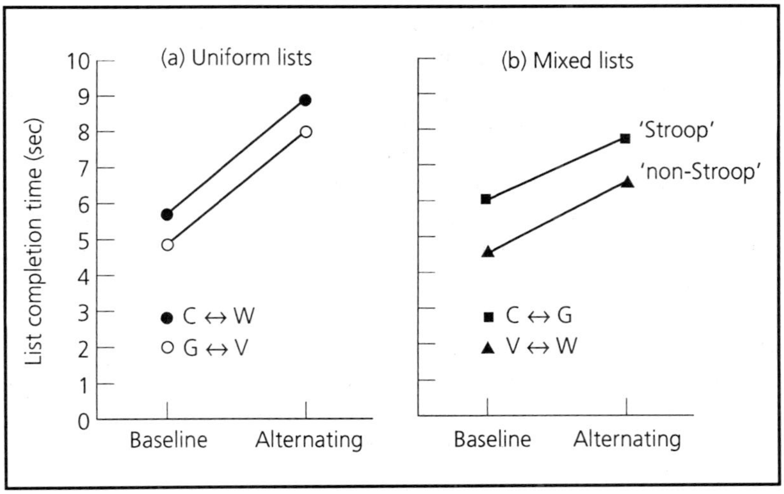

FIG. 9.3. List reading times for reading uniform and mixed lists. Subjects named words (W), ink colours (C), numeral value (V), or the number of numerals in a group (G), either as repeated tasks (baseline) or in pairwise alternation (reprinted from Allport et al., 1994, copyright © MIT Press).

both classes of stimuli. In the mixed lists, where responses might have been expected to be stimulus driven, we also observe smaller but still significant shift cost. Note, however, that the shift cost is no greater for the difficult shift between non-dominant (colour and group) tasks than for the easy dominant (value and word) tasks. The Stroop stimuli are slower to respond to, but this is an overall effect which does not increase when alternating. It looks as if more control does not result in greater shift costs. Also, the mixed lists, in which, according to Spector and Beiderman (1976), we might have expected no shift costs at all, do show a cost of task alternation.

One difference between the experiment reported here and those of Jersild (1927) and Spector and Beiderman (1976) is that our subjects were asked to perform all tasks in counter-balanced order several times. Thus all subjects did all tasks in all combinations. Sometimes the target task was "Name the ink, and ignore the word", sometimes the task was "Ignore the ink and name the word". Previous experimenters had used different groups of subjects, so subjects had not recently been responding to stimulus dimensions, which they now had to ignore. This difference between experiments is the same as that made by Shiffrin and Schneider (1977) when they distinguished between varied mapping and consistent mapping (see Chapter 8). Our subjects were in a varied mapping condition, whereas Jersild and Spector and Beiderman had used consistent mapping. Varied mapping never becomes automatic, always requiring deliberate control. Perhaps this is important (although our subjects and those of Jersild and Spector and Beiderman had had far less practice than Shiffrin and Schneider's): recently activated task schema may have remained primed, even though the subject was not intending to respond to that stimulus dimension on a particular trial.

In another experiment Allport, Styles, and Hseih (1994) looked at the effect of consistent stimulus response mapping and its reversal. Two groups of subjects were used and all lists were mixed. Remember that in mixed lists the stimuli specify the operation to be performed on them and no intentional control should be needed. The experiment was divided into three blocks each of eight successive runs, where a run consisted of three successive tasks (two baseline single tasks and one alternation). Half the subjects started the first block with the tasks *value* and *word*, the other half with *group* and *colour*. No mention of the other possible response mappings was made. At the end of the first block, subjects were told that their task was now changed. Those subjects who had previously been attending to *value* and *word* were to respond to *group* and *colour* and vice versa for the other half of the subjects. After another eight runs on the new task, subjects were told to revert to their original tasks.

The results are quite clear; see Fig. 9.4. At the beginning of the first block in the first run there is an extremely small cost of task shifting which soon disappears completely. However, when the tasks are reversed, so that previous target dimensions are now to be ignored, there is a large shift cost over the first two or three runs, which settles down to a small but persistent cost. The most interesting comparison is between performance at the beginning of the first block, where subjects have not, in the experiment at least, been responding to the to-be-ignored stimulus dimension, and performance at the beginning of block three, where exactly the same task is being performed, but immediately after responding to the alternative dimension. In the first run of block three there is a very large shift cost of several hundred milliseconds. It seems that the shift cost in mixed lists is not due to the time taken to operate a control process, but is due to interference from the preceding task.

Allport et al. interpreted these results as reflecting a phenomenon they called task set inertia (TSI), a kind of proactive interference. Proactive interference refers to cases where what you have just been doing interferes with what you do next. TSI suggests that the costs of shifting between tasks are not due to the operation of some executive controller, but are the result of the time taken for the information processing system to settle to a unique response after the next stimulus has arrived. In terms of the Norman and Shallice (1986) model, it is as if the conflict resolution process takes longer to sort out which schema is to win, if conflicting schemata have been recently active.

In their fifth experiment Allport et al. (1994) tested the effects of delaying the time between shifts. They hypothesised that if the shift cost represented the time for voluntary, executive control to set up the system for task execution, then delaying stimuli for longer than the known shift cost would allow a cost free performance. That is, provided there was enough time, the system would be ready to respond to the new stimulus immediately it was presented. However, even at a delay of over a second (much longer than any observed shift cost) the shift cost was not significantly different from that at 20ms. Thus, even if the next stimulus arrives long after the normal time required to shift, there is no benefit of the wait. This important result suggests that disengaging from one task must wait until the triggering action of the next stimulus. If this is the case, then what would usually be thought of as a control process, seems to be stimulus driven, which is one of the major properties of automatic processes.

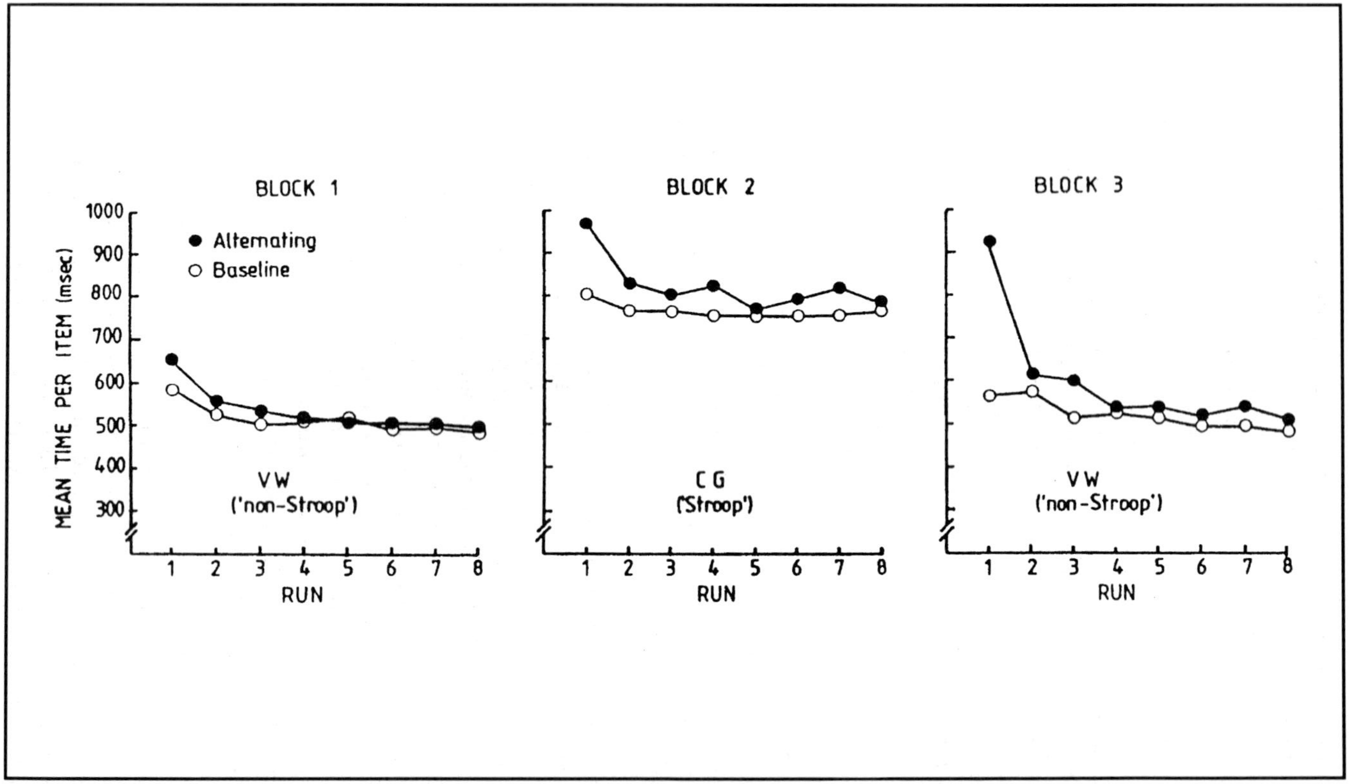

FIG. 9.4.
The results of changing task set, from Allport et al. (1994), copyright © MIT Press. Note that in the first block the shift costs are small, but, when the previously attended set becomes the ignored set in blocks 2 and 3, there is a large increase in cost on the first run of the new task.

Using a different experimental paradigm, this time a rapid serial visual presentation (RSVP) task, Allport et al. asked subjects to monitor rapidly presented words for particular categories. In the shift condition, subjects were given a visual indication (change of location) that they were to stop monitoring for one category, e.g. animals, and change to monitoring for "small things". Data showed that immediately after a criterion shift, subjects were very much less accurate at detection; and, more importantly, it took the arrival of between 5 and 7 more words before performance had recovered. Careful controls were carried out to ensure that the drop in performance was not simply due to the location changing. Of course, it takes time for 5 to 7 items to be presented, and it was important to know whether the shift cost recovered simply because of time, or whether it was the number of items that was important. By varying the rate of presentation we were able to show that it is indeed the number of items presented and not the passage of time that leads to shift cost recovery. This result is further evidence for a stimulus driven change. In sum, our results seem to cloud the distinction between controlled and automatic processing, as originally proposed by Shiffrin and Schneider (1977) and incorporated into the Norman and Shallice (1986) model of willed and automatic control of behaviour.

The basic assumption of these theories and many others, like Baddeley's (1986) working memory model, is that there is an "autonomous executive controller" which exerts control over other system(s), which without control will be purely stimulus driven. The controller, on the other hand, is not stimulus driven, but initiates its operation from within: "the subject does it". No external triggering should be necessary. The experiments by Allport et al. show quite clearly that what must by any account be considered an act of "will" (i.e. doing one task and then another) cannot be controlled entirely from within, endogenously, but is dependent upon exogenous triggering from environmental stimuli. You might, of course, want to argue that, even though the task requires an environmental trigger, the task must have been set up in the first place. This is exactly what Rogers and Monsell (1995) suggest.

Rogers and Monsell (1995), have also experimented on the costs of predictable switches between simple cognitive tasks and their results have led them to suggest that task set inertia (TSI) is insufficient to account for the whole phenomenon of the task shifting data. They propose that changing task set involves at least two components: an initial endogenous process which is done in anticipation of the task; and a second component which is exogenously triggered when the task relevant stimulus arrives. This second process, they propose, might well be subject to the kind of proactive interference, or TSI, suggested by Allport et al. (1994), but in addition there must be a stage-like, active process of endogenous task set configuration.

Rogers and Monsell (1995) used an alternating runs paradigm where, rather than alternating single tasks within a block of trials, subjects alternated between runs of two trials for the two tasks and were given a cue to remind them which task they were to do. In their experiments subjects were presented with pairs of characters and had to classify either the digit as odd or even, or the letter as a vowel or a consonant, by pressing one of two keys. The characters were presented close together side by side and the relevant character, which could be neutral or a member of the other stimulus set, was randomly on the left or right of the pair, on the assumption that this would mean the subject would be unable to avoid processing the irrelevant character. For the digit task, only one of the characters was a digit and for the letter task, only one of the characters was a letter. When subjects switched between tasks Rogers and Monsell found the expected shift cost, which Monsell (1996, p.135) interprets as reflecting the time for task set reconfiguration (TSR) which is "a process of enabling and disabling connections between processing modules and/or re-tuning the input–output mappings performed by these processes, so that the same type of input can be processed in a different way required by the new task". Although one would expect a subject to reconfigure tasks set in anticipation of the upcoming task, we have already seen (Allport et al., 1994) that the evidence is that, even when the delay between tasks is longer than the longest switch cost, anticipation does not remove the cost of task alternation. Some exogenous triggering seems to be necessary. Rogers and Monsell (1995) find similar results which show anticipation does not eliminate shift costs. When the interval between response to the last task and the next stimulus is randomly varied between 150ms and 1.2secs there is no reduction of shift cost. However, when the preparation time between tasks is kept constant over a whole block of trials, there is a significant reduction in shift costs as the time between tasks is increased, up to 500ms. Beyond this time there was no further reduction in costs. So, although in predictable circumstances shift cost cannot be eliminated, there is evidence that something the subject does—i.e. an endogenous effect—can reduce switch costs over about the first half second between tasks.

In addition, Rogers and Monsell looked at the effect of crosstalk interference between competing responses. There were two conditions: one, the no-crosstalk condition, where the irrelevant character was always a non-alphanumeric character from a neutral set, and the crosstalk condition, where the irrelevant character was from the neutral set on only one third of trials. Thus in the crosstalk condition there was a character associated with a currently inappropriate task on two thirds of the trials. In addition, there were congruent and incongruent trials, in which the response button for both the relevant and irrelevant character was the same (congruent) or different (incongruent). Rogers and Monsell found that when stimuli shared attributes with a competing task, both switch and non-switch trials are impaired relative to neutral; they call this the task-cueing effect. They also found that complete suppression of task irrelevant stimulus response mappings (congruent versus incongruent) was not possible, even if subjects performed accurately; they call this Stroop-like crosstalk. The Stroop-like crosstalk between attributes was less than the task-cueing effect. The task-cueing effects are taken as demonstrating that when a character in the display is associated with the task from which the subject must switch away, switching is much more difficult. Both these interference effects seem to point to exogenously triggered control. So, it seems that both an endogenous and an exogenous component of task switching are involved in producing the time cost of switching between tasks.

Rogers and Monsell (1995) believe their results are generally consistent with Norman and Shallice's (1986) model, described earlier. Activation of schema (or task sets as Rogers and Monsell prefer to call them) are triggered by external environmental stimuli and this activation is modulated by internal processes which ensure that the appropriate task set wins and the correct action made. They do, however, propose (p.229) that "substantial elaboration of the metaphor is required to account for the details". The control of task shifting is still not fully understood and significantly it is one of the topics chosen by Bruce (1996) in *Unsolved mysteries of the mind*. In this book Monsell (1996) reviews more of the evidence, but as yet the question of intentional control remains only barely researched.

How many controllers might there be?

The trouble with proposing any endogenous system in which "the subject" sets up the task, is that we are in danger of attributing processes to an unknown homunculus, SAS, or central executive. The question then is: does the executive responsible for task reconfiguration do other kinds of control as well, or is control delegated to a variety of dedicated subsystems? Remember that Spector and Beiderman (1976) thought that part of the problem in task shifting was remembering which task to do. Once the stimulus does not provide the cue for which task is to be performed, it is essential that the subject remembers for themselves the correct task reconfiguration in order to be prepared. In many of our own experiments we have observed that whenever possible subjects self-instruct themselves by repeating the task instruction. In everyday life we frequently find ourselves repeating lists of instructions to ourselves, especially when tasks are novel or difficult. Although shifting between long sequences of different actions has not yet received attention by researchers it is obviously important that we are able to remember our intentions. (We looked at memory for more everyday intentions, or prospective memory in Chapter 6.) It seems quite plausible that the articulatory loop in Baddeley's (1986) working memory model, could be used to maintain the task sequence in the sort of experiments we are considering here. Allport and Styles (1990) tested the effects on switch cost of increasing the number of tasks between which subjects were required to shift and also of adding a verbal memory load. We reasoned that, if a subject were concurrently rehearsing a list individually set at their maximum span, which would have to be recalled at the end of the task shifting, they would be unable to self-instruct themselves without forgetting the memory span. We compared shift costs between two tasks and four tasks, with and without a memory load. The only data included were from trials on which the memory load was accurately maintained and task shifting was correct. In these tasks subjects not only have to maintain the task shift sequence, or plan of intended actions, but they also have to maintain the memory load sequence at the same time as actually shifting task. We found that the shift cost was no greater for four tasks than for two and that the concurrent maintenance of the memory load did not interact with shift costs. This kind of evidence could be taken as evidence for a variety of intentional or executive processes able to run concurrently, and hence there might not be a single executive but a number of them each involved in different aspects of task control. Nevertheless, when possible, subjects do seem to use a verbal reminder of what they are to do. Possibly language plays an important role in control.

Linguistic and conceptual control of visual spatial attention

Logan (1995) proposes a theory of voluntary control of visual attention which involves the use of linguistic cues like "above", "below", "left", and "right" to direct attention from one spatial location to another. Although most psychology experiments have involved the use of a spatial cue to indicate a target for report (see Chapter 4), psychologists have not worked out how the subject actually directed attention to the target from the cue. We have seen that exogenous cues (Logan calls these "pull" cues, after Kahneman et al., 1992) can draw attention to a target involuntarily—e.g. Posner and Cohen (1984)—but an endogenous cue ("push" cue) is voluntary and needs attention to be directed firstly to the cue and secondly from the cue to the target. Logan argues that to explain this we need to take into account the literature on the linguistics of spatial representation.

Elementary spatial relations such as up–down, left–right are important in language because they express relational space, where something is relative to the location of something else. This relationship is, of course, exactly what a subject must compute in any experiment where a bar-marker cues a target. We have reviewed many such experiments in Chapters 3 and 4: in order to report the target letter, attention which has been directed to the cue must then be redirected to the letter indicated by the probe; alternatively, as in the experiment by Styles and Allport (1986) in which subjects were instructed to report a letter to the top, bottom, left, or right of a group of letters, the verbal instruction must be mapped in some way onto the visuo-spatial perceptual representation to allow selection of the target from its relative position within the group.

Logan identifies three classes of spatial relations:

1. *Basic relations* These specify where a single object is relative to the reference frame of the viewer. There is no information about where objects are relative to each other; for example, "My pen is there."
2. *Deictic relations* These specify the relations between a located object with respect to the reference object; for example, "My pen is next to the book." (Note that this relation focuses on pen; it does not mean the same as, "The book is next to my pen.")

3. *Intrinsic relations* These relations specify the position of the located object with respect to a reference object that has intrinsic axes, such as top, bottom, left, and right; for example, "My pen is on top of the table."

Deictic and intrinsic relations have the power, according to Logan, to be used as representations in attentional cueing. For attention to be directed from one object to another, two computations are necessary. First, the cue must be located; for this basic, deictic or intrinsic relations may be used depending on the task. Second, locate the target relative to the cue; for this computation, only deictic or intrinsic relations are useful. Both deictic and intrinsic relations require the subject to impose a reference frame before the relation can be computed but basic relations do not. A reference frame is a mechanism of spatial attention; while a spotlight directs attention to objects, reference frames orient attention to space. Logan's theory predicts reference frame effects when attention must compute a relation between two objects, but not when attention is directed to a single object. Using a version of the Eriksen task (see Chapters 3 and 4) Logan asked subjects to report the colour of a shape, indicated by a cue. There were four cueing relations: the cue could be *next to*, *opposite*, a step *clockwise* or *anti-clockwise* from the cue. These cues necessitate computing the relation between the cue and the target, and the relation differs in complexity. The distance (in visual angle) between the cue and the target was varied. It was predicted that if a spotlight had to move from the cue to the target, RT would increase with cue–target distance. On the other hand, if a spatial template can be applied simultaneously to all locations to determine relations, RT should not increase with cue–target distance. Results showed that distance had very little effect on RT, but the type of cue produced large effects. This, Logan argues, shows that the difference between the cues must be explained by the processes that compute the relation between the cue and the target. *Next to*, was computed most quickly, followed by *opposite*, with the *clockwise* instructions being the slowest. In further experiments using a variety of stimuli, including views of a head from above, in front, etc. Logan showed that subjects can use reference frames flexibly; they can move them across space, rotate them and align them with the intrinsic axis of attended objects, at will, voluntarily or deliberately.

How is it, then, that the verbal instruction of a speaker (the experimenter) can enable a listener (the subject) to direct attention from one object to another? In some way, the linguistic description activates conceptual representations which are then translated into a computation. Perhaps this could be achieved by activating nodes, as in a connectionist/neural network. Recent attempts to model attention—e.g. Phaf, van der Heijden, and Hudson (1990) (see Chapter 5) and Cohen, Dunbar, and McClelland (1990) (see Chapter 8)—run into trouble over what is known as "combinatorial explosion". If all possible properties of what we were to attend to and not attend to had to be represented in the network, the system would be unworkable. Logan suggests that language has the property of being able to specify relations in a constructive way, which makes it economical as it can build relations as they are needed, rather than needing to have them all computed beforehand. In language, an argument which is meaningful in itself can express a new argument when combined with another argument. The semantics of the arguments specify the computational goals of attention. Logan prefers to view attention as a behaviour that emerges from a number of interacting subsystems within the brain (Posner & Peterson, 1990) and considers that, in addition to physiological and psychophysical factors, language also may constrain attention.

Is intentional control an illusion?

SOAR is another cognitive theory based on a production system architecture, developed by Laird, Newell, and Rosenbloom (1987) and Newell, Rosenbloom, and Laird (1988). Like ACT* it is a symbolic, artificial intelligence architecture. In SOAR there is a single long-term memory, which is a production system, used for both procedural and declarative knowledge. There is also a working memory which holds perceptual information, preferences about what should be done, a goal hierarchy, and motor commands. This cognitive system uses a problem-solving principle to select the most appropriate course of action, given the current situation. When a decision is difficult, due to incomplete or inconsistent knowledge, the architecture automatically creates a new sub-goal and the problem solving goes back to resolve the impasse. This process of creating new sub-goals produces new goal hierarchies. In this way new productions are continuously being produced as a result of SOAR's experience in goal-based problem solving, a process called *chunking*.

It could be that, although it appears as if a person sets goals internally and intentionally (endogenous control), they are in fact activated by environmental stimuli such as an instruction from the experimenter, or by internal needs and desires that arise out of fundamental biological processes (exogenous control). So, the need for food may activate the goal "Make a sandwich". What appears to be free will and goal-directed behaviour, may be simply a complex behaviour pattern that emerges from a whole conspiracy of internal needs and external stimulation. Kelley and Jacoby (1993) argue that we cannot distinguish between what they call "conscious" control and "automatic" control by simply asking people whether they intended to do something or not, because intention is an attribution which may follow behaviour as well as direct it. When we feel the intention to stand up, for example, this feeling of intention may be *following* the beginning of the action rather than preceding it. That is to say, we may attribute our action to an intention, when in fact this was not so. Interpreting our actions in terms of intentions gives us the feeling of having rational, meaningful behaviour. Thus it may be dangerous to assume that the subjective experience of free will is evidence for its existence; and if, indeed, this is the case, the distinction between automatic and controlled processing—which relies on "the subject" applying strategic control—is immediately blurred.

Summary

In order to interact with the environment in a goal-directed manner, we must be able to select which response is appropriate at any given moment. Most stimuli have a number of possible actions appropriate to them, but depending on circumstances we sometimes choose one action and sometimes choose another. Patients with damage to their frontal areas show gross disorganisation of behaviour. They exhibit a bewildering variety of symptoms, from behavioural rigidity to extreme distractibility: planning ahead and goal-directed behaviour is compromised, patients often being unable to start or complete a task. Duncan (1986) believes these patients have difficulty setting up and using goal lists. Duncan has argued for the importance of setting up goal lists which are designed to meet our desires and needs. Goal lists are used to create action structures which are set up using the problem-solving heuristic of means–ends analysis. For goals to be achieved other potential actions have to be inhibited. Norman and Shallice (1986) have a theory in which the activation or inhibition of task relevant schema, or actions, can be intentionally controlled by the SAS. This system can bias the schema that are needed for intended actions so that, instead of the action which would normally be most active capturing control, the intended action can be made. The SAS has been equated with the central executive of working memory (Baddeley, 1986). If the SAS were damaged, behaviour would degenerate in the manner observed in frontal patients. To date there has been little experimental effort directed to exploring the voluntary control of tasks. Picking up on work by Jersild (1927), Allport, Styles, and Hseih (1994) and Rogers and Monsell (1995) have shown that, when a stimulus is ambiguous, or there is competing task information in the display, there is a large and reliable cost of intentionally switching from one task to another. This shift cost seems to depend on how recently the irrelevant task has been performed. However, even when the time between tasks is increased to be far longer than any shift cost, shift cost is not eliminated. Allport et al. interpreted the shift cost as the time required for conflict (or task set inertia) to be resolved after the next stimulus has arrived. Rogers and Monsell (1995) argue for an endogenous process that reconfigures the task set (TSR) as well as an endogenous process which acts as a trigger. The agent responsible for setting and shifting task may not be part of a single, unitary central executive, but one of a number. Logan (1995) thinks that visual spatial attention could be voluntarily controlled by linguistic descriptions which activate conceptual representations that can be translated into actions. However, our subjective feeling of intention may, according to Kelley and Jacoby (1993), follow the beginning of an action rather than precede it. If so, our feeling of control may be illusory.

Further reading

Baddeley, A.D. (1986). *Working memory*. Oxford: Oxford University Press.

Monsell, S. (1996). Control of mental processing. In V. Bruce (Ed.), *Unsolved mysteries of the mind*. Hove, UK: Psychology Press. This is an excellent chapter reviewing what is known to date and the controversies surrounding the mystery of control.

Norman, D.E., & Shallice, T. (1986). Attention to action: Willed and automatic control of behaviour. In R. Davison, G. Schwartz, & D. Shapiro (Eds.), *Consciousness and self-regulation: Advances in research and theory*. New York: Plenum. This is really quite approachable and lays out the evidence for their theory together with more details of how it works.

The problems of consciousness 10

Evidence from neurologically normal subjects

One of the major differences between automatic and controlled processing is that controlled processing is, by definition, said to be open to strategic, conscious control whereas automatic processing takes place outside consciousness. Although we may become aware of the outcome of automatic processing we are unable to consciously inspect the processing leading up to that outcome. By this account it sounds as if the difference between conscious and unconscious processing corresponds very closely to the distinction made between controlled/automatic processing. Some theorists have indeed tried to equate attentional processes with consciousness or awareness. To a large extent this is what Norman and Shallice (1986) have done in their model. But, beware, there is more than one meaning, or interpretation of *conscious* or *consciousness.* We shall return to arguments over the nature of consciousness after we have considered some experiments in which the fate of unattended (unconsciously processed?) information is examined. Despite the problems associated with deciding what we actually mean by conscious and unconscious processing, there is a large literature on the fate of unattended information, where experimenters usually take the term "unattended" to mean "unaware" or "without conscious identification". We shall consider what consciousness might be at the end of the chapter.

In our discussion of the early–late debate in Chapter 2, we saw that the ability of unattended information to bias responses given to attended information was taken as evidence for extensive pre-attentive (automatic, unconscious) processing. That is, prior to the selective, attentional stage, where information became consciously available, unconscious information processing was producing subliminal semantic priming effects. These results were taken as evidence for late selection.

Over the years there has been a long-standing debate about the validity of experiments said to provide evidence for semantic activation without conscious identification (SAWCI). There is argument about the best methodology to use, which criteria should be chosen to determine consciousness or awareness in the subject, and the right kind of thresholding techniques. Studies of SAWCI have been undertaken using three main experimental paradigms: *dichotic listening*, *parafoveal visual presentation*, and *visual masking*. As the unconscious is by any definition unable to be reported, all these paradigms involve looking for indirect evidence of unconscious processing. Holender (1986) provides a critical review in which he evaluates all experiments claiming to find SAWCI to that date. His review divides experiments into the three categories of tasks which we shall now examine.

Dichotic listening tasks. In this paradigm subjects are presented with two messages, one to each ear. They are instructed to repeat back, or shadow one message and ignore the other. Rather than repeat a number of experiments already discussed in Chapter 2, let's take one experiment as an example. Corteen and Wood (1972) had conditioned their subjects to expect an electric shock in association with particular words to do with the city. Then, in a dichotic listening experiment, while subjects shadowed the attended message, some of the shock associated words were presented on the unattended channel. Although subjects claimed to be unaware of anything on the unattended channel, they showed a clear galvanic skin response not only to the shock associated words but also to semantic associates of shock words. This result seemed to provide good evidence that the unattended message, although unconscious, was nevertheless processed to a semantic level. However, this experiment does not replicate easily. For instance, Wardlaw and Kroll (1976) did exactly the same experiment using Corteen and Wood's procedure, but were unable to find the same effect. They suggested that subjects in Corteen and Wood's experiment may have sometimes been aware, albeit briefly, of the unattended message. Unless we can be absolutely certain that subjects never become aware of the unattended channel the dichotic listening task cannot provide a sufficiently well-controlled experiment on which to base arguments about unconscious processing.

Parafoveal vision experiments. Experiments using stimuli presented in the parafovea are conceptually similar to dichotic listening experiments. Here the subject is instructed to focus attention on a central visual stimulus and to ignore any other stimuli which are presented toward the parafovea. Here again, let's look at one example. Underwood (1976) claimed to have demonstrated the unconscious, automatic semantic processing of unattended words which flanked a target. Each target word was flanked by other words which, although the subject was unable to explicitly report them, were shown to bias the semantic interpretation of the attended word. So, for example, an ambiguous target word like *palm* might be interpreted as to do with trees or with hands depending on what the unattended meaning was. This result was taken to suggest that the semantic information in the unattended stimuli was processed outside conscious awareness. Other researchers have shown that the semantics of unattended words in the periphery can influence the processing of fixated words, in the absence of eye movements. Lambert, Beard, and Thompson (1988) and Lambert and Voot (1993) showed that when an abrupt onset distractor appeared for 30ms in the periphery, response to the target was slowed by a semantically related distractor.

Holender (1986) provides an extensive, critical and sceptical review of experiments that claim to provide evidence for semantic activation without conscious identification (SAWCI). He concluded that both dichotic listening and parafoveal vision experiments were unsuitable for demonstrating SAWCI. To be certain that there is no chance of the subject having any possibility of conscious knowledge of the stimulus under test it is not safe to rely on the subject voluntarily ignoring it. In dichotic listening experiments subjects may indicate that they were unaware of the ignored message when questioned afterwards, but it could be that they were temporarily aware at the time but rapidly forgot. As SAWCI effects are typically small, it is possible that just the occasional switch to the unattended channel could be enough to give a significant result. The same is true in parafoveal vision experiments. Here, the words presented in the periphery may occasionally be attended and the experimenter would have no way of testing this. Quite rightly Holender suggests that if we are to find good evidence for SAWCI it will come from experiments using visual masking. Under severe pattern masking, a stimulus can be rendered unreportable because of data limitation (Norman & Bobrow, 1975; see Chapter 3) so, no matter how hard the subject tries, they are unable to report the stimulus. While it is the case that there have been many experiments in the dichotic listening and parafoveal vision paradigms that could be demonstrating SAWCI, uncertainty over when the biasing stimuli were or were not in some sense consciously processed means we must be cautious when interpreting the results.

Visual masking experiments. Some of the most striking examples of apparently unconscious processing of word meaning come from studies using backward visual masking. In some experiments the subject is shown a word immediately followed by a pattern mask and asked to guess what the word was; e.g. Allport (1977). Allport found that even when subjects could not report the meaning of the word, they would sometimes produce interesting errors when forced to guess. Given the word *jazz* the subject might respond *blues*, indicating that although there was no conscious perception of the stimulus, its semantics had been accessed. The subject was unable to determine exactly which of the semantically activated meanings corresponded to the stimulus word because the pattern mask prevented the possibility of integrating the physical, episodic features of the stimulus with the meaning (see the section on iconic memory, Chapter 3). The subject was therefore unaware that the stimulus had been presented and was left with only semantic activation on which to base a guess. Without any feeling of confidence, the guess turned out to be a "semantic paralexia", which means reporting a word semantically related to the target, as, for example, when "blues" instead of "jazz" is produced. Similar errors are made by patients with deep dyslexia (Coltheart, 1980). Unless we have a conscious experience of a stimulus, we are unlikely to try to act on it; and both Allport (1977) and Coltheart (1980) have suggested that it is the act of integrating physical and semantic information that gives rise to conscious awareness and confident report. These arguments were discussed in more detail in Chapter 3, when we looked at the way information, about *what* and *where* a stimulus is, appears to dissociate in iconic memory experiments. The visual masking experiments used to test for SAWCI are in a sense extreme versions of iconic memory experiments. In some iconic memory experiments the subject is shown a brief backward masked stimulus array (supraliminally) and the limits of report tested. In experiments on SAWCI, the procedure is just the same except the stimulus duration is so short that the stimulus is subliminal. If the stimulus duration is such that there is no time for any perceptual integration, there will be no possibility for confident report. Although there may have been semantic activation of *what* the stimulus was, any information about *where* it was has been disrupted by the mask. Hence, there can be semantic activation, without conscious identification. Umiltà (1988, p.334) suggests that the role played by consciousness is to allow voluntary organisation of unconscious operations that are going on in our minds. He proposes that "voluntary control over cognitive processes depends on the phenomenal experience of being conscious". Without this phenomenal experience we would not be able to act on otherwise unconscious processes. There are a variety of neurological syndromes that illustrate this. For example, patients with blindsight, visual neglect and amnesia all provide evidence that information is available within the processing system, but is below the level of conscious awareness. Using careful testing this information can be shown to influence behaviour. We shall evaluate the evidence from patient data at the end of this chapter.

If there really is semantic activation from stimuli that we are unable to report, then we should be able to look at the effect of that activation on a subsequent task. There have been a number of experiments that have attempted to use the semantic activation from unreportable words to prime subsequent stimuli. In these experiments the first (prime) stimulus is presented very rapidly, usually in a tachistoscope, and immediately followed by a mask. The speed with which the mask follows the stimulus can be set such that the subject is not even able to determine whether a word was presented at all, let alone what the word was. Subsequent presentation of another word (the probe) at a supraliminal level is usually used to test for any effects of the first word on the second. This priming paradigm has produced some of the most controversial experiments in the SAWCI literature. Under these conditions there seems to be little possibility that the subject could pay any conscious attention to the first, priming stimulus, even if they tried, so we can be more certain that any effects are due to unconscious processing. Of course, there is always the problem of determining what exactly we mean by "unconscious" together with the difficulty of setting the prime-mask duration so that we can be sure that the subject really was unconscious. We shall discuss these problems in more detail after we have looked at some examples of visual masking experiments, said to demonstrate SAWCI.

Marcel (1980, 1983) has provided some of the most controversial data on high level information processing below the level of conscious awareness. Using an associative priming paradigm based on that of Meyer and Shavaneveldt (1971), Marcel presented his subjects with a masked prime and then measured how long it took for the subjects to make a lexical decision. Lexical decision tasks involve asking subjects to say as quickly as possible whether the letter string they see is a word or not. In normal, supraliminal conditions, a prime such as BREAD will facilitate the lexical decision for an associated word like BUTTER, but will not facilitate an unassociated word such as NURSE. Marcel's priming stimuli were masked so severely that the subject could not detect their presence on more than 60% of trials. Would the same results be found in this subliminal condition? When the primes were masked by a pattern mask, there was evidence of facilitation (i.e. BREAD primed BUTTER) just as in supraliminal experiments. However, when the mask was a random noise mask, there was no priming. This is taken as evidence for two different kinds of masking (see Turvey, 1973 for a review), one produced by the noise mask, which degrades the stimulus input early in processing, and another produced by the pattern mask. Marcel proposed that the pattern mask does not prevent the automatic, unconscious access to stored semantic knowledge, but does prevent perceptual integration, and hence access to consciousness. This argument is similar to the one made by Allport (1977) and Coltheart (1980).

In another experiment Marcel looked at the Stroop effect. Here he presented his subjects with colour patches in which a colour word was written. Remember that with normal Stroop stimuli the colour word interferes with colour patch naming. Subjects were individually tested for the stimulus mask onset asynchrony (SOA) where they were able to detect the presence of the word 60% of the time; and then, using the same SOA, subjects were asked to name the colour patches with the word superimposed on them. Marcel found that there was the typical Stroop interference effect even though the words were not reportable. This looks like further good evidence for the unconscious processing of word meaning. However, there are problems. Why did Marcel choose a criterion of 60% rather than chance which would be 50%? How do we know that when a subject says they cannot detect a stimulus they are really telling the truth? Some subjects may be more or less willing to say there is or is not a stimulus there; so, what does it mean to ask a subject "Are you sure you couldn't see anything?"

Cheesman and Merikle (1984) argued that two kinds of threshold should be considered, subjective and objective. At the subjective threshold the experimenter has to rely on the subject's own subjective report of whether or not the prime was seen and subjects may vary in their confidence and willingness to report. Objective thresholds are those which can be set independently and objectively by the experimenter. Furthermore, a threshold should be set at statistical chance and many trials are needed to avoid the threshold changing with practice. Cheesman and Merikle admit that the most compelling evidence that words can be unconsciously perceived comes from studies involving backward pattern masking, but say that unless there is a direct measure of awareness the results of such experiments will remain equivocal.

Methodological problems

The question of what we mean by *conscious* is crucial to interpreting and explaining data. There have been two general approaches. Dixon (1971, 1981) advocates asking the subject whether they were "consciously aware" of the stimulus. If the subject says they were not consciously aware, then, by definition, that is taken as the evidence for lack of subjective awareness. However, the other approach, first advocated by Eriksen (1960), is that awareness is the ability to make a discriminatory response. Thus, if the subject reports lack of awareness but nevertheless is able to make a discriminatory response, the subject is objectively aware. According to Eriksen, the subject is unconscious of the stimulus only when they are unable to make a discriminatory response.

Cheesman and Merikle (1985) criticise the experiments of both Allport (1977) and Marcel (1983). They suggest that the semantic errors in Allport's study could have arisen by chance and unless it is known how many semantic errors might be expected to occur by chance, we cannot take his evidence as reflecting unconscious semantic processing. Later attempts to replicate Allport's experiment by Ellis and Marshall (1978) found approximately the same number of semantic errors. However, when the error responses were randomly assigned to masked words to establish baseline levels of semantic association, the proportion of semantic errors remained the same. Therefore, it would appear that Allport's results could have been due to chance association rather than being true semantic errors. Further problems are demonstrated in an experiment by Fowler, Wolford, Slade, and Tassinary (1981) who showed that response strategies were an important factor in priming experiments. Fowler et al. replicated one of Marcel's (1983) experiments in which, subjects were asked to decide: which of two alternatives was more similar in meaning to a masked word; which of two words was more graphemically similar to a masked word; or whether a word or a blank field had been presented. Marcel had manipulated SOA and monitored accuracy. He found that presence–absence decisions were less accurate than either the graphemic or semantic judgements and, as SOA decreased, the graphemic judgements reached chance levels before semantic judgements. Marcel interpreted these data as evidence for unconscious word recognition. Fowler et al. were able to produce exactly these results, but then proceeded to run the same experiment again but without presenting any words before the mask. Subjects were asked to make the same decisions about the similarity between the first stimulus (which of course did not exist) and the subsequently presented word. Fowler et al. found a similar pattern of results without there being any words presented for comparison. These effects were interpreted as evidence that response strategies, in the absence of any perceptual experience, could give rise to better than chance performance. However, there was a small difference, in that when words were actually present in the pre-mask phase, semantic judgements were slightly more accurate (63%) than when no words were presented (57%). So, although not all of Marcel's effects could be due to response strategies, at least some could be explained in those terms. Cheesman and Merikle suggest that unless response strategies can be eliminated from an explanation of subliminal semantic priming there will always be problems with this type of experiment.

Another problem, according to Cheesman and Merikle (1985), is that of determining the criterion for chance performance. Of course, Marcel had used 60% rather than 50% as his criterion for chance and as he used only a small number of threshold trials, performance may not have been stable prior to the beginning of the experiment. Furthermore, Marcel used subjective rather than objective thresholds. Cheesman and Merikle looked at Stroop colour word priming in an experiment similar to Marcel's, but used an objective threshold, where subjects were unable to give a discriminatory response between the colour words in a forced choice test. The SOA at which forced choice accuracy reached chance was shorter than that at which subjects were subjectively aware of the stimulus. Using the objective threshold as their criterion, Cheesman and Merikle found no evidence for unconscious processing of the colour words; i.e. there was no Stroop interference. As performance on the threshold task increased towards perfect performance the amount of Stroop interference also increased. However, between the objective threshold and the subjective threshold, there was evidence for Stroop interference. Cheesman and Merikle argue that in Marcel's study, although subjects were not subjectively aware of the masked stimuli, they would have shown a discriminatory response on forced choice. In line with this argument they propose that it is important to make an explicit distinction between objective and subjective thresholds in order to account for the relationship between word recognition and consciousness. In their experiments they found evidence for both conscious and unconscious processing only above the objective threshold. Below that level there was no evidence, either direct or indirect, that the information had been processed at all. Once the stimulus is processed sufficiently for discrimination responses to be made, the subjects may still be phenomenally unaware, but there is evidence for perceptual processing below the level of subjective awareness. According to Cheesman and Merikle, the subjective threshold is the point in perceptual processing when a stable, integrated percept is formed that allows conscious report and phenomenal awareness. This is the same argument made by Allport and by Marcel. However, Cheesman and Merikle argue that, rather than the pattern mask disrupting the visual record, as suggested by Allport and Marcel, the pattern mask actually disrupts all perceptual processing. At the objective threshold no perceptual records have been formed, but at the subjective threshold "sufficient" information has been accumulated for stable integrated percepts to be formed. Thus sensitivity to perceptual events can be found below the subjective threshold, although subjects claim to be unaware of them.

Cheesman and Merikle (1985) manipulated the percentage of trials on which Stroop colour words were congruent and incongruent. They found that, above the subjective threshold, interference effects indicated strategic processing by the subjects, in that when there was a high probability that the word and colour would be congruent, inconsistent stimuli showed greater interference than normal. However, when the stimuli were presented below subjective threshold, interference effects were independent of the probability that colour and word would be congruent. These results suggest there are qualitative differences between the processing operations that can be carried out on stimuli presented above and below the subjective threshold of conscious awareness. Conscious processing is open to strategic manipulation, but unconscious processing is not. In these results there seems to be a parallel between the conscious/unconscious distinction and the controlled /automatic distinction.

Although Cheesman and Merikle (1984) criticised Marcel for using subjective thresholds, they are able to use another of his experiments to provide further evidence for the qualitative difference between conscious and unconscious processing. Cheesman and Merikle assume Marcel was using the subjective threshold. Marcel (1980) presented his subjects with three successive letter strings and asked them to make lexical decisions to the first and third stimuli. On some trials the second letter string was a polysemous word, for example, PALM, and was either masked or unmasked. As an index of which meaning of the polysemous word had been accessed, Marcel had measured lexical decision time to the third letter string. When there was no masking and all three words were clearly visible, lexical decisions to the third word in a list like TREE - PALM - WRIST were slower than lexical decision for the third word in unrelated lists like CLOCK - RACE - WRIST. Thus, in the first list, TREE had biased PALM to be interpreted as "palm tree", not as "palm of the hand". This then slowed response to WRIST relative to the unrelated case. Lexical decisions were fastest to the third word in lists like HAND - PALM - WRIST when the meaning of the third word was consistent with the first. This pattern of results suggests that when all the words are consciously available to the subjects, the initial word in a list biases which meaning is accessed by the following word.

When the second word in the list was pattern masked to the point where subjects claimed to be unable to detect it, quite different results were obtained. Now all the meanings of the polysemous word seemed to be activated; lexical decisions to WRIST were equally facilitated whether they were in the sequence TREE - PALM - WRIST or HAND - PALM - WRIST, in comparison to an unrelated list like CLOCK - RACE - WRIST. These results from Marcel's (1980) experiment demonstrate a clear, qualitative difference between the kinds of processes initiated in conscious and unconscious processing. Another example of a qualitative difference between detected and undetected stimuli is given by Merikle and Reingold (1990, p.574). They argue that "if stimulus detection is an adequate measure of conscious awareness then any dissociation between stimulus detection and another measure of perception is sufficient to demonstrate perception without awareness". Subjects were presented with either words, non-words, or a blank field which was pattern masked. First, subjects had to make a detection decision and then make a forced choice recognition decision. Merikle and Reingold found that when subjects were unable to detect a non-word, no evidence of processing was found, but when the stimulus was a word, even when subjects were unable to detect it, they were better than chance on the subsequent forced choice recognition test. Thus, there were different patterns of results for words and non-words, and only words which had pre-existing memory representations were able to support recognition. When subjects were able to detect the stimuli there was no difference between words and non-words. This dissociation, they argue (p.582), shows that "the detect and non-detect states are qualitatively different", and therefore stimulus detection can be used as a measure of conscious awareness.

Priming below the objective threshold

According to Cheesman and Merikle (1985), once the objective threshold has been reached there can be no possibility of finding semantic priming effects because there are simply no perceptual records on which it could be based. Kemp-Wheeler and Hill (1988) agree that there is an important distinction to be made between the objective and subjective threshold, but suggest that Cheesman and Merikle's results do not provide sufficient evidence to prove there is no semantic priming below objective threshold. Picking up and modifying a number of methodological problems in the Cheesman and Merikle work, Kemp-Wheeler and Hill (1988) were able to demonstrate that semantic priming effects can be found when pattern masked primes were presented 10% below objective detection threshold. Kemp-Wheeler and Hill criticised the four-choice identity discrimination procedure used by Cheesman and Merikle in which subjects were to say which of four pattern masked colour words had been presented. They say that identity discrimination does not assess detection threshold, and furthermore, there are strong colour preferences when people are asked to produce colour names in free association. Simon (1971) found that 52% of college men gave *blue*, 11% gave *red*, 10% *green*, 8.5% *brown*, 5.5% *purple*, and 3% *yellow*. This bias in producing responses may have meant that when Cheesman and Merikle were setting thresholds, and subjects were in a state of great uncertainty as they approached "objective" threshold, the SOA may have been reduced more than necessary. Although Cheesman and Merikle told their subjects that all four colours were equally probable, Trueman (1979) found that even when subjects were told about colour preferences, this did not eliminate response bias.

Although critical of Cheesman and Merikle, Kemp-Wheeler and Hill accept the criticisms made of other work such as Marcel's. They suggest that for really good evidence to be found for priming at objective threshold it is necessary to:

1. Use detection rather than identity discrimination to determine thresholds.
2. Demonstrate non-discriminative responding at threshold using Merikle's (1982) criteria.
3. Demonstrate that the magnitude of any priming effect is not significantly related to detection performance.

Merikle's (1982) criteria are statistical guidelines involving the use of confidence limits to ensure that the response distribution is no different from chance and all types of response categories are used. Kemp-Wheeler and Hill carefully and individually measured the objective criterion and set prime mask SOA 10% below that level. They used the d′ measure from signal detection theory[1] to correlate with the priming effects if found, and sophisticated statistical analysis. They used dichoptic and binocular presentation and were careful to equate lighting conditions during threshold setting and during the experiment, in case light adaptation was different between threshold setting and the experiment (Purcel, Stewart, & Stanovitch, 1983). In sum, they believed that they were able to demonstrate (in very strict conditions, meeting as far as possible any criticism that could be made) that semantic priming could be found below objective threshold. More recently, Dagenbach, Carr, and Wilhelmsen (1989) and Greenwald, Klinger, and Liu (1989) have reported subliminal priming given certain (usually different) conditions are met.

There is so much evidence and counter-evidence, argument and counter-argument over the existence of SAWCI, how are we to determine the truth? Why do some experimenters find evidence and others do not? Research on "unconscious perception" is controversial and apparently inconclusive. Possibly the best evidence for SAWCI comes from patients who have suffered brain damage.

Evidence from neuropsychology

While there are numerous difficulties in determining whether or not normal subjects are aware or conscious of a stimulus at the time of presentation, patients with specific forms of neurological damage are never able to report certain stimuli, no matter how hard they try or how long the stimulus duration is. Studies on neuropsychological patients provide more evidence for the importance of consciousness in normal behaviour as well as evidence that stimuli which cannot be overtly recognised are, in fact, processed outside consciousness. In the literature there are a number of striking examples of the way in which attention and consciousness can break down following brain damage. Cognitive neuropsychologists study the behaviour of these patients in order to try to understand not only the damaged system, but also the normal cognitive system. Apart from throwing light on the processes underlying normal information processing, studies of patients demonstrate selective impairments of different varieties of consciousness.

One of the most important assumptions made by cognitive neuropsychologists is that the human brain is *modular*. This assumption stems from the very influential ideas of Marr (1976) and Fodor (1983). In a modular system, large and complicated computations are achieved by lots of *modules*. These modules perform particular processing operations on particular, domain specific, kinds of information. Together they form the whole system, but each module acts as an independent processor for its own particular purpose. Fodor (1983) argues that modules are innately specified, hard wired and autonomous in that the functioning of the module is not under conscious control. In a modular system the failure of one module does not prevent the other remaining modules from working. Such a system would seem advisable in terms of survival: we would be in deep trouble if damage to one small part of the brain resulted in all the rest of the undamaged brain ceasing to work. Not only is a modular system a sensible design, but there is good evidence that, when patients suffer local damage to particular brain regions, only certain computational functions are lost. If we assume attention and consciousness are important cognitive processes or states, then it seems likely that cognitive neuropsychology may throw light on them. Further, if there are varieties of attention and consciousness, we might expect to find patients who show deficits in just one or other variety.

Farah (1994) reviews disorders of perception and awareness following brain damage. She considers the relation between conscious awareness and other brain mechanisms and classifies the theoretical position occupied by consciousness in the view of a number of other authors. According to Farah, some psychologists give consciousness a "privileged role". For example, Schacter, McAndrews, and Moscovitch (1988) propose that the conscious awareness system is separate from the modules which process other, domain specific information in the brain. According to this view consciousness may almost be considered another module which can become dissociated from the rest of the modules responsible for perception, cognition, and action. Schacter et al. (1988) call their model DICE (dissociated interactions and conscious experience).

Another view which Farah considers as giving consciousness a privileged role is that proposed by Gazzaniga (1988), who suggests that the conscious/non-conscious distinction is related to which cerebral hemisphere is responsible for information processing of particular tasks. The left hemisphere has language and is conscious whereas the right hemisphere does not have language and is unconscious. Unconscious processing occurs when perceptual representations fail to access the language areas of the left hemisphere. Again, rather as in the DICE model, consciousness can become disconnected from other processing. Recall that in Chapter 9 Logan (1995) proposed that language could be an important factor in conscious control.

Farah (1994, p.39) groups together another set of theories about consciousness because they put forward the view that consciousness is a "state of integration amongst distinct brain systems". Kinsbourne's (1988) integrated field theory sees consciousness as a state of the brain which arises when all the concurrently active modality specific information is mutually consistent. Normally these systems will produce an integrated conscious output, but brain damage may result in a situation where processes become disconnected and do not form an integrated consciousness. In this state there can be a dissociation between processes and consciousness. Without the integrated state there can be processing but no conscious experience of that processing. The importance of binding and perceptual integration has arisen in earlier chapters. In Chapter 3, Allport (1977) and Coltheart (1980) postulated that identity and location needed to be stabilised for accurate, conscious report of stimuli from brief pattern masked displays; in Chapter 5, possible mechanisms for perceptual integration were discussed—for example, Treisman's (1993) feature integration theory and Singer's (1994) theory of temporal synchrony.

Similar views were put forward by Crick and Koch (1990) who consider that consciousness of visual stimuli arises from the binding together of different separately represented visual properties of a stimulus. Damasio (1990) has also theorised that binding gives rise to conscious awareness. In her review, Farah (1994) points out that in all the cases above, consciousness must be all or nothing, it is disconnected or not, domains are integrated or not. However, she argues that there is evidence for consciousness being a "graded property" (p.40). (See also Farah, 1990; Wallace & Farah, 1992.) The most popular metaphor for the brain in current psychology is that of a neural network, and we know from studies of artificial neural networks that information in this kind of system can be represented by partial activation. Farah argues that evidence from patients suggests a relationship between the "quality" of a patient's perceptual representation and the likelihood that they will have a conscious awareness of that percept. We shall pick up this notion of graded conscious experience as we examine next some of the neurological disorders.

Blindsight

The term *blindsight* is used to describe patients who have lesions in their visual cortex which give rise to apparent blindness in part of their visual field. If you ask the subject if they can see anything in the "blind" field, they report that they cannot. However, if the subject is induced to play a game , in which, despite not "seeing" anything they are asked to guess about the presence or absence of events in the "blind" field, it is clear that discriminatory responses are being made.

The first report of a patient who exhibited this phenomenon was by Poppel, Held, and Frost (1973). They found that, although patients had severe damage to primary visual cortex, they were nevertheless able to move their eyes to the location of a light presented to the "blind" field. A region of blindness caused by damage to visual cortex is called a *scotoma*. Patients reported no phenomenal awareness of any light falling on the scotomatous region. It was as if eye movements were directed in response to the light, but below the level of conscious awareness. Soon after this initial report, Weiskrantz, Sanders, and Marshall (1974) began in-depth studies of what they called *blindsight*.

Weiskrantz et al. (1974) investigated a patient D.B., who had been operated on for persistent migraine. Part of the right hemisphere was removed, particularly striate cortex and part of the calcarine cortex on the right-hand side. Not surprisingly, D.B. exhibited a post-operative hemianopia affecting most of the left visual field. Over time this blind area contracted to just the lower left quadrant. D.B. was shown to be able to make eye movements or point to the object he claimed he could not see. D.B. believed he was guessing, but in fact was surprisingly accurate. D.B. is not unique; several other similar patients have been reported. Stimuli in the "blind" field can be discriminated on a number of attributes: horizontal/vertical, simple shapes, moving/not moving, X or O (Weiskrantz, 1988).

Although D.B. is a well-documented case study, there is evidence for significant variations in preserved abilities between subjects. Most patients can detect and localise light sources and some can detect shape, direction of movement, flicker, and line orientation. Occasionally colour vision is preserved (Stoerig & Cowey, 1990). These authors examined the sensitivity of blindsight patients to light of different wavelengths. It was discovered that the spectral sensitivity function for the patients was the same shape as that for normals but the threshold for detection was higher. Thus, colour discriminations could be made, although the patients were phenomenally unaware of the colours. More recent studies by Marzi, Tassarini, Aglioti, and

Lutzemberger (1986) have demonstrated response priming effects where, like normal subjects, patients with blindsight respond more rapidly to two stimuli rather than one, even when one of those stimuli falls in the blind field.

It is clear, then, that these patients have preserved psychological capacities to process and discriminate environmental stimuli, but they have lost the ability to "know" about them and therefore to make voluntary actions in response to them. This lack of knowledge is severely disabling for the patient because the information available to the brain is not available to the patient's awareness: stimuli are being processed, but do not reach consciousness. The subject has no confidence in their guesses and remain phenomenally unaware of the stimuli presented. Weiskrantz (1993) believes that the phenomenon of blindsight is difficult to talk about without using the term "unconscious". Is the patient with blindsight similar to the normal subject who is shown a very brief, pattern masked stimulus which they fail to acknowledge but nevertheless show evidence of processing (e.g. Marcel, 1983)? Weiskrantz believes not. There are conditions in which D.B., for example, can in fact detect stimuli in the blind field better than in the good field. However, at the same visual location form is detected in the good field better than in his blind field, so normal vision and blindsight cannot be the same.

Campion, Latto, and Smith (1983) argued that blindsight was mediated either by the scattering of light within the eyeball, off the scotomatic region onto the good region, or by tiny areas of preserved primary visual cortex. This possibility could account for simple detection tasks, but would not easily explain more fine-grain discrimination tasks such as telling an X from an O. An interesting observation here is that Farah (1994, p.43) notes that when blindsight patients make discriminations like that between X and O, they may say they have a "feeling", or judge the shapes to be "jagged" or "smooth" which would be evidence for the graded nature of perception and consciousness.

Visual neglect

We have already met visual neglect, extinction and simultanangnosia, in Chapter 4. Evidence of unconscious processing of extinguished stimuli was discovered in several studies; for example, Volpe, LeDoux, and Gazzaniga (1979) and Berti et al. (1992). In these studies, extinguished stimuli can be shown to have reached a high level of processing, but as the patients were not conscious of the outcome of this processing, they were unable to overtly report the extinguished stimuli. Farah (1994) proposed that extinction occurs because the representations achieved in the damaged field are not strong enough to integrate properly with information from the good field into a "new" integrated brain state and consequently the representation in the good field dominates. Presumably, when there is no competing representation in the good field, the weakened representation is able to give rise to a stable brain state and so support conscious awareness.

Prosopagnosia

Prosopagnosic patients have a deficit which renders them unable to overtly recognise familiar faces. To them, all faces are unfamiliar. Even the patient's family, friends, and the patient's own face in a mirror cannot be named. However, given the person's voice, or biographical details, the person can be identified. Despite the inability to recognise faces, prosopagnosics can be shown to have unconsciously processed the faces which they are unable to overtly recognise. For example, skin conductance changes when the patient views a familiar face (Bauer, 1984). De Haan, Young, and Newcombe (1987a,b) report studies on their prosopagnosic patient, P.H. Although P.H. could not recognise people from their faces, he could recognise then from their names. De Haan et al. wanted to discover whether there would be interference between written names and faces. If the face of a personality was presented, together with the written name of that person, this was called the *same* condition. If the name was different from the face, but both the face and the other person's name were from the same category (say, politicians) this was called the *related* condition. The *unrelated* condition used a face from one category (say a politician) and the name from another category (for example, a television personality). P.H. was told to judge as quickly as possible whether each name belonged to a politician or a television personality. There was more interference in the incongruent (*unrelated*) condition; that is, when the face of a politician was presented together with the name of a television personality. Normal people show the same pattern of interference, because both the face and the name access semantics automatically. As the same pattern of interference is observed in people who cannot overtly name a face, the face must have accessed its semantic representation, which interferes with overt naming of the incongruent written word. Clearly then, despite their inability to overtly recognise faces, prosopagnosic patients show evidence of covert, unconscious face recognition. This deficit of "access consciousness" as Young and Block (1996, p.156) call it, is very selective.

Some prosopagnosic patients are able to achieve overt recognition of faces in certain circumstances. De Haan, Young, and Newcombe (1991) showed that, if enough semantic activation is provided by giving multiple exemplars of the semantic category, P.H. is sometimes able to overtly recognise a face. This result is consistent with the idea that overt conscious recognition requires activation to rise above a threshold. Below threshold, activation is sufficient to allow priming or interference but insufficient to endow the subject with overt recognition. Above threshold, overt recognition is achieved. Thus, as Farah (1994) suggested, it looks as if consciousness is a graded property and such effects could be (are) easily modelled in neural networks.

Amnesia

Whilst patients with amnesia are often considered to have lost the ability to learn new information, this would be an oversimplification of the facts. One of the most famous amnesics is H.M., reported by Milner (1966). Although H.M. was able to learn only six new words following his operation, he was able to show improvement on tasks such as the pursuit-rotor task, which involves hand–eye coordination, despite not being able to recall ever having done the pursuit-rotor task before. The difference between learning words and learning skills might be explained in terms of declarative and procedural memory, which we met when we considered ACT* in Chapter 8. Squire (1986) proposed that amnesics have a selective loss of declarative memory, which is where episodic and semantic memories are stored. Learning new words, a semantic task, or recalling that a test has been done before, which relies on episodic memory, is impaired; but performance and learning on a procedural task like pursuit-rotor is unimpaired. Schacter (1987) thought that the procedural/declarative distinction was unsatisfactory, as there was no independent measure of whether a task involved procedural or declarative memory, except to test the patient to see whether they could do the task or not. Schacter suggested that memory tasks should be defined in whether or not a task demands access to *explicit* or *implicit* memory for accurate performance. *Explicit* memory is required for any task that requires intentional, deliberate, conscious recall of the previous learning experience; for example, a personal experience or a word. An *implicit* memory task does not need the previous learning experience to be explicitly recalled. In fact, in tasks like pursuit-rotor and other skills it simply is not possible, either in normal people or amnesic patients to describe explicitly what is being done: this information is unconscious and cannot be made conscious. See Schacter (1989) for a discussion and review.

While skills like eye–hand coordination are preserved, so too are other effects which do not rely on conscious access to stored information. Amnesics demonstrate repetition and semantic priming by stimuli which they are unable to recall; see Ellis and Young (1988), and Parkin (1996), for a review. In the section on normal subjects, we discussed the difficulty in demonstrating that priming had taken place below the level of conscious awareness. With amnesics, this is easy, as they can never recall the priming stimulus. Despite this inability to consciously recall the prime, response to following stimuli is influenced by the relation between the prime and probe, giving clear evidence for unconscious processing which effects or modifies subsequent overt actions. In some sense, then, the processing system has "remembered" previously presented information, but this information has not accessed consciousness. The same type of effect was evident in the experiments on prosopagnosics where we saw that faces that could not be overtly recognised influenced word naming.

It is one matter to explain neuropsychological deficits by saying that these patients have selectively lost "consciousness". It is another matter to explain why it is that "conscious" processes have been lost or what it is that normally allows these unconscious levels of processing to give rise to conscious experience.

But what is consciousness?

Shallice (1988a, p.305) says that "the existence of consciousness is one of the greatest, if not the greatest, of the unsolved problems of science". So far we have talked about conscious and unconscious processing as if we knew what this distinction meant. At the subjective threshold a neurologically normal subject reports phenomenal awareness of a stimulus and can act upon it with confidence. A patient with blindsight has no awareness of stimuli which they can be shown to have knowledge of. Prosopagnosics and amnesics have no "conscious" representation or phenomenal awareness of stimuli which can be shown to affect their judgements. But what is this "phenomenal awareness"? Does it have a function and how can we determine if someone else is or was phenomenally aware? Could we make a machine that is conscious? Is consciousness of only one kind, or does it come in a variety of forms?

Over the past few years consciousness has come back into the field of psychological enquiry and two recent books, Marcel and Bisiach

(1988) and Davies and Humphreys (1993), draw together the currently most influential thinking on the subject. Both are collections of essays by psychologists and philosophers, and the fact that both disciplines have important contributions to make emphasises the fact that psychology has its roots in philosophy and that "consciousness" was one of the most important issues for early psychologists like William James and Sigmund Freud. As it became increasingly clear that consciousness was difficult to define and study it was temporarily banned by the behaviourists. However, as psychologists rejected behaviourism, consciousness began to creep back into psychology, both as an explanatory term (albeit undefined) and as the basis for a subject's experimental reports. In the past 20 years more and more psychologists have begun to try to account for some kinds of "consciousness" in information processing terms, including Shallice (1972) and Norman and Shallice (1986) whose model we looked at in the last chapter. In their model, consciousness was hypothesised as being involved in intentional control. Other theorists, like Allport (1977), Coltheart (1980) and Marcel (1983), have proposed that consciousness is the outcome of some kind of perceptual integration or stabilisation. This early idea fits well with more recent suggestions by Crick and Koch (1990), who advocate a neurophysiological approach to consciousness. Their suggestion is that what consciousness does is make available the results of underlying neuronal computations which have become linked together by synchronous neural activity. As different parts of the brain are specialised for the processing of different information, there is the problem of combining the different sources of information together; for example, the semantics of a word with its perceptual properties. One way of solving the "binding problem" would be by synchronising activity over the groups of neurons which are related to the same object. In Chapter 5 we considered one theory put forward by Singer (1994), who proposed a neurobiological explanation of binding, attention, and consciousness.

There is not the space here to give an exhaustive review of current thinking on consciousness: the interested reader should refer to the reading list at the end of the chapter for more ideas. Here we shall look at a selection of views to give a flavour of the area.

Umiltà (1988) discusses the proposition with which we started this chapter—that the conscious/unconscious distinction corresponds to the controlled/automatic distinction—together with four other propositions about the disputed nature of consciousness. Let's examine his arguments. First, he discusses the notion that consciousness is equivalent to our phenomenal experience of what is going on in the limited capacity "central processor"—the supervisory attentional system (SAS) proposed by Norman and Shallice (1986) or Baddeley's (1986) central executive. Remember, this central processor is said to be in control of attention allocation and contention scheduling of other unconscious processes. As we have said before, this idea is virtually the same as the homunculus and does not get us very far with respect to clearer understanding.

Second, Umiltà discusses the proposition that while controlled processing is under the control of the central processor, automatic processing proceeds without central processor control. However, there is evidence, that the central processor does influence automatic processes in that these can run off as a consequence of consciously activated goal states. Third, Umiltà discusses whether attention and consciousness are synonymous. He says that, although the properties of attention and consciousness appear similar in that they are both said, amongst other things, to be limited capacity, slow, serial processes and active in working memory, they are in fact conceptually different. Crucially, consciousness uses attention to control "lower order cognitive processes" (Umiltà, 1988, p.343). We are able to have the intention to attend to something; thus, as intention is the precursor of allocating attention, they cannot be the same thing. Lastly, Umiltà considers what self-awareness is. He says that this kind of consciousness gives us a feeling of being in control of our mind.

Johnson-Laird (1983, 1988) points out that this ability for self-awareness is crucial for the formation of intentions. Intentions are based on models of "what the world would be like" if you did so-and-so. Without some awareness of the possible outcomes, planning actions and making decisions would be severely impaired. Self-awareness also allows us to know what we know; this is called meta-cognition. If I ask you the name of the fifth king of Norway, you will probably know immediately that you do not have this knowledge. On the other hand if I ask you for the fifth king of England, you might think that it is possible that you know the answer and begin a memory search. Naming the fifth day of the week is trivial; you know immediately that you have that knowledge. Knowing what we know depends on having access to the system's capabilities.

In his computational analysis of consciousness, Johnson-Laird (1988) argues that one way of solving the problem of what consciousness might be is to consider what would be necessary to produce a computer that had a high-level model, or awareness of its own operations. First, he assumes (p.358) that "consciousness is a computational matter that depends on how the brain carries out certain computations, not on its physical constitution". As the physical constitution is irrelevant to the explanation, any being endowed with consciousness might be explained this way. In terms of Marr's (1982) levels of explanation, we are concerned here only with the computational level. That is, to describe what needs to be computed, not the physical hardware that actually does the computing.

According to Johnson-Laird, there are four problems which any theory of consciousness must solve. First, there is the problem of awareness; any theory must account for the difference between information that can and information that cannot be made available to awareness (i.e. the difference between the conscious and unconscious). The second problem is that of control; in Johnson-Laird's conception, this is equivalent to will-power and differs between individuals. Then, the third and fourth problems are ones discussed earlier, self-awareness and intention. Self-awareness, meta-cognition and intentions all depend on the same computational mechanism. The computational system that Johnson-Laird proposes is like the brain in that it is hierarchical and parallel. At the highest level in the hierarchy is the operating system, or working memory, which is relatively autonomous but does not have complete control over all the other processes. The contents of the operating system/working memory are conscious but all other levels in the hierarchy are not. The operating system needs to be conscious so that it can construct a mental model of itself and how it is performing. Johnson-Laird takes the example of visual perception. The visual system sends data about the locations and identities of an object, then the operating system uses other procedures to construct a model of itself perceiving the world. Now the working memory has a model embedded within a model. This "embedding" of models could in principle continue *ad infinitum*—you can be aware that you are aware that you are aware etc. Once a computation system can represent itself and what it knows, it can display self-awareness, or be "conscious", make plans, and exhibit intentional behaviour. While all this seems promising, we have no idea what a machine which had a high level model of itself would be like. The operating system still sounds rather like a homunculus, but with a clearer description of what it needs to do. Norman (1986) gives thoughtful consideration to the problem of control in parallel distributed processing (PDP) computer networks.

Phaf, Mul, and Wolters (1994) consider what kind of system could create conscious experience out of unconscious activation and suggest that conscious processing should be added to the general capabilities of PDP models. Some connectionist models of attention were described at the end of Chapter 5, where we considered how information concerning different attributes of an object are combined. Phaf et al. propose that, for conscious experience to arise, there must be an explicit construction process which is based on the process responsible for sequential recursive reasoning, and for temporarily joining together active representations in working memory. They suggest that the articulatory loop would be a suitable candidate for this. Working memory is not generally mentioned in PDP models; long-term memory is considered to be the slowly changing weights within the network, and short-term memory the currently decaying activation (Grossberg, 1988).

Phaf et al. (1994) describe an extension to their CALM model which has a sequentially recurrent network (SeRN), or external rehearsal loop, which feeds back single localised activations, or chunks, to unconnected nodes in the input module for CALM, so that the chunks do not interfere with each other. This model simulated serial position effects in short-term memory as well as primacy and recency effects. In addition, they claim to show that all the requirements of consciousness can be met within connectionist models, although, of course, you could never determine whether their model was conscious or not! The external rehearsal loop in SeRN is just one module in their model and activation in other modules must be transformed if it is to enter the loop. Activations which cannot, or do not, reach the recursive loop are unable to be part of the construction process which Phaf et al. (1994) propose is involved in conscious experience. A dissociable module for conscious experience can explain how processing in one part of the system can proceed without conscious awareness. It seems unlikely, however, that the recursive loop can be the sole explanation for conscious experience, especially if this is equated with the articulatory loop component of working memory. When the articulatory loop is fully occupied with, for example, a digit span task, subjects are still able to perform logical reasoning (Hitch & Baddeley, 1976) and are conscious of doing so.

So, from the preceding discussion it is evident that there may be many varieties of consciousness. We must, however be alert to the problem of using "consciousness" in any form of its meaning to explain another phenomenon, unless we can explain the phenomenon of consciousness itself. This pitfall and the problems associated with determining criteria for different uses of the term "conscious", are eloquently discussed by Allport (1988). We have seen that the trouble with experimenting on normal subjects is that we need some criterion for establishing whether or not the subject was consciously aware of the stimulus that was presented. What could we use for a criterion? Allport (1988) considers three possible options, all of which he finds to be seriously flawed. First, he considers the criterion of potential action. With much qualification of his arguments, Allport suggests that if a person was "aware" of an event, they should be able, in principle, to respond to or act upon that event. Of course, if the subject chooses not to overtly respond to the event, we have no way of knowing whether they were aware of it or not. By this definition, we would then have no way of knowing whether they were conscious or unconscious of that event. Allport discusses other possible behavioural indicators of awareness that might be useful for determining a person's state of awareness. Some of these are involuntary—for example, pupil dilation, an autonomic response. Such involuntary indicators often tell us something different from what the person is telling us verbally; for example, when someone is lying, involuntary indicators may give them away. So, Allport argues, the proposal that awareness can be indexed by voluntary actions immediately runs into another problem. He concludes that there may be no behavioural indicators which can be reliably used to determine awareness.

The next criterion for "conscious awareness" which Allport examines is whether the subject can remember an event. When a person can recall an event, it may be possible to say that the person was aware of that event. However, what if they are unable to recall an event? They may have been aware at the time, but have forgotten by the time you question them. There are further problems with the memory criterion in that we often exhibit absent-mindedness. We perform actions, presumably in response to the environment or internal goals, but do not remember doing them: does this mean we are not aware of these actions or the events that triggered them? How about the confidence criterion, proposed by Merikle and Cheesman (1985) and discussed earlier with respect to SAWCI experiments? The problem here is how much confidence is required for the acknowledgement of an event. Overall, it seems that there are a variety of indicators, which suggest that there is no unique form of consciousness, rather a variety of forms which may be indicated in different ways. We shall see this most clearly when we review neurological patients in the next section. Third, Allport suggests, "consciousness" might be related to selection for action and that objects selected for action are likely to form an episodic memory, which can be recovered explicitly. Objects that are not directly selected for action are only "in some sense" conscious. This idea, however, does not seem to explain how objects which are selected for action, acted upon, and integrated into a coherent routine (for example, lifting the sugar spoon and adding sugar in tea) may be acted on twice, or not at all. We may have been "conscious" in one sense, but do not have a retrievable episodic memory of our action which we can subsequently report.

Despite the difficulty of defining consciousness and ascertaining its presence or absence, there are psychologists who believe that psychology cannot ignore "phenomenal awareness". Marcel (1983b, 1988) believes that consciousness is central to mental life; and, as psychology is the science of mental life, to ignore it would reduce psychology to cybernetics or biology. In their experiments psychologists generally ask people to perform tasks which rely on a report based on a conscious percept: "Press a button as soon as you see a red light"; "Do you hear a high or low pitched tone?" and so forth. Thus, Marcel argues, the data derived in experiments are based on phenomenal experience. Unless the subject has a conscious experience of the stimulus, they are unwilling to make a response. Here again, we see how important it is that the subject has confidence in their experience if they are to make a voluntary action.

Shallice (1988a, p.307) agrees that consciousness is important because we rely on the phenomenal experience of our subjects in psychology experiments and because these experiments also depend on the subject's understanding the task instructions. As we treat subjects as if they were "responsible conscious agents", we are acknowledging something about what it is to be conscious. He suggests that a useful way of approaching the problem might be to try to make a link between information processing and experiential accounts of the same events. This was what was attempted by Shallice (1972) and Norman and Shallice (1986). We have already discussed Norman and Shallice's model of willed and automatic behaviour in the previous chapter, in which the supervisory attentional system (SAS) can bias schemata in order to allow intentional, willed behaviour. Shallice's (1988a) version of the flow of information between control systems included two additional modules, the language system and an episodic memory. However, within this model the problem arises as to what exactly corresponds to consciousness. Shallice identifies five levels within the model that might be candidates: input to the language system; the processing carried out by the SAS; the selection of schemata; the operation of some particular component of the system; or the episodic memory module.

Shallice argues that it is not easy to decide which part of the system might correspond to consciousness, first, because a definition of consciousness has not yet been worked out (Shallice lists fourteen possible varieties in his paper); second, the information-processing models are too loosely specified; and last, because, as information processing involves so many subsystems, it is difficult to know which ones are critical for producing awareness. Shallice suggests (p.327) that it would be misguided to attempt to find a one-to-one correspondence between any component of the information processing system and consciousness. Rather, control could be shared between subsystems, and as the control structures would be operating on information from the same schemata, "there would be a coherent pattern of control over all other subsystems, which is shared between those control systems that are active. Might not this shared control be the basis for consciousness?" We have met the idea that coherence between subsystems might be important for conscious experience at the beginning of our discussion of consciousness. As patterns of coherence might differ, so might conscious experience.

Summary

Experiments which claim to demonstrate semantic activation without conscious awareness have been criticised on a number of counts by Holender (1986). Dichotic listening and parafoveal vision tasks are suspect because they rely on the subject doing what they are told—that is, to ignore some stimuli which might become available if attention shifted. Experiments using visual stimuli and backward pattern masking are more reliable (for example, Marcel, 1980, 1983) because no stimuli have to be ignored. However, the problem here is that the parameters of the experiment have to be arranged so that the subject cannot consciously report the visually presented primes. Argument has centred on how best to determine whether or not the subject was consciously aware, and what, in fact, it means to be "consciously aware". Merikle and Cheesman (1984) proposed that there were two thresholds, subjective and objective. They claimed that most experiments showing SAWCI had used the subjective threshold and that below this, at the objective threshold, no semantic effects would be found. Some studies have shown SAWCI at or below the objective threshold (Kemp-Wheeler & Hill, 1988). Perhaps the most convincing evidence for processing without conscious awareness and for dissociations of consciousness comes from neuropsychological patients. Reviewing the evidence on blindsight, visual neglect, prosopagnosia and amnesia, we find there are a surprising number of selective dissociations between perceptual processing and conscious awareness, as well as good evidence for semantic activation and learning outside consciousness. A related issue here is the problem of what we mean by consciousness and whether psychologists should be concerned with it. Consciousness is seen by different people as having different properties, aspects, and functions. It is difficult to provide a coherent summary because, really, there is not one. However, a number of people (e.g. Marcel, 1988; Shallice, 1988a,b) have pointed out that, although consciousness may be difficult to define, it must have a place in psychology, because we use data from "consciously aware" subjects. The notion of some kind of stable brain state being responsible for the emergence of phenomenal awareness seems to have support from a number of quarters, as is evident in Shallice's ideas on coherence between control subsystems, Allport's suggestion of behavioural integration, and Crick and Koch's theory of neural synchronisation.

Note

1. d′ (called d prime) is a measure of the distance between the means of two distributions. One distribution represents background noise and the other distribution represents the signal (stimulus) plus noise. When the distributions overlap it is not possible for the subject to always be correct in knowing if a signal has occurred. By measuring the number of hits, misses, false alarms, and correct rejections it is possible to calculate d′. The greater the value of d′ the more likely it is that a signal will be detected accurately.

Further reading

Davies, M., & Humphreys, G.W. (Eds.) (1993). *Consciousness: Readings in mind and language*. Oxford: Blackwell.

Ellis, A.W., & Young, A.W. (1988). *Human cognitive neuropsychology*. Hove, UK: Lawrence Erlbaum Associates Ltd.

Marcel, A.J., & Bisiach, E. (Eds.) (1988). *Consciousness in contemporary science*. Oxford: Oxford University Press. Dissociations.

Parkin, A. (1996). *Explorations in cognitive neuropsychology*. Oxford: Blackwell.

Shallice, T. (1988). *From neuropsychology to mental structure*. Cambridge: Cambridge University Press.

Young, A.W., & Block, N. (1996). Consciousness. In V. Bruce (Ed.), *Unsolved mysteries of the mind*. Hove, UK: Psychology Press. This provides an easily accessible overview of biological, psychological, philosophical and neurophysiological thinking on consciousness.

Epilogue 11

At the very beginning of this book, I said that I did not have a simple definition of attention and tried to illustrate the wide variety of situations to which the term "attention" is applied in everyday usage. However, despite this lack of clarity, we set off on our journey through experiments which were said to be about "attention", hoping that as we went along we would discover, if not what "attention" is, at least some of its varieties. We journeyed through selective attention, the movement and allocation of attention, attention to objects, selection for action, divided attention, skill, automaticity, and control, etc. Along the way we met theories designed, successfully or otherwise, to account for all of these "attentional" tasks. Finally, we arrived at the end of the book to find ourselves engaged in a debate on the nature and function of consciousness, for which there is also no agreed definition. How did this happen?

When I quoted William James (1890, pp.403–404) at the beginning of the first chapter, I gave only a part of what he said: "Everyone knows what attention is". However, James continued:

> It is the taking possession by the mind, in clear and vivid form, of one out of what would seem several simultaneously possible objects or trains of thought. Focalisation, concentration, of consciousness are of its essence. It implies withdrawal from some things in order to deal effectively with others.

In this statement, James refers to the selectivity of attention, its apparently limited nature, and he brings consciousness into the explanation. James reflected carefully on attention and consciousness, but as long as we have no agreed definition for either "attention" or "consciousness", or for any of their varieties, we are in danger of trying to explain something we do not properly understand in terms of something else that we do not properly understand. In the chapters of this book I have probably been as guilty of this as anyone else.

A note of optimism

Despite the lack of agreed definitions and confusion of terms, progress has been made. Forty years ago, the abilities of the human operator were discussed in terms of information theory and a single channel limited capacity, general-purpose processor. The first theories of attention were general theories designed to account for general attentional phenomena. However, early theorists were alert to the problems of definition. If you look in the subject index of *Decision and stress* (Broadbent, 1971), there is no entry for *attention* or *consciousness* despite the book being considered by everyone else to be on attention. Even a decade later, Broadbent's (1982) paper was entitled "Task combination and the selective intake of information". Although he put forward a theory of attention he was, himself, wary of calling it that.

In the beginning, the prospect of considering psychological theories in terms of whole brain states was not on the horizon, the metaphor of mind was a communication channel. Forty years ago psychologists realised that far more information impinged on the senses than could be overtly responded to, and this is still the case. The original solution was to allow only a small amount of task relevant information to gain access to higher levels (Broadbent, 1958). Developments over the following 30 years made it increasingly evident that not only were the physical properties of task relevant objects concurrently available within the processing system, but so too were their higher level representations of conceptual and semantic properties. Further, task irrelevant information showed evidence of high levels of processing. As early as 1967, Fitts and Posner pointed out that "the concept of channel capacity as employed in information theory should not be confused with concepts regarding man's capacities and limitations. Man does have a limited capacity for many tasks ... However, there is not a single human channel capacity for all tasks and codes" (p.92). Fitts and Posner were not yet talking about brain states, but as we have seen through this book, as time has passed, it has become increasingly evident that the brain codes information using many different special-purpose processing systems. This specialisation has been demonstrated experimentally in laboratory experiments with neurologically normal subjects, by neurophysiological methods and by the analysis of the breakdown of behaviour following brain damage. While each specialised processing system might have its own limitations there is no evidence for a general overall limit on the processing capacity of the human brain. There may be limits within each specialised sub-system and there is good evidence from studies on the psychological refractory period for a limit at the level of response retrieval. This may be functional, as discussed in Chapter 6, in that it might maintain coherence of behaviour.

Once it was agreed that the apparent limit on performance might not be a result of a limit on overall processing capacity, the problem of "attention" could be redefined. The problem then became: given the amount of information concurrently available in separate codes in different parts of the brain, how is it all combined and controlled? How can one set of stimuli control one voluntary action in one circumstance and a different action in another circumstance?

Today, our improved understanding of the underlying neurophysiology of the brain, together with the powerful computer metaphor of mind—connectionism—allows a vision of information processing and decision making that was previously impossible. It is beginning to look as if our subjective feelings of "attending" or being "conscious" in any of the senses of these words, must be the outcome of a multiplicity of brain processes which cooperate and/or compete until a resolution is reached. The examples we have met are Crick and Koch (1990) and Singer (1994). The brain of a patient with damage to a particular process may not achieve an integrated brain state (Farah, 1994) and so render the patient "unconscious" or "inattentive to" information which, because it affects behaviour, must have been encoded. Therefore, although consciousness or attention might have the subjective property of being limited, the brain's computational capability is vast. Only a very small proportion of its computations, or their outcomes, are available for us to "know about". Just because we "know about" only a little of what is going on below the level of conscious awareness, this does not mean that nothing else is being processed. This is where our subjective "capacity" is most limited.

From what I have just outlined, it is evident that contributions to our understanding of attention and consciousness come from quite diverse disciplines. There is the neurophysiology of the brain, there are computer models, mathematical theories, data from experimental subjects and from neuropsychological patients. While evidence from all these sources must ultimately be important, and should constrain psychological theory, the difficulty of incorporating all the evidence from all the sources into a single theory arises. On a small scale, there is a good number of theories which account well for a part of the evidence. On the larger scale, the choice of agreed terms and level of explanation is difficult and probably impossible. At the very least, it must be clear that a single term for attention or consciousness is almost certainly inappropriate. It is possible that there are as many varieties of "attention" and "consciousness" as there are experiments to investigate them. If different tasks recruit different sub-sets of specialised brain areas, then every task will impose a different demand on the neural substrate. Furthermore, if this is the case, we must rule out the possibility of formulating a unified theory of either "attention" or "consciousness". I am sorry if this disappoints the reader, but to try to provide a unified theory of attention and/or consciousness would, at present, be misleading.

References

Adams, M.J. (1979). Models of word recognition. *Cognitive Psychology, 11*,136–176.

Albert, M.L. (1973). A simple test of visual neglect. *Neurology, 23*, 658–664.

Allport, D.A. (1977). On knowing the meaning of words we are unable to report: The effects of visual masking. In S. Dornic (Ed.), *Attention and performance VI*. Hillsdale, NJ: Lawrence Erlbaum Associates Inc.

Allport, D.A. (1980a). Attention and performance. In G. Claxton (Ed.), *Cognitive psychology: New directions*. London: Routledge & Kegan Paul.

Allport, D.A. (1980b). Patterns and actions. In G. Claxton (Ed.), *Cognitive psychology: New directions*. London: Routledge & Kegan Paul.

Allport, (D.)A. (1987). Selection for action: some behavioural and neurophysiological considerations of attention and action. In H. Heuer & A.F. Sanders (Eds.), *Perspectives on perception and action*. Hillsdale, NJ: Lawrence Erlbaum Associates Inc.

Allport, (D.)A. (1988). What concept of consciousness? In A.J. Marcel & E. Bisiach (Eds.), *Consciousness in contemporary science*. Oxford: Oxford University Press.

Allport, (D.)A. (1989). Visual attention. In M.I. Posner (Ed.), *Foundations of cognitive science*. Cambridge, MA: MIT Press.

Allport, (D.)A. (1993). Attention and control: have we been asking the wrong questions? A critical review of twenty-five years. In D.E. Meyer & S.M. Kornblum (Eds.), *Attention and performance XIV: Synergies in experimental psychology, artificial intelligence, and cognitive neuroscience*. Cambridge, MA: MIT Press.

Allport, D.A., Antonis, B., & Reynolds, P. (1972). On the division of attention: A disproof of the single channel hypothesis. *Quarterly Journal of Experimental Psychology, 24*, 25–35.

Allport, (D.)A., & Styles, E.A. (1990). *Multiple executive functions, multiple resources? Experiments in shifting attentional control of tasks*. Unpublished manuscript, Oxford University.

Allport, (D.)A., Styles, E.A., & Hseih, S. (1994). Shifting intentional set: Exploring the dynamic control of tasks. In C. Umiltà & M. Moscovitch (Eds.), *Attention and performance XV: Conscious and nonconscious information processing*. Cambridge, MA: MIT Press.

Allport, D.A., Tipper, S.P., & Chmiel, N.R.J. (1985). Perceptual integration and post-categorical filtering. In M.I. Posner & O.S.M. Marin (Eds.), *Attention and performance XI*. Hillsdale, NJ: Lawrence Erlbaum Associates Inc.

Anderson, J.R. (1983). *The architecture of cognition*. Cambridge, MA: Harvard University Press.

Atkinson, R.C., & Shiffrin, R.M. (1968). Human memory: A proposed system and control processes. In K.W. Spence & J.D. Spence (Eds.), *The psychology of learning and motivation (Vol.2)*. New York: Academic Press.

Avebach, E., & Coriell, A.S. (1961). Short-term memory in vision. *Bell System Technical Journal, 40*, 309–328.

Baddeley, A.D. (1986). *Working memory*. Oxford: Oxford University Press.

Bauer, R.M. (1984). Autonomic recognition of names and faces in prosopagnosia: A neuropsychological application of the guilty knowledge test. *Neuropsychologia, 22*, 457–469.

Baylis, G., Driver, J., & Rafal, R. (1993). Visual extinction and stimulus repetition. *Journal of Cognitive Neuroscience, 5*, 453–466.

Bechtel, W., & Abrahamsen, A. (1991). *Connectionism and the mind: An introduction to parallel processing in networks*. Oxford: Blackwell.

Beck, J. (1966). Effect of orientation and of shape similarity on perceptual grouping. *Perception and Psychophysics, 1*, 300–320.

Behrmann, M. (1996). Neglect dyslexia: Attention and word recognition. In M.J. Farah & G. Ratcliff (Eds.), *The neuropsychology of high-level vision* (pp.173–214). Hillsdale, NJ: Lawrence Erlbaum Associates Inc.

Behrmann, M., & Moskovitch, M. (1994). Object centred neglect in patients with unilateral neglect: Effects of left right coordinates of objects. *Cognitive Neuroscience, 6*, 1–16.

Behrmann, M., & Tipper, S.P. (1994). Object-based attentional mechanisms: Evidence from patients with unilateral neglect. In C. Umiltà & M. Moscovitch (Eds.), *Attention and performance XV, Conscious and nonconscious information processing*. Cambridge, MA: MIT Press.

Berger, R.C., & McLeod, P. (1996). Display density influences visual search for conjunctions of movement and orientation. *Journal of Experimental Psychology: Human Perception and Performance, 22*, 114–121.

Berti, A., Allport, (D.)A., Driver, J., Deines, Z., Oxbury, J., & Oxbury, S. (1992). Levels of processing for visual stimuli in an "extinguished" field. *Neuropsychologia, 30*, 403–415.

Bianchi, L. (1985). The functions of the frontal lobes. *Brain, 18*, 497–530.

Bianchi, L. (1922). *The mechanism of the brain and the function of the frontal lobes*. Edinburgh: Livingstone.

Bisiach, E., & Luzatti, C. (1978). Unilateral neglect of representational space. *Cortex, 14*, 128–133.

Bjork, E.L., & Murray, J.T. (1977). On the nature of input channels in visual processing. *Psychological Review, 84*, 472–484.

Bouma, H. (1970). On the nature of input channels in visual processing. *Nature, 226*, 177–178.

Briand, K.A., & Klein, R.M. (1987). Is Posner's "beam" the same as Treisman's "glue"? On the relationship between visual orienting and feature integration theory. *Journal of Experimental Psychology: Human Perception and Performance, 13*, 228–241.

Broadbent, D.E. (1952). Listening to one of two synchronous messages. *Journal of Experimental Psychology, 44*, 51–55.

Broadbent, D.E. (1954). The role of auditory localisation in attention and memory span. *Journal of Experimental Psychology, 47*, 191–196.

Broadbent, D.E. (1958). *Perception and communication*. London: Pergamon Press.

Broadbent, D.E. (1971). *Decision and stress*. London: Academic Press.

Broadbent, D.E. (1982).Task combination and selective intake of information. *Acta Psychologia, 50*, 253–290.

Broadbent, D.E. (1984). The Maltese Cross: A new simplistic model for memory. *Behavioural and Brain Sciences, 7*, 55–68.

Broadbent, D.E. (1985). A question of levels: Comment on McClelland and Rumelhart. *Journal of Experimental Psychology: General, 114*, 189–192.

Bruce, V. (Ed.) (1996). *Unsolved mysteries of the mind: Tutorial essays in cognition*. Hove, UK: Psychology Press.

Bundesen, C. (1990). A theory of visual attention. *Psychological Review, 97*, 523–527.

Bundesen, C., & Shibuya, H. (Eds.) (1995). *Visual selective attention: A special issue of Visual Cognition*. Hove, UK: Lawrence Erlbaum Associates Ltd.

Burgess, P.W., & Hitch, G.J. (1992). Toward a network model of the articulatory loop. *Journal of Memory and Language, 31*, 429–460.

Campion, J., Latto, R., & Smith, Y.M. (1983). Is blindsight an effect of scattered light, spared cortex, and near-threshold vision. *Behavioural and Brain Sciences, 3*, 423,447.

Carlson, N.R. (1994). *Physiology of behaviour* (5th ed.). Needham Heights, MA: Allyn & Bacon.

Carramazza, A., & Hillis, A.E. (1990). Spatial representation of words in the brain implied by studies of a unilateral neglect patient. *Nature, 346*, 267–269.

Carrier, L.M., & Pashler, H. (1995). Attentional limits in memory retrieval. *Journal of Experimental Psychology: Learning, Memory and Cognition, 21*, 1339–1348.

Castiello, U., & Umiltà, C. (1992). Splitting focal attention. *Journal of Experimental Psychology: Human Perception and Performance, 18*, 837–848.

Chase, W.G., & Ericsson, K.A. (1982). Skill and working memory. In G.H. Bower (Ed.), *The psychology of learning and motivation* (Vol.16, pp.1–58). New York: Academic Press.

Chase, W.G., & Simon, H.A. (1973). Perception in chess. *Cognitive Psychology, 4*, 55–81.

Cheesman, J., & Merikle, P.M. (1984). Priming with and without awareness. *Perception and Psychophysics, 36*, 387–395.

Cheesman, J., & Merikle, P.M. (1985). Word recognition and consciousness. In D. Besner, T.G. Waller, & G.E. MacKinnon (Eds.), *Reading research: Advances in theory and practice* (Vol.5). New York: Academic Press.

Cherry, E.C. (1953). Some experiments on the recognition of speech with one and two ears. *Journal of the Acoustical Society of America, 25*, 975–979.

Cohen, G. (1989). *Memory in the real world*. Hove, UK: Lawrence Erlbaum Associates Ltd.

Cohen, J.D., Dunbar, K., & McClelland, J.L. (1990). On the control of automatic processes: A parallel distributed processing account of the Stroop effect. *Psychological Review, 97*, 332–361.

Cohen, J.D., & Huston, T. (1994). Progress in the use of interactive models for understanding attention and performance. In C. Umiltà & M. Moscovitch (Eds.), *Attention and Performance XV: Conscious and nonconscious information processing*. Cambridge, MA: MIT Press.

Coltheart, M. (1972). Visual information processing. In P.C. Dodwell (Ed.), *New horizons in psychology, 2*. Harmondsworth, UK: Penguin.

Coltheart, M. (1980a). Iconic memory and visible persistence. *Perception and Psychophysics, 27*, 183–228.

Coltheart, M. (1980b). Deep dyslexia: A review of the syndrome. In M. Coltheart, K. Patterson, & J.C. Marshall (Eds.), *Deep dyslexia*. London: Routledge & Kegan Paul.

Coltheart, M. (1984). Sensory memory: A tutorial review. In H. Bouma & D.G. Bouwhuis (Eds.), *Attention and Performance X: Control of language processes*. Hove, UK: Lawrence Erlbaum Associates Ltd.

Compton, B.J., & Logan, G.D. (1993). Evaluating a computational model of perceptual grouping by proximity. *Perception and Psychophysics, 53*, 403–421.

Corbetta, M., Miezen, F.M., Shulman, G.L., & Peterson, S.E. (1993). A PET study of visual spatial attention. *Journal of Neuroscience, 13*, 120020–120026.

Corteen, R.S., & Dunn, D. (1973). Shock associated words in a nonattended message: A test for momentary awareness. *Journal of Experimental Psychology, 102*, 1143–1144.

Corteen, R.S., & Wood, B. (1972). Autonomous responses to shock associated words in an unattended channel. *Journal of Experimental Psychology, 94*, 308–313.

Craik, F.I.M. (1983). On the transfer of information from temporary to permanent memory. *Philosophical Transactions of the Royal Society of London, B302*, 341–359.

Crick, F. (1984). Function of the thalamic reticular complex. *Proceedings of the National Academy of Science, USA. 81*, 4586–4590.

Crick, F., & Koch, C. (1990). Towards a neurobiological theory of consciousness. *Seminars in the Neurosciences, 2*, 263–275.

Crick, F., & Koch, C. (1992). The problem of consciousness. *Scientific American, 9*, 111–117.

Dagenbach, D., Carr, T.H., & Wilhelmsen, A. (1989). Task induced strategies and near threshold priming: Conscious influences on unconscious perception. *Journal of Memory and Language, 28*, 412–443.

Damasio, A.R. (1990). Synchronous activation in multiple cortical regions: A mechanism for recall. *Seminars in the Neurosciences, 2*, 287–296.

Davies, M., & Humphreys, G.W. (1993). *Consciousness: Readings in mind and language*. Oxford: Blackwell.

De Haan, E.H.F., Young, A., & Newcombe, F. (1987a). Face recognition without awareness. *Cognitive Neuropsychology, 4*, 385–415.

De Haan, E.H.F., Young, A., & Newcombe, F. (1987b). Faces interfere with name classification in a prosopagnosic patient. *Cortex, 23*, 309–316.

De Haan, E.H.F., Young, A., & Newcombe, F. (1991). A dissociation between the sense of familiarity and access to semantic information concerning familiar people. *European Journal of Cognitive Psychology, 3*, 51–67.

DeJong, R. (1995). The role of preparation in overlapping-task performance. *Quarterly Journal of Experimental Psychology, 48A*, 2–25.

Deutsch, J.A., & Deutsch, D. (1963). Attention, some theoretical considerations. *Psychological Review, 70*, 80–90.

Dick, A.O. (1969). Relations between the sensory register and short term storage in tachistoscopic recognition. *Journal of Experimental Psychology, 82*, 279–284.

Dick, A.O. (1971). On the problem of selection in short-term visual (iconic) memory. *Canadian Journal of Psychology, 25*, 250–263.

Dick, A.O. (1974). Iconic memory and its relation to perceptual processing and other memory mechanisms. *Perception and Psychophysics, 16*, 575–596.

Dixon, N.F. (1971). *Subliminal perception: The nature of the controversy*. New York: McGraw Hill.

Dixon, N.F. (1981). *Preconscious processing*. New York: Wiley.

Downing, C.J., & Pinker, S. (1985). The spatial structure of visual attention. In M.I. Posner & O.S.M. Marin (Eds.), *Attention and Performance XI*. Hillsdale, NJ: Lawrence Erlbaum Associates Inc.

Driver, J., & Baylis, G.C. (1989). Movement and visual attention: The spotlight metaphor breaks down. *Journal of Experimental Psychology: Human Perception and Performance, 15*, 448–456.

Driver, J., & Halligan, P.W. (1991). Can visual neglect operate in object centred co-ordinates? An affirmative case study. *Cognitive Neuropsychology, 8*, 475–96.

Driver, J., & McLeod, P. (1992). Reversing visual search asymmetries with conjunction search of movement and orientation. *Journal of Experimental Psychology: Human Perception and Performance, 18*, 22–33.

Driver, J., & Spence, C.J. (1994). Spatial synergies between auditory and visual attention. In C. Umiltà & M. Moscovitch (Eds.), *Attention and performance XV: Conscious and nonconscious information processing*. Cambridge, MA: MIT Press.

Driver, J., & Tipper, S.P. (1989). On the non-selectivity of selective seeing: Contrasts between interference and priming in selective attention. *Journal of Experimental Psychology: Human Perception and Performance, 15*, 304–314.

Duncan, J. (1980). The locus of interference in the perception of simultaneous stimuli. *Psychological Review, 37*, 272–300.

Duncan, J. (1984). Selective attention and the organisation of visual information. *Journal of Experimental Psychology: General, 113*, 501–517.

Duncan, J. (1986). Disorganisation of behaviour after frontal lobe damage. *Cognitive Neuropsychology, 3*, 271–290.

Duncan, J. (1993). Selection of input and goal in the control of behaviour. In A.D. Baddeley & L. Weiskrantz (Eds.), *Attention: Awareness, selection, and control*. Oxford: Oxford University Press.

Duncan, J., & Humphreys, G.W. (1989). Visual search and visual similarity. *Psychological Review, 96*, 433–458.

Duncan, J., & Humphreys, G.W. (1992). Beyond the search surface: Visual search and attentional engagement. *Journal of Experimental Psychology: Human Perception and Performance, 18*, 578–588.

Egeth, H.E., Jonides, J., & Wall, S. (1972). Parallel processing of multi-element displays. *Cognitive Psychology, 3*, 674–698.

Eich, E. (1984). Memory for unattended events: Remembering with and without awareness. *Memory and Cognition, 12*, 105–111.

Ellis, A.W., Flude, B.M., & Young, A.W. (1987). Neglect dyslexia and the early visual processing of letters in words. *Cognitive Neuropsychology, 4*, 439–464.

Ellis, A.W., & Marshall, J.C. (1978). Semantic errors or statistical flukes? A note on Allport's "On knowing the meaning of words we are unable to report." *Quarterly Journal of Experimental Psychology, 30*, 569–575.

Ellis, A.W., & Young, A.W. (1988). *Human cognitive neuropsychology*. Hove, UK: Lawrence Erlbaum Associates Ltd.

Ericsson, K.A., & Kintsch, W. (1995). Long-term working memory. *Psychological Review, 102*, 211–245.

Ericsson, K.A., & Oliver, W. (1984, November). *Skilled memory in blindfold chess*. Paper presented at the annual meeting of the Psychonomic Society, San Antonio, TX.

Ericsson, K.A., & Staszewski, J. (1989). Skilled memory and expertise: Mechanisms of exceptional performance. In D. Klahr & K. Kotovsky (Eds.), *Complex information processing: The impact of Herbert A. Simon* (pp.235–267). Hillsdale, NJ: Lawrence Erlbaum Associates Inc.

Eriksen, C.W. (1960). Discrimination and learning without awareness: A methodological survey and evaluation. *Psychological Review, 67*, 279–300.

Eriksen, C.W. (1995). The Flankers task and response competition: A useful tool for investigating a variety of cognitive problems. *Visual Cognition, 2*, 101–118.

Eriksen, B.A., & Eriksen, C.W. (1974). Effects of noise letters upon the identification of a target in a non-search task. *Perception and Psychophysics, 16*, 143–149.

Eriksen, C.W., & Murphy, T.D. (1987). Movement of attentional focus across the visual field: A critical look at the

evidence. *Perception and Psychophysics, 42*, 299–305.
Eriksen, C.W., & Rohrbaugh, J.W. (1970). Some factors determining the efficiency of selective attention. *American Journal of Psychology, 83*, 330–343.
Eriksen, C.W., Pan, K., & Botella, J. (1993). Attentional distribution in visual space. *Psychological Research, 56*, 5–13.
Eriksen, C.W., & Shultz, T. (1979). Information processing in visual search: A continuous flow conception and experimental results. *Perception and Psychophysics, 25*, 249–263.
Eriksen, C.W., & St James, J.D. (1986). Visual attention within and around the field of focal attention: A zoom lens model. *Perception and Psychophysics, 40*, 225–240.
Eriksen, C.W., & Yeh, Y-Y. (1985). Allocation of attention in the visual field. *Journal of Experimental Psychology: Human Perception and Performance, 11*, 583–597.
Esslinger, P.J., & Damasio, A.R. (1985). Severe disturbance of higher cognition after bilateral frontal ablation: Patient E.V.R. *Neurology, 35*, 1731–1741.
Estes, W.K. (1972). Interaction of signal and background variables in visual processing. *Perception and Psychophysics, 12*, 278–286
Estes, W.K. (1974). Redundancy of noise elements and signals in visual detection of letters. *Perception and Psychophysics, 19*, 1–15.
Eysenck, M.W., & Keane, M.T. (1995). *Cognitive psychology: A student's handbook.* (3rd ed.). Hove, UK: Lawrence Erlbaum Associates Ltd.
Fagot, C., & Pashler, H. (1992). Making two responses to a single object: Implications for the central attentional bottleneck. *Journal of Experimental Psychology: Human Perception and Performance, 18*, 1058–1079.
Fagot, C., & Pashler, H. (1994). Repetition blindness: Perception of memory failure? *Journal of Experimental Psychology: Human Perception and Performance, 21*, 275–292.
Farah, M.J. (1988). Is visual imagery really visual? Overlooked evidence from neuropsychology. *Psychological Review, 95*, 307–317.
Farah, M.J. (1990). Visual agnosia: *Disorders of object recognition and what they tell us about normal vision.* Cambridge, MA: MIT Press.
Farah, M.J. (1994). Visual perception and visual awareness: A tutorial review. In C. Umiltà & M. Moscovitch (Eds.), *Attention and performance XV: Conscious and nonconscious information processing.* Cambridge, MA: MIT Press.
Fisk, A.D., & Schneider, W. (1984). Memory as a function of attention, level of processing and automatization. *Journal of Experimental Psychology: Learning, Memory, and Cognition, 10*, 181–197.
Fitts, P.M., & Posner, M.I. (1973). *Human performance*. London: Prentice Hall.
Fodor, J.A. (1983). *Modularity of Mind.* Cambridge, MA: MIT Press.
Fowler, C.A., Wolford, G., Slade, R., & Tassinary, L. (1981). Lexical access with and without awareness. *Journal of Experimental Psychology: General, 110*, 341–362.
Francolini, C.M., & Egeth, H.E. (1980). On the nonautomaticity of "automatic" activation: Evidence of selective seeing. *Perception and Psychophysics, 27*, 331–342.
Fox, L.A., Schor, R.E., & Steinman, R.J. (1971). Semantic gradients and interference in naming colour, spatial direction and numerosity. *Journal of Experimental Psychology, 91*, 59–65.
Gazzaniga, M.S. (1988). Brain modularity: Towards a philosophy of conscious experience. In A.J. Marcel & E. Bisiach (Eds.), *Consciousness in contemporary science*. Oxford: Oxford University Press.
Gentilucci, M., & Rizzolatti, G. (1990). Cortical motor control of arm and hand

movements. In M.A. Goodale (Ed.), *Vision and action: The control of grasping.* Norwood, NJ: Ablex.

Gillie, T., & Broadbent, D.E. (1989). What makes interruptions disruptive? A study of length, similarity and complexity. *Psychological Research, 50,* 243–250.

Goldberg, M.E., & Wurtz, R.H. (1972). Activity of superior colliculus in behaving monkey: II. Effect of attention on neuronal responses. *Journal of Neurophysiology, 35,* 560–574.

Goodale, M.A., & Milner, A.D. (1992). Separate visual pathways for perception and action. *Trends in Neuroscience, 15,* 20–25.

Gopher, D, (1993). The skill of attentional control: Acquisition and execution of attentional strategies. In S. Kornblum & D.E. Meyer (Eds.), *Attention and performance XIV: Synergies in experimental psychology, artificial intelligence and cognitive neuroscience.* Cambridge, MA: MIT Press.

Graves, R.S. (1976). Are more letters identified than can be reported? *Journal of Experimental Psychology, Human Learning and Memory, 2,* 208–214.

Gray, C.M., & Singer, W. (1989). Stimulus specific neuronal oscillations in the cat visual cortex: A cortical functional unit. *Proceedings of the National Academy of Sciences, USA, 86,* 1698–1702.

Gray, J.A., & Wedderburn, A.A. (1960). Grouping strategies with simultaneous stimuli. *Quarterly Journal of Experimental Psychology, 12,* 180–184.

Greenwald, A.G., Klinger, M.R., & Liu, T.J. (1989). Unconscious processing of dichotically masked words. *Journal of Experimental Psychology: General, 110,* 341–362.

Greenwald, A.G., & Shulman, H.G. (1973). On doing two things at once: II. Elimination of the psychological refractory period. *Journal of Experimental Psychology, 101,* 70–76.

Grossberg, S. (1980). How does the brain build a cognitive code? *Psychological Review, 87,* 1–51.

Hécaen, H., & Albert, M.L. (1978). *Human neuropsychology.* New York: Wiley.

Hampson, P.J., & Morriss, P.E. (1996). *Understanding cognition.* Oxford: Blackwell.

Harlow, J. (1868). Recovery after severe injury to the head. *Publications of the Massachusetts Medical Society, 2,* 327–36.

Harris, J.E., & Morris, P.E. (Eds.) (1984). *Everyday memory, actions and absent-mindedness.* New York: Academic Press.

Hasher, L., & Zacks, R.T. (1979). Automatic and effortful processes in memory. *Journal of Experimental Psychology: General, 108,* 356–388.

Hebb, D.O. (1949). *The organisation of behaviour.* New York: Wiley.

Heuer, H., & Sanders, A.F. (Eds.) (1987). *Perspectives on perception and action.* Hillsdale, NJ: Lawrence Erlbaum Associates Inc.

Hick, W.E. (1952). On the rate of gain of information. *Quarterly Journal Of Experimental Psychology, 4,* 11–26.

Hinton, G., & Anderson, J.R. (1981). *Parallel models of associative memory.* Hillsdale, NJ: Lawrence Erlbaum Associates Inc.

Hinton, G., & Shallice, T. (1991). Lesioning an attractor network: Investigations of acquired dyslexia. *Psychological Review, 98,* 74–95.

Hintzman, D.L., Carre, F.A., Eskridge, V.L., Owens, A.M., Shaff, S.S., & Sparks, M.E. (1972). "Stroop" effect. Input or output phenomenon. *Journal of Experimental Psychology, 95,* 458–459.

Hirst, W. (1986). The psychology of attention. In J.E. LeDoux & W. Hirst (Eds.), *Mind and brain: Dialogues in cognitive neuroscience.* Cambridge: Cambridge University Press.

Hirst, W., Spelke, E.S., Reeves. C., Caharack, G., & Neisser, U. (1980).

Dividing attention without alternation or automaticity. *Journal of Experimental Psychology: General, 109*, 98–117.

Hitch, G.J., & Baddeley, A.D. (1976). Verbal reasoning and working memory. *Quarterly Journal of Experimental Psychology, 28*, 603–631.

Hochhaus, L., & Moran, K.M. (1991). Factors in repetition blindness. *Journal of Experimental Psychology: Human Perception and Performance, 17*, 422–432.

Holender, D. (1986). Semantic activation without conscious identification in dichotic listening, parafoveal vision and visual masking: A survey and appraisal. *Behaviour and Brain Sciences 9*, 1–66.

Humphreys, G.W. (1981). Flexibility of attention between stimulus dimensions. *Perception and Psychophysics, 30*, 291–302.

Humphreys, G.W., & Bruce, V. (1989). *Visual cognition: Computational, experimental and neuropsychological perspectives*. Hove, UK: Lawrence Erlbaum Associates Ltd.

Humphreys, G.W., & Müller, H.J. (1993). SEarch via Recursive Rejection (SERR): A connectionist model of visual search. *Cognitive Psychology, 25*, 43–110.

Humphreys, G.W., Romani, C., Olson, A., Riddoch, M.J., & Duncan, J. (1994). *Nature, 372*, 357–359.

Huppert, F.A., & Piercy, M. (1976). Recognition memory in amnesic patients: Effect of temporal context and familiarity of material. *Cortex, 12*, 3–20.

Jacoby, L.L. (1994). Measuring recollection: Strategic versus automatic influences of associative context. In C. Umiltà & M. Moscovitch (Eds.), *Attention and performance XV: Conscious and nonconscious information processing*. Cambridge, MA: MIT Press.

Jacoby, L.L., Woloshyn, V., & Kelley, C.M. (1989). Becoming famous without being recognised: Unconscious influences of memory produced by dividing attention. *Journal of Experimental Psychology: General, 118*, 115–125.

James, W. (1890). *The principles of psychology*. New York: Holt.

Jeannerod, M. (1984). The timing of natural prehension movements. *Journal of Motor Behaviour, 16*, 235–254.

Jeannerod, M. (1997). *The cognitive neuroscience of action*. Oxford: Blackwell.

Jersild, A.T. (1927). Mental set and shift. *Archives of Psychology, 9*, Whole issue.

Jonides, J. (1981). Voluntary versus automatic control over the mind's eye. In J. Long & A. Baddeley (Eds.), *Attention and Performance IX* (pp.187–203). Hillsdale, NJ: Lawrence Erlbaum Associates Inc.

Jonides, J., & Gleitman, H. (1972). A conceptual category effect in visual search: O as a letter or a digit. *Perception and Psychophysics, 12*, 457–460.

Johnson, J.C., & McClelland, J. (1976). Experimental tests of a hierarchical model of word recognition. *Journal of Verbal Learning and Verbal Behaviour, 19*, 503–524.

Johnson-Laird, P.N. (1983). A computational analysis of consciousness. *Cognition and Brain Theory, 6*, 499–508.

Johnson-Laird, P.N. (1988). A computational analysis of consciousness. In A.J. Marcel & E. Bisiach (Eds.), *Consciousness in contemporary science*. Oxford: Oxford University Press.

Johnston, W.A., & Dark, V.J. (1986). Selective attention. *Annual Review of Psychology, 37*, 43–75.

Johnston, W.A., & Heinz, S.P. (1979). Depth of non-target processing in an attention task. *Journal of Experimental Psychology, 5*, 168–175.

Jordan, M.I., & Rosenbaum, D.A. (1989). Action. In M.I. Posner (Ed.), *Foundations of cognitive science*. Cambridge, MA: MIT Press.

Kahneman, D. (1973). *Attention and effort*. Englewood Cliffs, NJ: Prentice Hall.

Kahneman, D., & Chajczyk, D. (1983). Tests of the automaticity of reading: Dilution of Stroop effects by colour-irrelevant stimuli. *Journal of Experimental Psychology: Human Perception and Performance, 9*, 497–509.

Kahneman, D., & Henik, A. (1981). Perceptual organisation and attention. In M. Kubovy & J.R. Pomerantz (Eds.), *Perceptual organisation*. Hillsdale, NJ: Lawrence Erlbaum Associates Inc.

Kahneman, D., & Treisman, A.M. (1984). Changing views of attention and automaticity. In R. Parsuraman & D.R. Davies (Eds.), *Varieties of attention*. Orlando, FL: Academic Press.

Kahneman, D., Treisman, A., & Gibbs, B. (1992). The reviewing of object files: Object-specific integration of information. *Cognitive Psychology, 24*, 175–219.

Kanwisher, N. (1987). Repetition blindness: Type recognition without token individuation. *Cognition, 27*, 117–143.

Kanwisher, N. (1991). Repetition blindness and illusory conjunctions. *Journal of Experimental Psychology: Human Perception and Performance, 17*, 404–421.

Kanwisher, N., Driver, J., & Machado, L. (1995). Spatial repetition blindness is modulated by selective attention to colour or shape. *Cognitive Psychology, 29*, 303–337.

Kelley, C.M., & Jacoby, L.L. (1990). The construction of subjective experience: Memory attributions. *Mind and Language, 5*, 49–61.

Kemp-Wheeler, S., & Hill, A.B. (1988). Semantic priming without awareness: Some methodological considerations and replications. *Quarterly Journal of Experimental Psychology, 40A*, 671–692.

Kinsbourne, M. (1988). Integrated field theory of consciousness. In A.J. Marcel & E. Bisiach (Eds.), *Consciousness and contemporary science*. Oxford: Clarendon Press.

Kinsbourne, M., & Warrington, E.K. (1962). A variety of reading disability associated with right hemisphere lesions. *Journal of Neurology, Neurosurgery and Psychiatry, 25*, 339–344.

Klein, R.M. (1988). Inhibitory tagging system facilitates visual search. *Nature, 334*, 430–431.

Knowles, W.B. (1963). Operator loading tasks. *Human Factors, 5*, 151–161.

Kramer, A.F., Tham, M.P., & Yeh, Y-Y. (1991). Movement and spatial attention: A failure to replicate. *Perception and Psychophysics, 17*, 371–379.

LaBerge, D. (1983). Spatial extent of attention to letters and words. *Journal of Experimental Psychology: Human Perception and Performance, 9*, 371–379.

LaBerge, D., Brown, V., Carter, M., Bash, D., & Hartley, A. (1991). Reducing the effect of adjacent distractors by narrowing attention. *Journal of Experimental Psychology: Human Perception and Performance, 17*, 65–76.

LaBerge, D., & Buchsbaum, J.L. (1990). Positron emission tomography measurements of pulvinar activity during an attention task. *Journal of Neuroscience, 10*, 613–619.

Lackner, J.R., & Garrett, M.F. (1972). Resolving ambiguity: Effect of biassing context in the unattended ear. *Cognition, 1*, 359–372.

Laird, J.E., Newell, A., & Rosenbloom, P.S. (1987). Soar: An architecture for general intelligence. *Artificial Intelligence, 33*, 1–64.

Lambert, A.J., Beard, C.T., & Thompson, R.J. (1988). Selective attention, visual laterality, awareness and perceiving the meaning of parafoveally presented words. *Quarterly Journal of Experimental Psychology, 40A*, 615–652.

Lambert, A.J., & Voot, N. (1993). A left visual field bias for semantic encoding of unattended words. *Neuropsychologia, 31*, 67–73.

Lavie, N. (1995). Perceptual load as a necessary condition for selective

attention. *Journal of Experimental Psychology; Human Perception and Performance, 21*, 451–468.
Law, M.B., Pratt, J., & Abrams, R.A. (1995). Colour-based inhibition of return. *Perception and Psychophysics, 57*, 402–408.
Lewis, J.L. (1970). Semantic processing of unattended messages using dichotic listening. *Journal of Experimental Psychology, 85*, 225–228.
Lhermitte, F. (1983). Utilisation behaviour and its relation to lesions in the frontal lobes. *Brain, 106*, 237–255.
Logan, G.D. (1995). Linguistic and conceptual control of visual spatial attention. *Cognitive Psychology, 28*, 103–174.
Logan, G.D. (1996). The CODE theory of visual attention: An integration of space-based and object-based attention. *Psychological Review, 103*, 603–649.
Luna, D., Marcos-Ruiz, R., & Merino, J.M. (1995). Selective attention to global and local information: Effects of visual angle, exposure duration and eccentricity on processing dominance. *Visual Cognition, 2*, 183–200.
Luria, A.R. (1966). *Higher cortical functions in man*. London: Tavistock.
MacKay, D.G. (1973). Aspects of the theory of comprehension, memory and attention. *Quarterly Journal of Experimental Psychology, 25*, 22–40.
MacLeod, C.M. (1991). Half a century of research on the Stroop effect: An integrative review. *Psychological Bulletin, 109*, 163–203.
MacLeod, C.M., & Dunbar, K. (1988). Training and Stroop-like interference: Evidence for a continuum of automaticity. *Journal of Experimental Psychology: Learning, Memory and Cognition, 14*, 137–154.
McClelland, J.L., & Rumelhart, D.E. (1981). An interactive activation model of context effects in letter perception: Part 1. An account of basic findings. *Psychological Review, 85*, 375–407.
McClelland, J.L., Rumelhart, D.E., & Hinton, G.E. (1986). The appeal of parallel distributed processing. In D.E. Rumelhart & J.L. McClelland (Eds.), *Parallel distributed processing: Explorations in the microstructure of cognition*. (Vol.1, pp.2–44). Cambridge, MA: MIT Press.
McKonkie, G.W., & Zola, D. (1979). Is visual information integrated across successive fixations in reading? *Perception and Psychophysics, 25*, 221–224.
McLeod, P.D. (1977). A dual task response modality effect: Support for multi-processor models of attention. *Quarterly Journal of Experimental Psychology, 29*, 651–667.
McLeod, P.D. (1978). Does probe RT measure central processing demand? *Quarterly Journal of Experimental Psychology, 30*, 83–89.
McLeod, P., & Posner, M.I. (1984). Privileged loops from percept to act. In H. Bouma & D.G. Bouwhuis (Eds.), *Attention and performance X: Control of language processes*. Hove, UK: Lawrence Erlbaum Associates Ltd.
McLeod, P., & Driver, J. (1993). Filtering and physiology in visual search: A convergence of behavioural and neurophysiological measures. In A.D. Baddeley & L. Weiskrantz (Eds.), *Attention: Awareness, selection, and control*. Oxford: Oxford University Press.
Marcel, A.J. (1980). Conscious and preconscious recognition of polysemous words: Locating the selective effects of prior verbal context. In R.S. Nickerson (Ed.), *Attention and performance VII*. Hillsdale, NJ: Lawrence Erlbaum Associates Inc.
Marcel, A.J. (1983). Conscious and unconscious perception: An approach to the relations between phenomenal experience and perceptual processes. *Cognitive Psychology, 15*, 238–300.
Marcel, A.J., & Bisiach, E. (Eds.) (1988). *Consciousness in contemporary science*. Oxford: Oxford University Press.

Marr, D. (1976). Early processing of visual information. *Philosophical Transactions of the Royal Society of London, B207*, 187–217.
Marr, D. (1982). *Vision*. San Francisco, CA: Freeman.
Martin, M. (1979). Local and global processing: The role of sparsity. *Memory and Cognition, 7*, 479–484.
Marzi, C.A., Tassinari, C. Aglioti, S., & Lutzemberger, L. (1986). Spatial summation across the vertical meridian in hemianopics: A test of blindsight. *Neuropsychologia, 24*, 749–758.
Maylor, E. (1985). Facilitatory and inhibitory components of orienting in visual space. In M.I. Posner & O.S.M. Marin (Eds.), *Attention and performance XI*. Hillsdale, NJ: Lawrence Erlbaum Associates Inc.
Merikle, P.M. (1980). Selection from visual persistence by perceptual groups and category membership. *Journal of Experimental Psychology: General, 109*, 279–295.
Merikle, P.M. (1982). Unconscious perception revisited. *Perception and Psychophysics, 31*, 298–301.
Merikle, P.M., & Reingold, E.M. (1990). recognition and lexical decision without detection: Unconscious perception? *Journal of Experimental; Psychology: Human Perception and Performance, 16*, 574–583.
Mewhort, D.J.K. (1967). Familiarity of letter sequences, response uncertainty and the tachistoscopic recognition experiment. *Canadian Journal of Psychology, 21*, 309–321.
Mewhort, D.J.K., Campbell, A.J., Marchetti, F.M., & Campbell, J.I.D. (1981). Identification, localisation and "iconic memory": An evaluation of the bar-probe task. *Memory and Cognition, 9*, 50–67.
Meyer, D.E., & Kornblum, S. (Eds.) (1993). *Attention and performance XIV: A Silver Jubilee*. Hillsdale, NJ: Lawrence Erlbaum Associates Inc.
Meyer, D.E., & Schvaneveldt, R.W. (1971). Facilitation in recognising pairs of words: Evidence of a dependence between retrieval operations. *Journal of Experimental Psychology, 90*, 227–234.
Miller, J. (1991). The flanker compatibility effect as a function of visual angle attentional focus, visual transients and perceptual load: A search for boundary conditions. *Perception and Psychophysics, 49*, 270–288.
Milner, B. (1963). Effects of different brain lesions on card sorting. *Archives of Neurology, 9*, 90–100.
Milner, B. (1966). Amnesia following operation on the temporal lobes. In C.W.M. Whitty & O.L. Zangwill (Eds.), *Amnesia*. London: Butterworths.
Monsell, S. (1996) Control of mental processes. In V. Bruce (Ed.), *Unsolved mysteries of the mind: Tutorial essays in cognition*. Hove, UK: Psychology Press.
Moray, N. (1959). Attention in dichotic listening: Affective cues and the influence of instructions. *Quarterly Journal of Experimental Psychology, 11*, 56–60.
Moray, N. (1967). Where is capacity limited? A survey and a model. *Acta Psychologia, 27*, 84–92.
Morton, J. (1969). Interaction of information in word recognition. *Psychological Review, 76*, 165–178.
Morton, J. (1979). Facilitation in word recognition: Experiments causing change in the logogen model. In P.A. Kohlers, M. Wrolstead, & H. Bouma (Eds.), *Processing of visible language* (Vol.1). New York: Plenum Press.
Mountcastle, V.B., Lynch, J.C., Georgopoulos, A., Sakata, H., & Acuna, C. (1975). Posterior parietal association cortex of the monkey: Command functions for operations within extrapersonal space. *Journal of Neurophysiology, 38*, 871–908.
Mozer, M.C. (1987). Early parallel processing in reading: A connectionist

approach. In M. Coltheart (Ed.), *Attention and performance XII: The psychology of reading*. Hove, UK: Lawrence Erlbaum Associates Ltd.

Mozer, M.C. (1988). *A connectionist model of selective attention in visual attention* (Tech. Rep. CRG-TR-88-4). Toronto: University of Toronto, Department of Computer Science.

Müller, H.J., & Found, A. (1996). Visual search for conjunctions of motion and form: Display density and asymmetry reversal. *Journal of Experimental Psychology: Human Perception and Performance, 22*, 122–132.

Müller, H.J., & Maxwell, J. (1994). Perceptual integration of motion and form information: Is the movement filter involved in form discrimination? *Journal of Experimental Psychology: Human Perception and Performance, 20*, 397–420.

Müller, H.J., & Rabbitt, P.M.A. (1989). Reflexive orienting of visual attention: Time course of activation and resistance to interruption. *Journal of Experimental Psychology: Human Perception and Performance, 15*, 315–330.

Murray, D.J., Mastroddi, J., & Duncan, S. (1972). Selective attention to "physical" versus "verbal" aspects of coloured words. *Psychonomic Science, 26*, 305–307.

Navon, D. (1977). Forest before trees: The precedence of global features in visual perception. *Cognitive Psychology, 9*, 353–383.

Neill, W.T. (1977). Inhibitory and facilitatory processes in attention. *Journal of Experimental Psychology: Human Perception and Performance, 3*, 444–450.

Neisser, U. (1967). *Cognitive psychology*. New York: Appleton Century Crofts.

Neisser, U. (1976). *Cognition and reality*. New York: W.H. Freeman.

Neuman, O. (1984). Automatic processing: A review of recent findings and a plea for an old theory. In W. Printz & Sanders, A. (Eds.), *Cognition and motor processes*. Berlin: Springer.

Neuman, O. (1987). Beyond capacity: A functional view of attention. In H. Heuer & A.F. Sanders (Eds.), *Perspectives on selection and action*. Hillsdale, NJ: Lawrence Erlbaum Associates Inc.

Newell, A., Rosenbloom, P.S., & Laird, J.E. (1989). Symbolic architectures for cognition. In M.I. Posner (Ed.), *Foundations of cognitive science*. Cambridge, MA: MIT Press.

Norman, D.A. (1968). Towards a theory of memory and attention. *Psychological Review, 75*, 522–536.

Norman, D.A. (1981). Categorization of action slips. *Psychological Review, 88*, 1–15.

Norman, D.A. (1986). Reflections on cognition and parallel distributed processing. In J.L. McClelland & D.E. Rumelhart (Eds.), *Parallel distributed processing: Explorations in the microstructure of cognition. Vol.2: Psychological and Biological models*. Cambridge, MA: MIT Press.

Norman, D.A., & Bobrow, D.G. (1975). On data-limited and resource-limited processes. *Cognitive Psychology, 7*, 44–64.

Norman, D.A., & Shallice, T. (1986). Attention to action: Willed and automatic control of behaviour. In R.Davison, G.Shwartz, & D.Shapiro (Eds.), *Consciousness and self regulation: Advances in research and theory*. New York: Plenum.

Pardo, J,V., Pardo, P.J., Janer, K.W., & Raichle, M.E. (1990). The anterior cingulate cortex mediates processing selection in the Stroop attentional conflict paradigm. *Proceedings of the National Academy of Science of the USA, 87*, 256–259.

Parkin, A.J. (1996). *Explorations in cognitive neuropsychology*. Oxford, UK: Blackwell.

Pashler, H. (1984). Processing stages in overlapping tasks. Evidence for a central bottleneck. *Journal of Experimental Psychology: Human Perception and Performance, 10*, 358–377.

Pashler, H. (1990). Do response modality effects support multi-processor models of divided attention? *Journal of Experimental Psychology: Human Perception and Performance, 16*, 826–842.

Pashler, H. (1993). Dual-task interference and elementary mental mechanisms. In D.E. Meyer & S.M. Kornblum (Eds.), *Attention and performance XIV: Synergies in experimental psychology, artificial intelligence and cognitive neuroscience.* Cambridge, MA: MIT Press.

Patterson, K.E., & Wilson, B. (1990). A ROSE is a ROSE or a NOSE: A deficit in initial letter recognition. *Cognitive Neuropsychology, 7*, 447–477.

Perenin, M.T., & Vighetto, A. (1988). Optic ataxia: A specific disorder in visuo-motor coordination. In A. Hein & M. Jeannerod (Eds.), *Spatially oriented behaviour*. New York: Springer.

Perret, E. (1974). The left frontal lobe of man and the suppression of habitual responses in verbal categorical behaviour. *Neuropsychologia, 12*, 323–330.

Petersen, S.E., Fox, P.T., Miezen, F.M., & Raichle, M.E. (1988). Modulation of cortical visual responses by direction of spatial attention measured by PET. *Association for Research in Vision and Opthalmology, Abstracts, 22*.

Petersen, S.E., Robinson, D.L., & Morris, J.D. (1987). Contributions of the pulvinar to visual spatial attention. *Neuropsychologia, 25*, 97–105.

Phaf, R.H., van der Heijden, A.H.C., & Hudson, P.T.W. (1990). SLAM: A connectionist model for attention in visual selection tasks. *Cognitive Psychology, 22*, 273–341.

Phaf, R.H., Mul, N.M., & Wolters, G. (1994). A connectionist view on dissociations. In C. Umiltà & M. Moscovitch (Eds.), *Attention and performance XV: Conscious and nonconscious information processing.* Cambridge, MA: MIT Press.

Poppel, E., Held, R., & Frost, D. (1973). Residual visual function after brain wounds involving the central visual pathways in man. *Nature, 243*, 2295–2296.

Posner, M.I. (1978). *Chronometric explorations of mind.* Hillsdale, NJ: Lawrence Erlbaum Associates Inc.

Posner, M.I. (1980). Orienting of attention. *Quarterly Journal of Experimental Psychology, 32*, 3–25.

Posner, M.I. (1993). Attention before and during the decade of the brain. In D.E. Meyer & S.M. Kornblum (Eds.), *Attention and performance XIV: Synergies in experimental psychology, artificial intelligence and cognitive neuroscience.* Cambridge, MA: MIT Press.

Posner, M.I., & Boies, S.J. (1971). Components of attention. *Psychological Review, 78*, 391–408.

Posner, M.I., & Cohen, Y. (1984). Components of visual orienting. In H. Bouma & D.G. Bouwhuis (Eds.), *Attention and Performance X* (pp.531–556). Hove, UK: Lawrence Erlbaum Associates Ltd.

Posner, M.I., & Petersen, S.E. (1990). The attentional system of the human brain. *Annual Review of Neuroscience, 13*, 25–42.

Posner, M.I., & Snyder, C.R.R. (1975). Attention and cognitive control. In R.L. Solso (Ed.), *Information processing and cognition: The Loyola symposium.* Hillsdale, NJ: Lawrence Erlbaum Associates Inc.

Posner, M.I., Snyder, C.R.R., & Davidson, B.J. (1980). Attention and the detection of signals. *Journal of Experimental Psychology: General, 109*, 160–174.

Posner, M.I., Walker, J.A., Friedrick, F.J., & Rafal, R.D. (1984). Effects of parietal injury on covert orienting of visual attention. *Journal of Neuroscience, 4*, 1863–1874.

Poulton, E.C. (1953). Two-channel listening. *Journal of Experimental Psychology, 46*, 91–96.

Poulton, E.C. (1956). Listening to overlapping calls. *Journal of Experimental Psychology, 52*, 334–339.

Pratt, J., & Abrams, R.A. (1995). Inhibition of return to successively cued spatial locations. *Journal of Experimental Psychology: Human Perception and Performance, 21*, 1343–1353.

Pratt, J., & Abrams, R.A. (1996). Spatially diffuse inhibition affects multiple locations: A reply to Tipper, Weaver, & Watson (1996). *Journal of Experimental Psychology: Human Perception and Performance, 22*, 1294–1298.

Prinzmetal, W. (1981). Principles of feature integration in visual perception. *Perception and Psychophysics, 30*, 330–340.

Purcell, D.G., Stewart, A.L., & Stanovitch, K.K. (1983). Another look at semantic priming without awareness. *Perception and Psychophysics, 34*, 65–71.

Quinlan, P. (1991). *Connectionism and psychology: A psychological perspective on new connectionist research*. Hemel Hempstead, UK: Harvester Wheatsheaf.

Rafal, R.D., & Posner, M.I. (1987). Deficits in human spatial attention following thalamic lesions. *Proceedings of the National Academy of Science, 84*, 7349–7353.

Ramachandran, V.S. (1988). Perceiving shape from shading. *Scientific American, 259*, 76–83.

Reason, J. (1979). Actions not as planned: The price of automatization. In G. Underwood & R. Stephens (Eds.), *Aspects of consciousness* (Vol.1). London: Academic Press.

Revelle, W. (1993). Individual differences in personality and motivation: 'Non-cognitive' determinants of cognitive performance. In A.D. Baddeley & L. Weiskrantz (Eds.), *Attention : Awareness, selection, and control*. Oxford: Oxford University Press.

Rizzolatti, G., & Carmada, R. (1987). Neural circuits for spatial attention and unilateral neglect. In M. Jeannerod (Ed.), *Neurophysiological and neuropsychological aspects of spatial neglect*. Amsterdam: North Holland.

Rizzolatti, G., & Gallese, V. (1988). Mechanisms and theories of spatial neglect. In F. Boller & J. Grafman (Eds.), *Handbook of neuropsychology* (Vol.1). Amsterdam: Elsevier.

Rizzolatti, G., Gentilucci, M., & Mattelli, M. (1985). Selective spatial attention: One centre, one circuit or many circuits. In M.I. Posner & O. Marin (Eds.), *Attention and performance XI*. Hillsdale, NJ: Lawrence Erlbaum Associates Inc.

Rizzolatti, G., Riggio, L., & Sheliga, B.M. (1994). Space and selective attention. In C. Umiltà & M. Moscovitch (Eds.), *Attention and Performance XV: Conscious and nonconscious information processing*. Cambridge, MA: MIT Press.

Robertson, L.C., Lamb, M.R., & Knight, R.T. (1988). Effects of lesions of temporal parietal junction on perceptual and attentional processing in humans. *Journal of Neuroscience, 8*, 3757–3769.

Robinson, D.L., & Peterson, S.E. (1986). The neurobiology of attention. In J.E. LeDoux & W. Hirst (Eds.), *Mind and brain: Dialogues in cognitive neuroscience*. Cambridge: Cambridge University Press.

Rogers, R.D., & Monsell, S. (1995). Costs of a predictable switch between simple cognitive tasks. *Journal of Experimental Psychology: General, 124*, 207–231.

Roland, P.E. (1985). Cortical organisation of voluntary behaviour in man. *Human Neurobiology, 4*, 155–167.

Rolls, E.T., & Baylis, G.C. (1986). Size and contrast have only small effects on the responses of face neurons in the cortex of the superior temporal sulcus of the monkey. *Experimental Brain Research, 65*, 38–48.

Rumelhart, D.E. (1989). The architecture of mind: A connectionist approach. In

M.I. Posner (Ed.), *Foundations of cognitive science*. Cambridge, MA: MIT Press.
Rumelhart, D.E., & McClelland, J.L. (1986). *Parallel distributed processing: Explorations in the microstructure of cognition: Vol.1. Foundations*. Cambridge, MA: MIT Press.
Rumelhart, D.E., & Norman, D.A. (1982). Simulating a skilled typist: A study of skilled cognitive-motor performance. *Cognitive Science, 6*, 1–36
Rylander, G. (1939). *Personality changes after operations on the frontal lobes: A clinical study of 32 cases*. Copenhagen: E. Munksgaard.
Sandson, J., & Albert, M.L. (1984). Varieties of perseveration. *Neuropsychologia, 22*, 715–732.
Santee, J.L., & Egeth, H.E. (1980). Interference in letter identifications: A test of feature specific inhibition. *Perception and Psychophysics, 27*, 321–330.
Santee, J.L., & Egeth, H.E. (1982). Do reaction time and accuracy measure the same aspects of letter recognition? *Journal of Experimental Psychology: Human Perception and Performance, 8*, 489–501.
Schacter, D.L. (1987). Implicit memory: History and current status. *Journal of Experimental Psychology: Learning, Memory and Cognition, 13*, 501–518.
Schacter, D.L. (1989). Memory. In M.I. Posner (Ed.), *Foundations of cognitive science*. Cambridge, MA: MIT Press.
Schacter, D.L., McAndrews, M.P., & Moscovitch, M. (1988). Access to consciousness: Dissociations between implicit and explicit knowledge in neuropsychological syndromes. In L. Weiskrantz (Ed.), *Thought without language*. Oxford: Oxford University Press.
Schacter, D.L., & Tulving, E. (1982). Amnesia and memory research. In L.S. Cermak (Ed.), *Human memory and amnesia*. Hillsdale, NJ: Lawrence Erlbaum Associates Inc.
Schneider, W., & Shiffrin, R.M. (1977). Controlled and automatic human information processing: I. Detection, search and attention. *Psychological Review, 84*, 1–66.
Schneider, W.X. (1993). Space based visual attention models and object selection: Constraints problems and possible solutions. *Psychological Research, 56*, 35–43.
Schneider, W.X. (1995). VAM: A neuro-cognitive model for visual attention, control of segmentation, object recognition and space-based motor action. *Visual Cognition, 2*, 331–375.
Sejnowski, T.J. (1986). Open questions about computation in cerebral cortex. In J.L. McClelland & D.E. Rumelhart (Eds.), *Parallel distributed processing: Explorations in the microstructure of cognition, Vol. 2: Psychological and biological models.* Cambridge, MA: MIT Press.
Shaffer, L.H. (1975). Multiple attention in continuous verbal tasks. In P.M.A. Rabbitt & S. Dornic (Eds.), *Attention and performance V*. New York: Academic Press.
Shallice, T. (1972). Dual functions of consciousness. *Psychological Review, 79*, 383–393.
Shallice, T. (1982). Specific impairments of planning. *Philosophical Transactions of the Royal Society of London, B298*, 199–209.
Shallice, T. (1988a). Information processing models of consciousness. In A.J. Marcel & E.Bisiach (Eds.), *Consciousness in contemporary science*. Oxford: Oxford University Press.
Shallice, T. (1988b). *From neuropsychology to mental structure*. Cambridge: Cambridge University Press.
Shallice, T., & Burgess, P.W. (1993). Supervisory control of action and thought selection. In A.D. Baddeley & L. Weiskrantz (Eds.), *Attention : Awareness, selection, and control*. Oxford: Oxford University Press.

Shallice, T., Burgess, P., Schon, F., & Baxter, D. (1989). The origins of utilization behaviour. *Brain, 112*, 1587–1598.

Shallice, T., & Warrington, E.K. (1977). The possible role of selective attention in acquired dyslexia. *Neuropsychologia. 15*, 31–41.

Shannon, C.E., & Weaver, W. (1949). *The mathematical theory of communication*. Urbana, IL: University of Illinois Press.

Shiffrin, R.M. (1988). Attention. In R.C. Atkinson, G. Lindzey, & R.D. Luce (Eds.), *Handbook of experimental psychology: Vol. 2. Learning and cognition* (2nd ed., pp.738–811). New York: Wiley.

Shiffrin, R.M., & Schneider, W. (1977). Controlled and automatic information processing: II. Perception, learning, automatic attending and a general theory. *Psychological Review, 84*, 127–190.

Shulman, G.L., Remington, R.W., & McLean, J.P. (1979). Moving attention through visual space. *Journal of Experimental Psychology: Human Perception and Performance, 5*, 522–526.

Simon, W.E. (1971). Number and colour responses of some college students: Preliminary evidence of the blue and seven phenomena. *Perception and Motor Skills, 33*, 373–374.

Singer, W. (1994). The organisation of sensory motor representations in the neocortex: A hypothesis based on temporal coding. In C. Umiltà & M. Moscovitch (Eds.), *Attention and performance XV: Conscious and nonconscious information processing*. Cambridge, MA: MIT Press.

Sinott, J.D. (1989). General systems theory: A rationale for the study of everyday memory. In L.W. Poon, D.C. Rubin, & B.A. Wilson (Eds.), *Everyday cognition in adulthood and late life*. Cambridge: Cambridge University Press.

Smyth, M.M., Collins, A.F., Morris. P.E., & Levy, P. (1994). *Cognition in action* (2nd ed.). Hove, UK: Lawrence Erlbaum Associates Ltd.

Spector, A., & Beiderman, I. (1976). Mental set and mental shift revisited. *American Journal of Psychology, 89*, 669–679.

Spelke, E., Hirst, W., & Neisser, U. (1976). Skills of divided attention. *Cognition, 4*, 215–230.

Spence, C., & Driver, J. (1996). Audio-visual links in endogenous covert spatial attention. *Journal of Experimental Psychology: Human Perception and Performance, 22*, 1005–1030.

Sperling, G. (1960). The information available in brief visual presentations. *Psychological Monographs, 74*, (Whole No. 498).

Sperling, G., & Melchner, M.J. (1978). Visual search, visual attention and the attention operating characteristic. In J. Requin (Ed.), *Attention and performance VII*. Hillsdale, NJ: Lawrence Erlbaum Associates Inc.

Squire, L. (1987). *Memory and brain*. New York: Oxford University Press.

Stern, L.D. (1981). A review of theories of human amnesia. *Memory and Cognition, 9*, 247–262.

Stoerig, P., & Cowey, A. (1990). Wavelength sensitivity in blindsight. *Nature, 242*, 916–918.

Stoffer, T.H. (1993). The time course of attentional zooming: A comparison of voluntary and involuntary allocation of attention to the levels of compound stimuli. *Psychological Research, 56*, 14–25.

Stroop, J.R. (1935). Studies of interference in serial-verbal reaction. *Journal of Experimental Psychology, 18*, 643–662.

Styles, E.A., & Allport, D.A. (1986). Perceptual integration of identity, location and colour. *Psychological Research, 48*, 189–200.

Tipper, S.P. (1985). The negative priming effect: Inhibitory effects of ignored primes. *Quarterly Journal of Experimental Psychology, 37A*, 571–590.

Tipper, S.P., & Behrmann, M. (1996). Object-centred not scene-based visual neglect. *Journal of Experimental Psychology: Human Perception and Performance, 22,* 1261–1278.

Tipper, S.P., & Cranston, M. (1985). Selective attention and priming: Inhibitory and facilitatory effects of ignored primes. *Quarterly Journal of Experimental Psychology, 37A,* 591–611.

Tipper, S.P., & Driver, J. (1988). Negative priming between pictures and words: Evidence for semantic analysis of ignored stimuli. *Memory and Cognition, 16,* 64–70.

Tipper, S.P., Brehaut, J.C., & Driver, J. (1990). Selection of moving and static objects for the control of spatially based attention. *Journal of Experimental Psychology: Human Perception and Performance, 16,* 492–504.

Tipper, S.P., Driver, J., & Weaver, B. (1991). Object-centred inhibition of return of visual attention. *Quarterly Journal of Experimental Psychology, 43A,* 289–298.

Tipper, S.P., Lortie, C., & Baylis, G.C. (1992). Selective reaching: Evidence for action centred attention. *Journal of Experimental Psychology: Human Perception and Performance, 18,* 891–905.

Tipper, S.P., Weaver, B., & Houghton, G. (1994). Behavioural goals determine inhibitory mechanisms of selective attention. *Quarterly Journal of Experimental Psychology, 47A,* 809–840.

Tipper, S.P., Weaver, B., Jerreat, L., & Burak, A. (1994). Object-based and environment-based inhibition of return of visual attention. *Journal of Experimental Psychology: Human Perception and Performance, 20,* 478–499.

Tipper, S.P., Weaver, B., & Watson, F.L. (1996). Inhibition of return to successively cued spatial locations: Commentary on Pratt and Abrahams (1995). *Journal of Experimental Psychology: Human Perception and Performance, 22,* 1289–1293.

Townsend, V.W. (1973). Loss of spatial and identity information following a tachistoscopic exposure. *Journal of Experimental Psychology, 8,* 113–118.

Treisman, A.M. (1960). Contextual cues in selective listening. *Quarterly Journal of Experimental Psychology, 12,* 242–248.

Treisman, A.M. (1964a). Monitoring and storage of irrelevant messages in selective attention. *Journal of Verbal Learning and Verbal Behaviour, 3,* 449–459.

Treisman, A.M. (1964b). Verbal cues, language and meaning in selective attention. *American Journal of Psychology, 77,* 206–219.

Treisman, A.M. (1964c). Effect of irrelevant material on the efficiency of selective listening. *American Journal of Psychology, 77,* 533–546.

Treisman, A.(M.). (1969). Strategies and models of selective attention. *Psychological Review, 76,* 282–299.

Treisman, A.(M.) (1986, November). Features and objects in visual processing. *Scientific American, 106–115.*

Treisman, A(M.). (1988). Features and objects: The fourteenth Bartlett memorial lecture. *Quarterly Journal of Experimental Psychology, 40A,* 201–237.

Treisman, A.(M.) (1993). The perception of features and objects. In A.D. Baddeley & L. Weiskrantz (Eds.), *Attention: Awareness, selection, and control.* Oxford: Oxford University Press.

Treisman, A.M., & Gelade, G. (1980). A feature-integration theory of attention. *Cognitive Psychology 12,* 97–136.

Treisman, A.(M.), Kahneman, D., & Burkell, J. (1983). Perceptual objects and the cost of filtering. *Perception and Psychophysics, 33,* 527–532.

Treisman, A.(M.), & Schmidt, H. (1992). Illusory conjunctions in the perception of objects. *Cognitive Psychology, 14,* 107–141.

Trueman, J. (1979). Existence and robustness of the blue seven phenomena. *Journal of General Psychology, 101*, 23–26.

Tsal, Y. (1983). Movements of attention across the visual field. *Journal of Experimental Psychology: Human Perception and Performance, 9*, 523–530.

Turvey, M.T. (1973). On peripheral and central processes in vision: Inferences from information processing analysis of masking with patterned stimuli. *Psychological Review, 80*, 1–52.

Turvey, M.T., & Kravetz, S. (1970). Retrieval for iconic memory with shape as the selection criterion. *Perception and Psychophysics, 8*, 171–172.

Umiltà, C. (1988). The control operations of consciousness. In A.J. Marcel & E. Bisiach (Eds.), *Consciousness in contemporary science*. Oxford: Oxford University Press.

Underwood, G. (1976). Semantic interference form unattended printed words. *British Journal of Psychology, 67*, 327–338.

Ungerleider, L.G., & Mishkin, M. (1982). Two cortical systems. In D.J. Ingle, M.A. Goodale, & R.J.W. Mansfield (Eds.), *Analysis of visual behaviour*. Cambridge MA: MIT Press.

Van der Heijden, A.H.C. (1981). *Short-term visual information forgetting*. London: Routledge & Kegan Paul.

Van der Heijden, A.H.C. (1993). The role of position in object selection in vision. *Psychological Research, 56*, 44–58.

Van Essen, G.W., & Maunsell, J.H.R. (1983). Hierarchical organisation and functional streams in the visual cortex. *Trends in Neuroscience, 6*, 370–375.

Van Oeffelen, M.P., & Vos, P.G. (1982). Configurational effects on the enumeration of dots: Counting by groups. *Memory and Cognition, 10*, 396–40.

Van Oeffelen, M.P., & Vos, P.G. (1983). An algorithm for pattern description on the level of relative proximity. *Pattern Recognition, 16*, 341–348.

Volpe, B.T., LeDoux, J., & Gazzaniga, M.S. (1979). Information processing of visual stimuli in the "extinguished" field. *Nature, 228*, 722–24.

Von der Malsburg, C. (1985). Nervous structures with dynamical links. *Bre. Bunsenges. Phys. Chem., 89*, 703–710.

Von Wright, J.M. (1969). Selection in visual immediate memory. *Quarterly Journal of Experimental Psychology, 20*, 62–68.

Von Wright, J.M. (1970). On selection in immediate memory. *Acta Psychologia, 33*, 280–292.

Wallace, M.A., & Farah, M.J. (1992). Savings in learning face–name associations as evidence for "covert recognition" in prosopagnosia. *Journal of Cognitive Neuroscience, 4*, 150–154.

Wardlaw, K.A., & Kroll, N.E.A. (1976). Automatic responses to shock associated words in a non-attended message: A failure to replicate. *Journal of Experimental Psychology: Human Perception and Performance, 2*, 357–60.

Weiskrantz, L. (1986). *Blindsight: A case study and implications*. Oxford: Oxford University Press.

Weiskrantz, L. (1993). Search for the unseen. In A. Baddeley & L. Weiskrantz (Eds.), *Attention: Selection, awareness, and control*.Oxford: Oxford University Press.

Weiskrantz, L., Sanders, M.D., & Marshall, J. (1974). Visual capacity in the hemianopic visual field following a restricted occipital ablation. *Brain, 97*, 709–728.

Welford, A.T. (1952). The psychological refractory period and the timing of high speed performance: A review and a theory. *British Journal of Psychology, 43*, 2–19.

Welford, A.T. (1967). Single channel operation in the brain. *Acta Psychologia, 27*, 5–22.

Wickens, C.D. (1984). Processing resources in attention. In R. Parsuraman

& D.R. Davies (Eds.), *Varieties of attention*. Orlando, FL: Academic Press.

Wolfe, J.M., Cave, K.R., & Franzel, S.L. (1989). Guided search: An alternative to feature integration model for visual search. *Journal of Experimental Psychology: Human Perception and Performance, 18*, 34–49.

Wolfe, J.M., & Pokorny, C.W. (1990). Inhibitory tagging in visual search: A failure to replicate. *Perception and Psychophysics, 48*, 357–362.

Wolford, G. (1975). Perturbation model for letter identification. *Psychological Review, 82*, 184–199.

Wolford, G., & Hollingsworth, S. (1974a). Lateral masking in visual information processing. *Perception and Psychophysics, 16*, 315–320.

Wolford, G., & Hollingsworth, S. (1974b). Retinal location and string position are important variables in visual information processing. *Perception and Psychophysics, 16*, 437–442.

Wood, N., & Cowan, N. (1995). The cocktail party phenomenon revisited: How frequent are attention shifts to one's name in an irrelevant auditory channel? *Journal of Experimental Psychology, Learning Memory and Cognition, 2*, 255–260.

Yantis, S., & Johnston, J.C. (1990). On the locus of visual selection: Evidence from focused attention tasks. *Journal of Experimental Psychology: Human Perception and Performance, 16*, 135–149.

Yerkes, R.M., & Dodson, J.D. (1908). The relation of strength of stimuli to rapidity of habit-information. *Journal of Comparative Neurology and Psychology, 18*, 459–82.

Young, A.W., & Block, N. (1996). Consciousness. In V. Bruce (Ed.), *Unsolved mysteries of the mind*. Hove, UK: Psychology Press.

Zeki, S. (1980). The representation of colours in the cerebral cortex. *Nature, 284*, 412–418.

Zeki, S., Watson, J.D.G., Leuck, C.J., Friston, K.L., Kennard, C., & Frackowiak, R.S. (1991). A direct demonstration of functional specialisation in human visual cortex. *Journal of Neuroscience, 11*, 641–649.

Author index

Subject index